I Should Have
Just Stayed Home

I Should Have Just Stayed Home

Award-Winning Tales of Travel Fiascoes

Edited by
Roger Rapoport
Bob Drews
& **Kim Klescewski**

RDR Books
Oakland, California

I Should Have Just Stayed Home

RDR Books
4456 Piedmont Avenue
Oakland, CA 94611
Phone: (510) 595-0595
Fax: (510) 595-0598
E-mail: read@rdrbooks.com
Website: www.rdrbooks.com

First Edition
Copyright 2003 by RDR Books
All Rights Reserved

ISBN: 1-57143-096-2
Library of Congress Catalog Card Number: 2002091342

Editors: Roger Rapoport, Bob Drews and Kim Klescewski
Cover Photograph: Ed Kashi
Cover Design: Paula Morrison and Bryan Knapp
Text Design: Paula Morrison
Proofreader: Sayre Van Young

Distributed in Canada by Starbooks Distribution,
100 Armstrong Way, Georgetown, ON L7G 5S4

Distributed in the United Kingdom and Europe by
Roundhouse Publishing Ltd., Millstone, Limers Lane,
Northam, North Devon EX39 2RG, United Kingdom

Distributed in Australia and New Zealand by
Wakefield Press (Aust) Pty Ltd
1 The Parade West, Kent Town, Adelaide, South Australia 5071

Printed in Canada

Dedicated to the memory of J. Richard Lombardi
who knew how to make people laugh.

Table of Contents

Introduction

NOT EVERY STORY that reaches our desk makes it into the pages of the *I Should Have Stayed Home* series. Consider the midwestern science teacher who lectured audiences around the country on barnyard science. When various plates in his limbs began setting off metal detectors at airports around the country, delays compounded one another. Arriving two hours early for his flight was not good enough.

Unable to verify that he wasn't a human timebomb, security screeners began bringing in supervisors who scratched their heads as their alarms kept going off. He was wanded so many times by suspicious gatekeepers that he began carrying cards from surgeons charting his medical history. There was one for the plate in his knee, another for his shoulder and even a bit of metal in his sternum. But some officious screeners weren't satisfied and so much time was lost he began missing flights. The last straw took place at the Philadelphia Airport. Totally frustrated with the wanding of his midsection, he removed his belt and dropped his trousers. The security staff wasn't quite sure what to do about this man in the boxer shorts.

"Well, you've certainly got nothing to hide," huffed the woman behind him.

That was the day the science teacher decided to quit flying. Now he drives to his appearances and no doubt other passengers like him are one of the reasons why airlines are losing so much money.

When RDR books launched this series in 1994, it never occurred to us that people like Mark Cerulli, an HBO editor, would console themselves on a disastrous trip through Africa with the realization that their miserable experience would fit perfectly in one of our books. With five books in the series and translations appearing around the world, it's obvious that Cerulli and our other contributors have learned an important lesson. As the late Susannah McCorkle put it one of her memorable recordings, "It Ain't Safe To Go Nowhere Anymore."

Despite the difficulties, few of us are willing to surrender our God-given right to explore the remotest corner of our planet. Even the tragic outbreak of Sudden Acute Respiratory Syndrome has not stopped people from hitting the road. When problems arise in one area, they simply rebook and head somewhere else. As I write these words, scheduled airline service has been announced to Antarctica. Instead of cutting back, more travelers are seeking out remote destinations confident in the assumption that lost continents are safer than brand name destinations.

With my colleagues Bob Drews and Kim Klescewski, I have had the pleasure of reading hundreds of stories submitted to contests our company has run in collaboration with booksellers around the country. One held at Books Inc. in San Francisco attracted over 100 entries, and cheers from a standing -room-only crowd of fellow travelers. Another at Chickering Bookstore in Laramie, Wyoming, turned into a collaborative effort with a statewide public radio call for entries and submissions funneled in by bookstores across the state. And, thanks to scores of radio shows, travelers who thought they would have to suffer in silence have learned otherwise.

As you read and enjoy the pieces in this new collection, we are already busy working on the next volume in the series. The international success of these books raises an important question. Although many people want to know how they can make it into these pages, no one ever asks how they can stay out. Here are a few rules of the road highly recommended to you and your loved ones.

1. Don't leave on schedule. Leave ahead of schedule. For example, if your cruise leaves from Miami on Monday night, get to Miami the day before.

2. Don't take the last flight of the day. If anything goes wrong you won't have a backup.

3. Whenever possible try to avoid renting cars in countries where you don't speak the language. The cost of a car and driver in many parts of the world is reasonable and well worth it.

4. The quickest route to the emergency room is through the bar.

5. Avoid carrying things you can't afford to lose.

6. Take a day off from your vacation now and then—you may need the rest. Try to avoid arriving home at 5:30 A.M. on the morning you have to go back to work.

7. Lower your expectations. It's amazing how much fun you can have reading a book or going for a walk, instead of driving an extra 100 miles to see one more sightseeing highlight.

8. Buy a guidebook. If you're spending, say, $1,500 on your vacation, maybe more, a $15 or $20 guidebook is a wise investment. If you save $50 with one of the book's hotel recommendations you have enough left over for a good meal, not to mention avoiding the overrated and the overpriced.

9. Bring your own babysitter. Not only will your kids thank you, you won't have to worry about language difficulties or lowering your standards.

10. If you're not sure about a restaurant, ask for a restaurant

kitchen tour before you sit down to dinner.

11. In the airline business, fourteen hours is considered a duty day. If a pilot can't finish an assignment within the time allotted, another pilot takes over. If you begin your day at 6 A.M., you should stop driving around 8 P.M.

On a personal note I would like to thank a few of the people who have been instrumental in the continued success of this series. They include my colleagues Linda Cohen, Bryan Knapp, Paula Morrison, Sayre Van Young, John Ferriby, Anu Hansen and L.D. Klepper. Special thanks to Martha and William Ferriby, Elizabeth and Jonathan Rapoport and Calvin Goodman.

Finally, you the reader deserve a special nod. Embracing this series from the start, making sure that good stories keep coming our way and supporting the bookselling community and public libraries has made it possible to introduce many fine new voices. At a time when many publishers won't even look at unsolicited material, we welcome submissions for future volumes in this series. Details are found at the end of this book. Be sure to let your friends know their submissions are also welcome.

Bon voyage to each and every one of you. All of us here at RDR Books hope you have great trips in the months and years ahead. And if you don't, we want to hear all about it.

—Roger Rapoport

Bavarian Creamed

by Brian Abrahams

THERE ARE TWO THINGS about Germany that Americans assume to be fact: the Autobahn has no speed limits, and Oktoberfest in Munich is one big jolly party. The Autobahn does have speed limits because I got a ticket on it as I was driving to Oktoberfest, where I was almost choked to death.

The fun began on the highway to Munich in my rented Audi. I was going to be a cool American and finally realize my full driving potential on the legendary road. I didn't make it very far. To begin with, the Autobahn is a myth. It's a bunch of boring highways like the Oklahoma Interstate, except the speed limit is higher in Oklahoma and the law is a lot friendlier.

True, there are a few speed-limit-free sections left, but the wild and open Autobahn ended years ago. Seems we never got that memo in America.

I was outside Munich getting on the highway, just merging into traffic, visions of driving freedom in my head when suddenly an unmarked car pulled in front of me and an arm came out the window holding a sign that said "Police—STOP" with an LED sign in the back window in German reading "Police … Follow me." I pulled over into a rest area behind him and realized that a second unmarked car was following me. That's when I got a little nervous. I had an American friend with me who said during the eight years he'd been living in Germany, he'd never seen a car actually pulled over by police

1

on the Autobahn. (They normally use cameras and radar guns, mailing you the ticket later.)

Two plainclothes police officers got out of the front car and another one emerged from the car behind me. I told my friend Ed, who is fluent in German, not to indicate that he spoke the language, attempting to see if I could get away with the dumb American tourist bit that had served me well in legal encounters elsewhere around the world. One of the officers unleashed a torrent of German invective, and Ed immediately began translating. So much for the trusty dumb tourist routine.

All along the Autobahn, even the few stretches with no speed limits, there are severely reduced speeds at the entrances and exits to cities. What ticked me off, and I say this as a dedicated speeder who will admit when he's really flying, was that I was truly only trying to merge into fast-moving traffic while getting on. They offered to let me see a videotape of myself speeding but I thought it would anger them if I challenged their credibility. At this point, the goal was to get away from them into the merry beer halls of Oktoberfest as soon as possible.

On the spot they fined me 230 deutschmarks, about $150. I didn't have it on me, but fortunately Ed did. He told me later that if you can't pay on the spot they impound your car until you cough up the dough.

Following that expensive lesson on modern Germany, I dropped Ed off and was free to head to Oktoberfest. Of course my problems were only beginning.

To begin with, my office in Munich had a hard time finding a hotel for me. When Oktoberfest is on in Munich, the hotels are packed. The decent ones anyway. Eventually they came up with a room in a *pension*. I checked into my hotel for the first revelation. "Pension" means the same thing across

Europe: "Don't stay here unless you are a poor student with a high threshold for noise, dirt and a constant looming danger that you will be robbed and murdered in your sleep." There were empty beer bottles scattered around the room, but I pretended that these were festive decorations to put guests in the mood for the world's biggest drinking party. The same went for the smell of old fermented beer that rose up from the carpet, something I haven't slept with since college days. Undeterred and glad to just have a place to lay my naïve head, I called my German employees and asked them to entertain me. Being native Bavarians and proud to show off the bountiful fruits of their region, they were glad to host me. Or if they weren't, they certainly kept it to themselves. Unlike French employees who will let you know how strongly they disagree with your decision to be in business at all, German employees have a well-ingrained sense of hierarchy and seniority.

Oktoberfest is very impressive but not quite as colorful as it sounds. More like the biggest carnival you've ever seen plus beer halls, but still it is unique. The beer halls in particular are amazing. I had always wondered about the Beer Hall Putsch, Hitler's first attempt to seize power that landed him in jail with enough time and privacy to dictate *Mein Kampf* and really get his operation ginned up. When I read about the Beer Hall Putsch I could never imagine how rousing a group of people in a bar would allow a guy to almost take over an entire city. (The site of the original beer hall where he launched the attempted coup is very near the site where Oktoberfest is held today.)

Of course when the Germans throw up a beer hall, it's much more than a local pub. They erect these enormous buildings, all built *temporarily* for Oktoberfest, each resembling a *Cheers* bar on steroids.

Each hall is sponsored by a particular brand of beer for promotional purposes. Picture the biggest high school or college basketball arena you've ever seen, on two to three levels, filled with thousands of people seated on benches at long wooden tables all getting stone drunk. In every hall there are at least two or three different oompah-type bands, each trying to outplay the others. The noise is at jet take-off levels, and the halls are packed tight with swaying bodies. If you've never spent an evening jammed into a mass of 3,000 large, sweaty Bavarians, don't rush into the experience. Seeing this I understood how an emotional speaker could rouse such a crowd and challenge a government. The second-hand smoke was thick, and I'm sure an evening spent in a beer hall is equal to smoking at least a pack and a half of unfiltered Camels. However, it *is* fun. The beer comes in a huge stein called a *maas* that holds a good two to three liters. My guys laughingly said that no American lightweight could drink more than two. The honor of my nation was challenged, and I went on to prove them wrong.

We ordered dinner, but the options are limited. They brought each of us half a chicken on a bare plate. No vegetable, no starch and no utensils. Just half a chicken to be eaten with bare hands. Primitive but filling.

One of the festive group aspects of Oktoberfest is that during the evening everyone stands up on the benches every ten minutes to sing favored songs. What is the absolute number one Oktoberfest song in tradition-minded Germany?

"Country Roads" by John Denver.

While Oktoberfest isn't for everyone, you shouldn't pass from this vale of tears until you've heard 3,000 plastered Bavarians sing the words "Mountain Mama" with a heavy German accent. They don't know what the song is about or even what a Mountain Mama is, but baby do they love that ditty. You can leave America, but wherever you go, America never leaves you.

As we stood on our benches during about the tenth rendition of John Denver's song, someone a few benches away shoved the person next to them. The tables are very tight, and by that point in the evening, balance is not anyone's strong point. The person who was shoved pitched across the table, knocking over a few people across from *him*. Those people fell backward into the people behind them, who then went across their table into the people across from them. This Bavarian domino effect inevitably reached our table, and several of the people sitting next to us fell backwards into the table behind us, causing a rather large gentleman to spill his *maas*. Red-faced and enraged, he grabbed the guy who had been sitting next to me and began to berate him in German, undoubtedly about the spilled lager.

One thing Americans are famous for in Europe is our sweet innocent willingness to be helpful in situations when no one wants our help. I think Europeans are sort of annoyed by this— we are the Boy Scouts of the world, always anxious to be helpful in any situation be it the Balkans or at a pub. Watching my tablemate in trouble with a man who outweighed him by a good hundred and fifty pounds, I decided to uphold the helpful traditions of my native land.

"Excuse me, sir," I said, in English, which he almost certainly didn't understand, "let me explain." I placed a gentle hand on his arm. "You see," I continued in a reasonable voice, "this started several tables away and this man here had nothing. . . ." Suddenly the man had a new focus for his anger and grabbed me around the neck with ten thick and powerful fingers.

"No … you … don't … understand…," I croaked out through my constricted windpipe. I tried to pull his hands off, but his grip was like steel. My guys were yelling at him in German and frantically trying to pry his hands from my throat, but he was no weakling. I could just imagine them trying to explain to the home office how they let their boss get killed during some festive business entertaining. You try expensing the cost of photocopying a coroner's report.

"Wait … let … me … explain …," I tried, my voice getting weaker, not that he probably heard it in the din. It felt like my face was blowing up. Fortunately the alcohol was dulling some of the pain.

He was only getting angrier and was now shaking me in addition to choking me. I'm a pretty big guy, but I felt myself starting to go limp like a rag doll, and there was no possibility of bouncers coming to my rescue. The beer halls are way too crowded and huge. They take a Darwinian approach to it, letting the customers sort things out with each other. I started to feel lightheaded and realized I might die for a guy I didn't even know.

I understood that the main issue was the spilled beer, so I managed to get my hand into a pocket and came up with a damp crumpled wad of Deutschmarks, which I waved in his face. God bless the departed but once reliable German mark. He released his grip without taking his eyes off my money. Coughing and rubbing my throat I motioned for a waitress and in short order he had a new *maas*. He shook my hand, happy again, and minutes later everyone was back singing John Denver songs like nothing happened, although my throat remained bruised for several days.

I decided to take a break from the crowd and call my wife on the cell phone to tell her how I'd nearly become a manslaughter statistic. To escape the roar I went to leave the hall, but it was obvious that the bouncers, blocking the crowd outside from entering, would not stamp my hand and let me back in.

I decided to squeeze myself into the doorway and make the call. As I shouted into the phone and tried to hear my spouse, the bouncers were blocking entry to a clearly drunken patron. Outraged, he stepped back from the door and flung the contents of his *maas* into the bouncers' faces. They immediately began to beat the stuffing out of the guy and his friends. Their knot of bodies slammed me back into the doorjamb, immobilizing me between the ball of red-faced brawling Germans and the solid construction of those efficient German engineers. The phone flew out of my hands and once again I found myself trying to protect my neck and face. Eventually they beat the guy to the ground, and I was released. Scrambling on my knees I found the phone in a puddle of beer and scurried back to the table, deciding to take my chances with the crazies already inside.

I treasure the Oktoberfest experience, but once is definitely enough. Later I returned to my hotel, having drunk a goodly amount of beer, and discovered my room had no bathroom. It was a jolly and festive night of running down the hall past my fellow "pensioners." Nothing like business travel on an expense account.

A few days later on the highway heading back to the airport, I stayed in the right-hand lane and took it *very* slow.

In Search of Mongolian Pie

by Larry Jer

*"Just sit right back and you'll hear a tale,
A tale of a fateful trip . . ."*

THE LYRICS STRETCHED OUT across the grasslands, powered by alcohol and punctuated by the tortured wail of the family watchdog. Everyone's a critic. We sang for our dinner: a feast of lamb, slain by our host, spiced and simmered in a cauldron over coals, served in washbasin buckets. Life was good.

We five had come to Inner Mongolia belting out the *Gilligan's Island* theme song in search of Mongolian Pie: An American, an Englishman and me, a Canadian joining two Chinese ladies for a day trip.

We worked in Shenyang, northeast China, all teachers but at different locations and at various points in our tenure. Ben, from Wisconsin, and Robert, of Oxford, had been in China about one year and I was the grand old man, hailing from Vancouver, coming to the end of my two-year hitch. The ladies lived in the industrial city. We became friends through a potpourri of circumstances, but one thread that wove its way through our personalities was the desire to eat the varied foods of the region.

This latest episode started when my colleague, a Chinese teacher, asked if I had eaten Mongolian Pie. Her boyfriend raved about it, so she suggested we gather some friends and travel to Huolinguole, an Inner Mongolian town about eight hours by train northwest of our home city and track some down.

It was fun.

We made some fast friends in Huolinguole, the way you know foreigners can if you've ever traveled in China. A Mr. Wong chauffeured our group into the vast grasslands where we stopped to chat with a few Mongolian families.

Through nods and smiles, the patriarch of one clan suggested I hop on one of his horses so we could go rope dinner, an unsuspecting lamb quietly grazing with the rest of the family's flock. I declined. In Vancouver's inner city, chasing dinner on horseback wasn't taught in public schools.

We stayed for hours, exchanging songs when conversation faltered. The day was full of goodwill and when we finally said our goodbyes, the entire group buzzed from the connection. We made our way back to the train station where our bags had been stored. Our contentment was short-lived.

The police met us with some bad news: We were traveling in a "restricted" military area. Our bags were held ransom and through a mishmash of English and Chinese, we were told we must pay a fine or be arrested. It was just a matter of how much or for how long.

Nice business the local gendarmerie ran.

They changed the rules or set them as they pleased. Prospecting for Mongolian Pie would cost us. For each foreigner, it was 5,000 *yuan* ($625), the cost of a ski weekend in, say, Utah, but several months' wages in China.

We refused to pay and were put under "house arrest," sequestered in the local hotel and forced to cough up for the "best" rooms. My four-star had no working lights, a backed-up toilet and cockroach carcasses in a few of the darker crannies.

We didn't take the detention seriously, even less so when ordered to write a self-criticism. Robert wrote in Latin (who said it was a dead language?), and I submitted an essay on what we had for lunch that day. Ben wrote bawdy lyrics to a rugby song. We knew the translator's English was lacking and that he probably had, like so many others in these positions, secured his job through nepotism—ill-qualified for the task. He put up a decent front, staring in great concentration at the sheets of paper, nodded knowingly at appropriate intervals and ceremoniously discarding the self-criticisms one by one. One speed bump over and done with.

We had two choices for dinner: 1. Have one, or 2. Don't have one. We chose option 1 thinking what the hell, maybe we'll finally get some Mongolian Pie since it hadn't been on the menu at our meal with the clan. Official pumping of our pockets of cash continued as Y25 each was charged. Dinner bell at six.

Y25 could easily have paid for all of us at any local restaurant, but that wasn't the kick. When we arrived promptly for dinner, the police were sitting at a huge, round table having a banquet, laughing raucously, red-faced from drinking. They were having a good time at our expense.

Between swigs of *baijiu*, the costliest alcohol in China, we were told that due to our tardiness, they had to eat the meal as our treat. We went back to our respective rooms to stew overnight, hungry and angry.

I fell asleep listening to the party extend into the night. As day broke, I noticed my room faced a fenced courtyard where there was an enormous sow wallowing in the makeshift pen. I thought at first it was a half-buried VW Beetle, but when it suddenly got agitated, I was surprised at how agile it could be.

The source of stress? The well-fed police had decided today

was the day the giant pig was to be sacrificed and divided up for their families. Through my window, it was a one-channel horror film. At once the cops were adept at graft and blackmail and with the flip of a new day they were in gumboots and aprons pig-wrestling.

We gathered before the next tribunal. Robert had read in a guidebook that though this sticky situation happens on occasion, don't get flustered, negotiate a fee that satisfies all, and within a few hours you will be free to move on, your wallet thinner, your load generously lightened by a small Huolinguole hospitality surcharge. Ben wouldn't have any of that. He put in an anxious call to the American Consulate, but the cold voice on the other end did nothing to quell our concerns. "Let us know if they move you." Click.

More ideas were tossed around. The best brainchild was, "Just tell them we don't have the money and that we'll pay off our time in prison," knowing full well that the Chinese wouldn't send foreigners to jail.

If nothing else, we gave the police a stitch from laughing too hard.

"Don't have the money?" the cops questioned. "Prison?" grins widening fast. "We'll put the women in jail and escort one of you to Shenyang to get the money you owe." Forty-eight hours of cat-and-mouse negotiations later and the matter was decided. Their ace was the simple mantra: "The longer we stay, the better food they will eat at our expense."

The cost for our adventure? Two days of bloated hotel fees, meals we paid for but didn't eat, limited and monitored movement, having to watch a giant pig's demise, a fine that plummeted from the astronomical Y5,000 down to an irritating Y140 (17 USD) but worst of all—still no Mongolian Pie.

It's Such a Comfort to Take the Bus

by Audra Crane

When our Kim's Café tourist mini-bus pulled up in front of our hotel at 5 A.M. on a wet morning in Nha Trang, Viet Nam, my friend Pricilla and I were as pleasantly surprised as it is possible to be at that time in the morning. The bus was on time and looked to be in decent shape. Pricilla got on first and quickly found a seat, which left me with the last one in the house, right next to a large Australian. I walked down the aisle and stood next to him, smiling through my sleep-swollen eyes and asked, "Is anyone sitting here?"

He leaped to his feet with something perilously close to a snap of his heels. Throwing out his chest, he bellowed, "No! Would you like the window seat? I don't mind where I sit. I'm so tall I can see right over your head and out the window! I'm Craig! From Australia!"

I introduced myself as I squeezed by his lanky 6 foot 5 inch frame and slid onto the seat. "Hi, I'm Audra. Thanks, I will take the window seat if you really don't mind."

I was surprised to hear how quiet and contained my voice sounded, but next to him almost anything would pale in comparison. He had red hair and a beard and wore a beaten akubra, the Australian bush hat. As the bus left, the rain beat steadily on, as did his voice.

We made it through his present circumstances, an ecologically aware tree farmer whose chief hobby is the study of arboreal marsupials, in short order. We had a break at that point, when the bus coasted to a halt. We had run out of gas before even leaving town—this is not in any way an unusual happening. I got off the bus to stretch my legs, and Craig eagerly followed to fill me in on the over 600 species of eucalyptus. The driver returned with an open, tub-like container of gasoline and a cigarette dangling precariously from his lip. I backed away from the bus as he leaned over to slop the gas into the tank, the burning cigarette wavering an inch above the tub of gasoline. Craig was kind enough to explain that it's the fumes— not the actual gasoline—that ignites so it didn't really matter if the cigarette dropped into the gasoline. In fact, that would probably extinguish it.

When the death-defying cigarette stunt was completed, we re-boarded and I attempted to respond to Craig's stream of talk for about an hour. Out of desperation I finally tried putting my head against the window, closing my eyes and explaining I had to take a nap. No dice. By the time I borrowed a novel off a sympathetic fellow passenger I knew enough about tree farming to open one.

The rest of the bus paid dearly for the book owner's sympathy. As the book rose higher and higher to cover my face and my replies became vague, Craig simply chose to continue his monologue to the bus at large. Mind you, he didn't need to tax his voice further as he'd already been easily audible to the rice field workers we were passing. Now he simply directed questions at random people, hoping they'd turn around and appear interested.

I was so firmly buried behind the book that it was a good hour into the developing storm before I became aware of the murmurs, relative to Craig's booming voice, of the others. When I risked a peep away from my book and out the window,

I was alarmed to see how the storm had progressed. We'd left at 5 A.M. and I had not noticed that the dawn's early light had failed to materialize as we headed north. I did notice that I'd never seen palm trees blown horizontally before.

I thought it was high time to get an expert opinion. "Ah, Pricilla?" I called to my Texan traveling companion who was sitting several rows up from me.

"Yeah?"

"Isn't this what a hurricane looks like?"

She turned in her seat to look at me and replied with a tight "Yep."

"Should we be driving in it?"

"No."

After the initial headline flashed across my mind, "Twenty Tourists Plummet off Cliff," I settled down. Actually there was lots to see: a couple of three-wheeled tuk-tuks upended and floating in the swollen river next to the road, and roofs that I'm reasonably certain were attached to houses under the water. The best part was watching for oncoming vehicles. We became numbed to seeing them when they were about a yard from our grill. Luckily traffic was moving so slowly that it was only a matter of lightly touching the brakes before backing off and driving around.

The first portion of flooded-out road we cleared brought a few cheers, but we soon came to almost expect the old bus to ford the floods. Finally we hit a huge flooded-out section, blocked by buses and trucks attempting a crossing. When a committee went to the driver with our cowardly decision to wait, something was lost in the sign language. I think he took it as a unanimous decision to "go for it." We all groaned as our bus slid down the road and joined the line on the flooded roadway. The water became deeper. I hung my head out the window and saw that the wheels were covered and that the trucks ahead of us were in even deeper.

I cursed myself for not having extra rolls of film as I clicked away at the unfolding scene. Foraging in backpacks became rampant and some pretty mean deals were being struck between the film-less and those with film to spare. Then the truck in front of us stalled, we ground to a halt, and the water lapped at our headlights and started to come in the lower stair of the door. The engine died.

Craig began to explain in excruciating detail why a diesel engine is particularly prone to croaking in these conditions. Apparently we would need to get to dry land, take most of the engine and fuel tank apart and let it dry before we could get started again. I didn't see any likelihood of getting to dry land in the near future. Indeed, I began to realize that our road was not simply flooded, it had been overtaken by the river that flooded the levee and tumbled around the bus.

Communal consternation began to rise along with the waters. When small waves began to break on the side of the bus, I decided it was time to abandon ship. Walking up the aisle, I collected Pricilla, unsuccessfully tried to calm two hysterical Danish girls and got myself out of the potential coffin.

Five of us stepped off and were mustered further up the road by the bus driver's assistant. Looking back I saw others trailing off. The assistant insisted that we make a break for high ground. Now we were in the water. It was chest deep, there was a strong current, and small waves were breaking over my head. Our band grabbed hands, forming a haphazard human chain, and made our way up what we hoped was the road with bad jokes and nervous, laughing sobs. None of us was sure whether we were following the road or were veering off into the angry, deep river alongside our path.

Each of us lost our footing at some point and would have been washed down the river were it not for the buddy system. Hand in hand we moved deliberately out of harm's way. Looking back I saw a similar chain following us. Craig was with them and I could see his mouth moving. Doubtless he was explaining the dynamics of flooding or discussing water rats; I struggled between annoyance and amusement for a lightened moment. Finally the water stopped pulling at my legs. The road began to rise.

We all laughed and hugged as we reached water only knee deep and nearly still. We'd made it. Continuing up the rise and around a bend in the road, I saw why all the buses and trucks had stopped. There was a café doing land office business in hot cocoa and coffee.

We couldn't see the road from the café, but other passengers from our bus trickled in. A couple of people were sobbing. We were dripping wet, cold and more than a little anxious about going back for the bus. The café was full of other refugees, mostly from another minivan; they were all pragmatic-looking older men. I walked over to speak to the middle-aged Vietnamese woman in charge and asked if their bus had broken down, blatantly angling for a ride in case mine turned out to be beyond repair.

She turned to me and said, "No, our bus is fine. You need to go get yours though. What happened to it?"

She and her husband, who gave a smile and a wave from across the café, were running tours for American Vietnam War veterans. Their customers lack of panic or impatience made sense now.

A cheer from my group interrupted our conversation. The last stragglers from the bus had just arrived. It turned out the driver wanted everyone off, allowing him and a few others to push it to safety. The terrified Danes had been two of the last forced off the bus and had been roped into pushing it.

The rain and wind had lessened considerably, not that it mattered to our drenched party. The driver and his assistant played with the engine for about an hour while Craig ambled up to each huddled group of survivors to propound his theories of what needed to be done to the engine and gas/water mix to get the bus running again. When he tired of mechanics, he entertained himself with collecting empty film canisters to house his new and burgeoning collection of Vietnamese beetles. The driver, convinced the bus was ready to go, asked us to push it up and over the rise. On a roll, the driver popped the clutch. Everyone cheered, forgetting that we didn't really want to be on the road in the storm.

We tumbled back onto the bus and started foraging for dry clothes. I was one of the lucky ones with a bag near the top. The packs on the bottom were soaked with all the water that had come into the bus. Wet clothes slapped and flopped, modesty disappeared, and everyone who could changed into warm clothes. After a depressingly short period, the engine died again.

The bus stalled in front of a farmhouse, apparently the only habitation for miles. We paraded down the aisle and out of the bus to stretch our legs as the driver, his assistant and a few passengers began investigating the engine again. I was desperate for a bathroom by this time and decided to approach the small house. Husband and wife came out and after a few failures with sign language I squatted and grimaced. I was ushered into the house with commiserating smiles and giggles and led straight out the backdoor. After a short study I found the only possible method, outside of wetting the porch, was to drop trou, tiptoe to the brick ledge over the river, pivot, hang onto the enormous clay water pot and do my business while staring down two penned chickens and three free-range toads.

By the time I returned from my little adventure, I found we had guests. I don't know where they came from, but within the next half an hour, 200 people came out of the rice paddies and trickled down the road to see the foreigners. It was a surreal experience. Someone came up with the idea of dancing but our attempts to teach waltzing and square dancing were met with howls of laughter. They thought we were, literally, a scream, but were only comfortable darting forward to touch a hairy forearm or blonde head before screaming again and backpedaling. All our attempts at sign language prompted nothing but laughter. The driver eventually got the bus running and we said goodbye and pushed it down the road again. Some of the kids must have chased the bus for a kilometer.

I managed to finish Roddy Doyle's *The Van* before dark but was distressed to find that it ended with the title character surrendering to the sea. Coincidence?

Our adventures had exhausted everyone but Craig. The weather was letting up, however, and we figured we'd surely run the gamut. What we didn't count on was nightfall, the total breakdown of the windshield wipers, and a strained battery. Goodbye wipers, so long headlights. Then an engineering type collected a couple of laundry lines and tied them to the wiper.

We all took turns standing at the front of the bus with a line in each hand, manually swishing the wiper. The thought of remaining invisible to oncoming traffic mobilized another passenger into digging his cyclists' headlamp out of his backpack. We attached it to the grill with a hope and a prayer. Our group was well into our fifteenth hour when someone mentioned that the driver's assistant was just that, an assistant, and had never actually driven. We were able to convey our concern about the driver's state of exhaustion, but he wouldn't give the driving up to anyone else, or stop short of Hoi An.

Taking a really good look at him, I saw that his eyes were bloodshot and swollen. Unable to get him to stop completely, we suggested a short stop to buy coffee, hot water and cigarettes. When each of us finished our windshield wiper shift, we took our place as coffee and cigarette holder. A "NO!" and a shake were enough to rouse him when he began to nod.

Craig's verbal barrage never subsided. Hours of monologue recapped every moment of the day and what should be done. He was a living, breathing non-stop passenger comment card, continuing to work on his beetle collection even after several escaped and adventured within the bus. It turned out he knew nearly as much about beetles as he did about arboreal marsupials and felt compelled to share everything. He traced his own family lineage back three generations. He ran out of comments and reminiscences at 1 A.M. Luckily he had managed to buy a bottle of Vietnamese whiskey at one of our breakdown spots and with its aid was able to fetch from his memory lesser-known nineteenth-century Australian bush poetry he had learned in high school. It is very lyrical and works well at top volume and slurred. I thought there might be a lynching at any moment.

We arrived in Hoi An 22 hours after leaving Nha Trang. It had been an adventure, but all I wanted were silence and dry clothes. It all seemed to be coming together until Pricilla and I heard Craig being led into the room next door, loudly apologizing in advance for his "world record breaking" snoring. He wasn't kidding. Between the rain, humidity and lack of a single tumble dryer in the entire country, it was a damp month. My clothes never did dry out.

The Otor Odge

by Erica Etelson

CARRIZO PLAINS was designated a National Monument in one of the final acts of the Clinton administration. There is only one lodge near the monument, and we're headed for it.

Doug has planned on camping in the monument, but it's beginning to look like rain. Carrizo Plains is high desert that gets only nine inches of rain a year, so Doug hasn't packed any foul-weather gear. And, although it is normally one of the most blazing hot places in California, on this day it is bone chillingly frigid, the kind of raw, damp cold that gives new meaning and texture to goose bumps.

Rose and I have a reservation at the California Valley Motor Lodge. At $65 a night, it isn't cheap and yet, the proprietor, Freddy, has forewarned me, "This isn't the Holiday Inn."

We miss the turn-off to the lodge by three or four miles. Doubling back, we are alerted to it when Rose notices the half-burned-down billboard on the side of the road: "alifornia alley otor odge" announces the sign.

The lodge has a one-level horseshoe layout with a drained pool in the center and a faded, rutted shuffleboard lane alongside it. The lodge looks like it was built in 1955, abandoned in 1956, and reopened without renovation after a 40-year hiatus. Across the unpaved road is a ramshackle barn with spray painting on the window, "Restaurant Closen Down."

"You must be Erica," says a short man with a slight limp as

he ambles toward us. We are shivering next to our car, which, I notice, is the only one in the grassy lot.

"Freddy?" I ask.

Freddy has dyed black hair with a one-inch strip of grey stretching from ear to ear. He has black, bushy eyebrows and skin that is not so much wrinkled as peeling off. He looks to be between 50 and 80.

Freddy welcomes us to the lodge and wastes no time telling us he operates it at a loss as a tax write-off. He lives in Los Angeles during the week, where he engages in other unspecified business enterprises.

I always enjoy patronizing businesses whose goal it is to lose money. The service is what keeps me coming back.

Dinner is at the restaurant across the road. Tonight's menu is all-you-can-eat fish and corned beef. And, Freddy adds, he will provide us with all the vodka we can drink, on the house. Good vodka, he promises. Russian vodka.

It has started to drizzle so we quickly transfer our luggage into Room Twelve. The first thing I notice is the room's dank, fungal smell that I would have thought impossible in a desert climate. Three of the walls are made of fake wood paneling and the fourth is nothing more than rough, discolored plywood. The beds are so old and dilapidated that the undersides of the mattresses sag almost to the floor.

It's cold, and the room is equipped with a circa-1950 wall heater that blasts blazing hot air across the room with the force of a rocket launcher. I'm grateful for the heat but wary of the Legionnaire's disease or whatever other lethal molecules are surely breeding inside the heating unit and blowing directly into my face.

I go into the bathroom to wash up. The faucet is so rusted shut that I need a washcloth to pad my grip as I crank it open.

Yellow water comes splashing into the sink, and I recall reading an article about how tap water in California's Central Valley is so contaminated with pesticides that only someone very crazy or very poor would drink it.

Doug is having second thoughts about camping. He read on the Carrizo Plains web site that when it rains, the dirt roads in the park quickly become impassable without a four-wheel drive. We agree that my Geo Metro would not perform well in mud. We also agree that because Doug snores like an avalanche, he cannot room with us. Rose suggests that given the lack of clientele, Freddy might be willing to cut Doug a deal.

Doug goes off to negotiate and returns with these options: He can pitch his tent for $10, sleep in one of the rooms described as "without furniture" or, if he can beat Freddy in a game of shuffleboard, sleep in a room without furniture for free.

The room without furniture turns out to be a room lacking in certain other amenities, such as a roof. Rain dribbles down in two corners, and clumps of furry, green mold decorate most of the ceiling. The reek is so overpowering that Rose and I won't set foot inside. We stand in the doorway advising Doug that if he sleeps here he'll probably die. Doug shrugs and says it will be fine.

Back in our room, Rose points out that the toilet tank is leaking considerable quantities of water. I discuss the matter with Freddy. His response is, "If it doesn't bother you, it doesn't bother me."

"Well, you see, it *does* bother me, Freddy."

"Okay, I'll take care of it."

"By the way, what's the deal with the tap water here? Can you drink it?" I ask.

"Of course."

Five minutes later, Freddy appears at our door with a small bucket that he wedges between the toilet and the wall. Dinner, he reminds us, is in 15 minutes.

At 7:15, we sprint across the muddy road under heavy rain and enter the Closen (sic) Down Restaurant. The lodge has filled up somewhat with rained-out campers, and all have assembled for dinner. The guests, seated at a long table in the center of the restaurant, have actually been *waiting* for us, the latecomers of Room Twelve, to arrive and are baring their teeth at us in an expression that could indicate hunger, camaraderie, the early stages of pesticide poisoning and/or a desire to see us dive headfirst into the empty pool.

Dinner is a sumptuous feast of poached salmon, saffron rice and roasted potatoes prepared by a woman who lives nearby and caters all meals at the *Closen* Down Restaurant. Freddy's role is to refill his guests' plastic cups of vodka, whether they want more or not. Toward the end of the dinner hour, Freddy overhears me exclaim "Oh, God" in response to a story told by Doug.

"Why do you call me God?" Freddy giggles.

Freddy is drunk.

After refusing a final refill and an offer to take the bottle of vodka back to our room, we retire for the evening.

"Tomorrow night, we're having vodka chicken for dinner," Freddy calls out after us.

Rose and I rifle through the chipped night table. It's home to an assortment of magazines from the early 1980s, including the *Vegetarian Times* and the *Journal of Longevity.*

Though I am in no position to complain about my sleeping accommodations compared to Doug's, I must say that the bed itself appears to approximate the torture racks used during the Spanish Inquisition. Each corner of the mattress slopes down, meeting in a kind of bottomless pit in the center. No position I can arrange myself in allows multiple limbs to rest in the same plane. And, to make matters worse, the pillow is about a foot high so that my neck, emerging from the pit and straining to meet the pillow, is pretty much vertical.

By morning, my back has stiffened into a rod roughly the consistency of hardened lava. Pulling my knees toward my chest for my morning stretch, the dozen or so cracks that ripple up my spine are loud enough to awaken Rose, or so I thought until Rose informs me that she hasn't slept for the past six hours, give or take an hour.

We return to the Closen Down Restaurant for breakfast, stopping on the way to pick up Doug, who has come down overnight with a respiratory infection unrelated, he insists, to the mold.

"How's it going, Freddy? How was your night?" Doug slaps Freddy across the back.

"When the drink wore off, I had to get up and walk around for a couple of hours to clear my head out," Freddy explains.

I picture Freddy staggering around in the pitch-black night, at times teetering perilously close to the edge of the empty pool.

Over lukewarm dishwater coffee and an amazingly wonderful breakfast prepared by the same angel of mercy who cooked last night's dinner, we discuss our predicament. It's still raining. It's still cold. And only Doug is willing to sleep in the same place as last night.

Freddy approaches our table with a bottle of vodka and offers a splash in our orange juice.

"I'm good with coffee," says Rose.

Freddy shrugs dismissively, grimaces and says something to the effect of "Bah."

I also decline the vodka.

Freddy turns finally to Doug, "How about you, school-teacher? A little hair of the dog?"

Doug clears his throat and says, "I'll just have tea."

Freddy makes a gesture of disgust with his free hand, then decides to pull up a chair and join us.

"Doug here's a schoolteacher. What about you?" Freddy nods toward me.

"I'm a lawyer."

"Ah, a lawyer! What kind of lawyer?"

"Human rights."

"Human rights." The words roll over his tongue as though becoming acquainted with them for the first time. "Have I told you what my plans for this place are?" he asks.

Burn it down for insurance money would be my advice. We shake our heads no.

"I'm going to fix it up very nice. It will be a resort and a drug and alcohol treatment center."

This is quite a plan. I can just see Freddy wandering around drunk in the night, offering recovering alcoholics a little night-cap.

"That's an ambitious idea," I respond.

Freddy nods.

The time has come to broach with Freddy the subject of our imminent departure and recovering any of our money for the second night. Since he's operating the place at a loss, I'm cautiously optimistic.

"Freddy," I begin, "since it's still raining and all, we've decided just to head back to Berkeley, and we were wondering what the refund policy is."

The refund policy, Freddy informs us, is credit to be used within 90 days. He looks forward to seeing us back at the Otor Odge soon.

Freddy recommends that, on our way home, if it has stopped raining, we head for Pismo Beach. He assures us it's spectacularly beautiful.

The sky is clear as we approach the coast. We stop at a small supermarket where I ask for hummus and the clerk asks me what it is. When I explain that it is a Middle Eastern chick pea dip, he glares as though he recognizes me from the FBI's Most Wanted Terrorists list. The market carries a wide variety of beef jerky and luncheon meats and we leave with a jar of peanut butter and a box of Chicken-in-a-Basket crackers.

We bundle up against the sharp wind and wander through the parking lot to the beach, except that there is little to distinguish parking lot from beach.

Pismo Beach, we learn, is a State Vehicular Recreation Area, which means that some state agency has decided that having SUVs tearing through the sand dunes and fish-tailing through the tide is an entirely appropriate and responsible use. Rose and I briefly touch on several legal theories that could be used to force the state to close it to vehicles while Doug lunges out of the erratic path of a Ford Explorer. We dub the beach "Highway Zero."

I lick the specks of artificial flavor off a cracker, and the tang makes my eyes water.

The Shoes of Kilimanjaro

by Cameron Burns

There, ahead, all he could see, as wide as all the world, great, high, and unbelievably white in the sun, was the square top of Kilimanjaro.

—Ernest Hemingway, *The Snows of Kilimanjaro*

IF YOU EVER GET to the foot of Kilimanjaro in East Africa, there are two sights that will take your breath away. First there's the mountain itself. The looming hulk of this huge, seemingly out-of-place extinct volcano hovers above the East African plain like a gigantic, otherworldly space craft, quietly poised to nab hundreds of unsuspecting humans for exotic experiments on the far side of the Universe.

The second sight that will take your breath away—and leave you simultaneously gasping in awe and scratching your head—are the shoes worn by the locals. That's right, the shoes.

I'm not talking about just any local, however, as there are tens of thousands of friendly Tanzanians inhabiting the towns, villages and farmlands surrounding Kilimanjaro who seem to have a fairly normal range of footwear for a dry, dusty eco-tone sitting astride the equator. I'm talking about the shoes worn by the porters and guides on the mountain. They are, to put it mildly, one of the most astonishing things you will ever see.

My odd relationship with Kilimanjaro's shoes began in late

1996 when I landed a job to write a climbing guide for an American publishing company about climbing the mountain. My wife, Ann, was to accompany me on the trip, and, sometime around October, we began planning our mini-expedition.

Although Kilimanjaro requires little more than some steep hiking by its most popular routes, we took our planning seriously, as if we were mounting an assault on K2, Fitzroy or Mt. McKinley. We started out by making lists because, after all, lists keep you organized. Or at least make you think you're organized. We had lists of things to do, lists of people to call, lists of arrangements to make with bill collectors, lists of diseases you can catch. We also made endless lists of gear to bring: tents, warm clothes, ropes, gear, accessories.

Nearly every item on our gear list was a simple matter of yes or no. Yes, we need it, no we don't. But things got awfully fuzzy when it came to footwear. Would river rafting sandals or sneakers be better in the hot, dry towns we'd travel through? Would sneakers be adequate for walking through the jungles on the lower part of the mountain? Would I need plastic mountaineering boots at the top, or would leather boots suffice?

In the end, after much profound soul searching, I packed up some sandals, a pair of sneakers, a pair of high-topped canvas boots and a pair of mid-weight leather mountaineering boots. I also threw in a pair of down booties for around camp and in the tent. Six pairs altogether. Once my pile of footgear was combined with Ann's flotilla of sandals, boots and loafers, we had 12 pairs—24 individual shoes all told, enough to fill one of our duffel bags entirely. Enough to make Imelda Marcos nervous.

At the airport, we paid $50 for our extra baggage (i.e. shoes), and once we landed in Nairobi, my wife and I found we had to tip taxi drivers and tour operators extra because we had so much stuff. It's quite amazing the amount of stuff the average Westerner brings along on a mountain experience.

On January 2, we began the first of six routes we would climb on the mountain.

A rented Land Rover dumped Ann and me, along with our required guide and four porters, at the Kilimanjaro National Park gate. After the porters had organized their loads, we started walking through the montane forests that occupy the first thousand meters of elevation on Kilimanjaro's slopes. I was in my sandals; Ann was in her walking shoes.

Our guide William wore a pair of Adidas sneakers, at least six sizes too big and looking remarkably like clown shoes. I later learned they had been donated by a German tourist. They looked like knock-offs—you know, cheap shoes manufactured illegally in China or Indonesia but made to look like the real thing. William couldn't have cared less—his clown shoes were a status symbol. Meanwhile, our porters—Michael, Alan, Mohammed and John—wore beach thongs.

Beach thongs!? I did a double-take and stared at the dusty, cracked brown heels in front of me. Wow! Are these guys nuts? I watched the clip-clapping shoes as I followed Michael through the forest. This took a while to get used to: beach thongs on a mountain nearly 6,000 meters high.

Regardless of the state of their footwear, none of the porters—nor William, for that matter—seemed the least bit handicapped by their footwear. Indeed, while Michael deftly maneuvered over slick, wet tree roots with the precision of a ballerina, Ann and I tripped over every log. When John nimbly tiptoed around and over sections of bog, we stumbled straight through, the mud up to our ankles. While Alan danced up short cliff bands encountered along the trail, we quavered in fright on the crumbling hand and footholds. And as

Mohammed sped along the rough gravel slopes below the southern glaciers, we skidded and fell, unsure of ourselves on the rhyolite gravel.

Not only did Michael, Alan, Mohammed and John do all this with 35 kilos on their back (Ann and I had day packs that might as well have been filled with Styrofoam peanuts), we were cheating by using trekking poles for balance.

That evening, when we reached the first of many camps we'd make on Kili, I exchanged my sandals for my camp booties and Ann put on some lightweight hiking boots. The next morning, I switched to sneakers, and Ann put on her walking shoes again.

As the days drifted by and we crept ever higher on the mountain, Ann and I changed shoes every half day or so. Sneakers to canvas boots. Canvas boots to walking shoes. Sneakers to leather mountaineering boots. Leather mountaineering boots to canvas boots, and so on—a foot fetish equal to the best of perversions.

As we fussed over our feet, our Tanzanian friends—in their beach thongs—watched in amusement. We were obviously appeasing some strange Western deity who had bestowed our weird religion with meticulous rules regarding feet.

On January 4, we reached the highest camp on the mountain, and the porters finally changed their footgear. Michael put on a pair of brown leather penny loafers. The seams were split and re-sewn with white string and the soles looked slick as ice. Alan and Mohammed both put on pairs of ripped sneakers. The treads were more suited to a grassy football field or a basketball court than a rocky trail. Meanwhile, John put on a pair of worn leather wingtips, the kind a bum in New York City's old Bowery might wear. (And, come to think of it, John looked like he belonged in the old Bowery.)

We sat around a small fire that night, the night before our final day of the climb, eating, laughing and sipping mugs of tea. Secretly, we were regarding each other's feet.

In all the world's societies, shoes are an important symbol of wealth and class. Imelda, the wife of the late Filipino ruler Ferdinand Marcos, acquired some 3,000 pairs of shoes while her husband was in power. Her status as one of the wealthiest women in the world was defined, in part, by her shoes. The famous children's fairy tale, "Cinderella", tells of a poor cinder maid who shoots straight to queenhood after her foot is found to fit a glass slipper that a charming prince is toting around the countryside while searching for an appropriately sized foot.

But shoes are more than symbols of status. They are icons of change, improvement and escape.

Since the beginning of human evolution, shoes have represented mobility. By using their feet (and thus their shoes) ancient human races were able to run away from saber-toothed tigers and advancing ice sheets. Nomadic peoples could migrate in search of water and game. Shoes represented the ability to get out of a bad situation and hopefully into a better one. Shoes allow us to change our circumstances, the circumstances of our progeny and the circumstances of entire civilizations, so for thousands of years they have been given special, sometimes magical, attributes.

"Throughout history footwear has figured widely in mythology, folk stories and superstition," wrote shoe aficionado Richard N. DeCost, a professional shoemaker from Massachusetts—obviously a guy as nutty about footwear as myself. "The Greek god Mercury wore winged sandals, and there are very few Europeans who do not remember childhood tales of 'Puss in Boots,' the 'Seven League Boots,' 'Cinderella' and 'The

Old Woman Who Lived in a Shoe,' and most cultures have stories where shoes play a starring role."

Ponder L. Frank Baum's book *The Wonderful Wizard of Oz* for a moment.

This book is often described as a fairy tale, but it's actually a story about shoes. Much of the plot details the Wicked Witch of the West's quest for Dorothy's silver shoes, which hold immense magical power. (Incidentally, the shoes started out belonging to the Wicked Witch of the West's sister, the Wicked Witch of the East, but were taken by Dorothy after Dorothy's house flattened the Eastern-dwelling sorceress.) In 1939, Metro-Goldwyn-Mayer screenwriter Noel Langley decided that for the film based on the book, Dorothy's silver shoes would be red slippers. Today, Langley's version of the shoes, those ruby slippers, are a world-recognized icon.

As we all remember, it's the ruby slippers that hold the power to correct all Dorothy's problems—namely, get her back home to Kansas.

"There's no place like home" is one of the most-quoted lines of movie script anywhere in history, and it's all centered around Dorothy's red pumps and their magical powers. (On May 24, 2000, Hollywood movie memorabilia collector David Elkouby paid $600,000 for the shoes worn by Judy Garland in the film version, *The Wizard of Oz,* at a Hollywood auction in New York City.)

Shoes are more than icons of change. They're symbols of power, good luck and control. Think of all the songs that have been written about shoes. Nancy Sinatra's "These Boots Were Made for Walking" told of her ability to walk out on a man as well as to "walk all over" him, equating boots to a powerful weapon of revenge. Elvis Presley's "Blue Suede Shoes" told the story of a man who would let another fellow "knock me down, step on my face, slander my name all over the place ... burn my house, steal my car, drink my liquor from my old fruit jar." Pretty much anything was okay, just as long as the antagonist did not "step on my blue suede shoes."

Shoes have even changed our language. Consider the following ideas and expressions: "give him the boot," "on a shoestring," "fill one's shoes," "put yourself in my shoes," "the shoe is on the other foot now," "goody two-shoes," "bet your boots," "die with your boots on," "lick his boots," "pull yourself up by your bootstraps," "walk a mile in my shoes," "heart in your shoes," "well-heeled" and "put on your dancin' shoes."

Ruth Tanenhous, author of "The Great American Foot," wrote that "in an average lifetime, our feet carry us over 65,000 miles, more than two and a half times around the world," so why wouldn't we consider our shoes important?

Indeed, a web page that no longer exists used to list Emma Peel's boots as the most important attraction at the Planet Hollywood restaurant in Las Vegas. Who was Emma Peel, you ask? She was the saucy, martial arts-kicking female do-gooder of *The Avengers* TV show fame—but that doesn't really matter. What matters is that her shoes were cited ahead of James Bond's trick car devices and Theda Bara's headdress in a description of Las Vegas museums on the Internet.

Anyway, you get my point. Shoes are pretty darn important.

They get us out of trouble, they carry us off to better places, they let us see new horizons and they allow us to know our world. And they accessorize with everything!

In the morning—if 1 A.M. counts as morning—Ann, William and I arose and toiled up five kilometers of frozen gravel to the summit of Kilimanjaro, where, predictably, we ran smack into a crowd, all milling about in the dawn light and celebrating their few minutes of glory on top of Africa.

Three German tourists wearing huge, neon-green Koflach plastic mountaineering boots stood side-by-side with local guides wearing leather street shoes. A British couple in $200-a-pair leather hiking boots and gaiters, slapped the backs of a Tanzanian porter—an apprentice guide who was wearing a pair of lightweight vinyl cross-country skiing shoes. And I hung around with William, in his knock-off Adidas boats six sizes too big and now that I really studied them hideously ugly.

We descended back to camp, packed up and then turned our attention to the descent through the forests. Our mini-expedition was an enormous success, and we were ready to celebrate our incredible, historic achievement—even though we were just three of 70 who submitted that day.

One of the most important aspects of mountain climbing is bragging rights. Mountain climbers dote on their ability to report not only making a summit, but making it by "fair means," or in a way that is more challenging than the way most other climbers have made the ascent.

In 1968, two one-legged Austrians, Otto Umlauf and Thomas Karcher, who were crippled during World War II, climbed Kilimanjaro. In 1981, Swiss mountaineer Fritz Lortscher reported that he had climbed Kilimanjaro at least 33 times.

But these achievements seem small when one considers that many of the guides and porters from the village of Marangu have not only climbed the mountain over 200 times, they've also done it in totally junk footwear.

And here, perhaps, is the kicker—they choose to climb the mountain in their crappy shoes.

A few days after our first climb up the mountain, Ann and I bumped into Mohammed on the streets of Moshi, the small town sitting at the base of the mountain. He was with a group of fellow locals, all vying for a job portering for the next round of tourists.

We noticed Mohammed was wearing very nice, very new hiking boots, a far cry from the beach thongs and crummy sneakers he'd worn on the mountain. We pulled him aside and politely grilled him about his footwear.

"These?" he asked in response to our accusatory fingers. "These are my good shoes. I wouldn't want to take them up on the mountain. I wouldn't want to ruin them. I use my old shoes up there, where it doesn't matter if they get damaged."

As I watched Mohammed walk back across the street to rejoin the group of porters all vying for a week's employment, something similar to what Ernest Hemingway had written 60 years ago came to mind.

"There, ahead, all he could see, as crappy as any product in all the world, tragic, worthless, and unbelievably flimsy on the trail, were the shoes of Kilimanjaro."

Taking Off with Buddha

by Thomas E. Stazyk

OUR NINTH WEDDING ANNIVERSARY was celebrated in the tiny national airport of Bhutan. It was not, shall we say, a piece of cake.

Unless you are in a nomadic tribe, you can only enter Bhutan via the national airline, Druk Air. *Druk* means dragon in Bhutanese but Dreck Air might be more like it. The one city in Bhutan with an airport is Paro, a farming community of 18,000 selected because it is in the only place reasonably close to the capital, Thimphu, where the weather and mountains make an airport possible. And that's pushing it. To quote from the user friendly Druk Air in-flight magazine:

"Owing to the unique conditions under which we operate, we at Druk Air felt the need to suggest a few tips to our valued clients to make their journey a pleasant and comfortable experience.

"As we operate from an airport that is 'daylight restricted' and totally dependent on weather, flights can sometimes be delayed. It is suggested that passengers keep at least 24 hours transit time for connecting flights out of Paro. It is also advisable to travel on non-restricted tickets so that if a connection is missed, it can be re-routed or 'endorsed' onto another carrier on the first available flight.

"Flights into Paro can also at times be disrupted due to unfavorable weather conditions. Under such circumstances, the flight halts the night at transit stations. In order to be prepared for such an event, it is advised to carry essential personal items like medicines, toiletries, minimum change, etc. in the hand baggage at the transit station."

My wife Mahrukh and I like to consider ourselves experienced travelers. But this was even more than we bargained for, particularly since Bhutan was just one stop on a trip that was to take us to Nepal, India, Hong Kong, Tokyo and New Zealand to mark our nine years of wedded bliss. It was early May, 2001.

The evening before we left Kathmandu for Paro we got a call from Druk Air advising us that our flight was being changed from 10:45 A.M. to 7:30 A.M. to beat some bad weather. It sounded a little odd, but we went ahead and called the travel agent to arrange for an early trip to the airport.

The next morning we learned what really had happened. Two days earlier, a flight out of Paro had been canceled due to weather. In attempting to put the plane in the hangar for the night the ground crew missed the door and knocked a piece off one of the wings.

So the mighty dragon had its wings clipped, literally and figuratively. But not to fear. Our friends at Druk Air had friends at Buddha Air and they were going to get us from Katmandu to Paro in an 18-seat shuttle service over the Himalayas. Lovely!

We met a number of fellow travelers at the airport. One was a German with UNICEF who was a veteran Bhutan traveler. He told us about a group of tourists who were once stranded in Bhutan for ten days. He also informed us that Druk Air's other plane (it has a fleet of two) was also out of commission. Hence Buddha Air to the rescue.

Much to our amazement, the 7:30 flight actually left about 8. Even more to our amazement, there was a snack and drink service and the stewardess and pilot pointed out the different

Himalayan peaks as we flew over them.

"Uh, this *is* the way to Paro, isn't it?" I wanted to ask the pilot as we threaded our way among some of the world's highest mountains. Our 90-minute flight was actually pretty pleasant until we landed. Paro is on a plateau in a valley and (we didn't know it at the time) the plane has to thread its way among the peaks during approach, sort of like the opening credits of *Where Eagles Dare*. The landing gear was out and the plane was definitely descending. I looked out the front windows—there was no separation between us and the cockpit—and we were heading straight toward a mountain. At what seemed like the last minute we made a 90-degree turn and started heading at another mountain. Hairpin turns in an airplane are not like in a car—it actually felt like we were going forward and sideways at the same time. This went on until finally I saw a runway about the size of a driveway. The plane bounced along and did a U-turn at the end to get to the terminal since there are no taxiways. Some passengers clapped. Religious artifacts were in wide evidence.

We had a fantastic five-day holiday in Bhutan and never ceased to be impressed with the country, its people and their culture. Bhutan is about the size of Switzerland and has a population of 770,000. Bhutan only opened for tourists in the 1980s and currently there is a quota of 7,000 tourists per year. To give you an idea of what the scale of the country is like, we learned that tourism is the largest industry. There is almost no industry and consequently no pollution. The country is very isolationist, which is understandable, being stuck between India and China, but everyone we met was unfailingly polite and friendly (even the cops). Clothing and architectural styles are mandated and enforced by the government. According to our guide, locals can be fined if they don't wear the national

costume in public. The men's costume is known as *gho*. It con-
sists of a knee-length robe tied at the waist, black socks up to
the knees, dark shoes and a shawl draped over the shoulder.

Our guide told us many interesting things. For example, it
is the duty of the husband to look after his wife's family. In
addition, polygamy is accepted as long as all parties agree to
it. There are women with several husbands as well as men with
several wives. Marriage is basically considered a formality. For
example, the king has four wives (four sisters), and he married them all on the same day. Apparently, the king, who is
about 49, does not live with any of the wives. They each have
their own palace, and he stays in a small cottage near the official government offices.

The current king is only the fourth they have had since
Bhutan becoming independent. English is the official language,
and we had no problem communicating with the locals.
Mahrukh and I thoroughly enjoyed Bhutan as one of the most
unique places we've visited. It was clean, beautiful, serene and
we felt as if we had stepped back in time. But all good things
must come to an end. On the day of our anniversary we headed
back to Paro airport for our trip to Delhi. We were scheduled
to leave on Sunday, May 6, at noon and by 10:30 A.M. I was
feeling pretty good. We were all checked in, the plane was there
and we met up with a number of the people we had gotten to
know during our trip. (Bhutan has limited hotels and tourist
spots, so you make acquaintances quickly.) Perhaps things
would go right after all.

We were chatting with our new friends when Mahrukh
pointed out a balding, older gentleman and a younger man,
both dressed in Buddhist monk robes. We had seen a lot of
Buddhist monks during the trip, and these guys were definitely not locals. The older man was French and told us with

an "I know something you don't know" tone that he had been a scientist and became a Buddhist monk in his 30s. The younger one was German and was attached to a Vietnamese Buddhist monastery in Germany. We were all having a great conversation when boarding began. We all shook hands and got in line at the door, waited about 20 minutes and then heard an announcement that the flight would be delayed a half-hour because of "excessive heat."

No one quite understood that, since it was warm and sunny outside, but definitely not hot. We assumed that the engines had overheated on the flight in or something. This was the first of many rumors that would swirl around us during the day.

We sat down and the older monk joined us. I couldn't resist asking him, "What do you do all day?" The answer was vague but distilled down to, "Pretty much whatever I feel like." His teaching, praying and other duties seemed fairly light. A number of people drifted over to listen in on the conversation. One was a bearded French man who sat quietly for a while, then excitedly burst in with a question. He called the monk "Your Excellency" or "Your Grace" or something like that. His question was hostile and argumentative. Our friend did a great job of managing the situation. Unfortunately, this only excited the guy even more, so he kept asking the same question in different ways. I was thinking, "Oh boy, a religious war in a Third World airport" when the monk finally got fed up and cut him off with, "Well, that's one way to look at it."

Oh, but if it were only so easy to ignore all adversity!

The announcer came on again. The flight would be delayed another half an hour. Anyone who travels by air and has been on a delayed flight knows this is a Very Bad Sign. Those half-hour increments have a way of adding up to a really nasty delay. Plus, who does the airline think it's kidding? I believe everyone would prefer if they would just say, "Ladies and gentlemen, we have no idea what's going on and don't know when or if the plane will leave so sit down, shut up and stop bothering us."

The travelers settled into that twilight/limbo/purgatory/hell that all people on delayed flights endure—people watching, clock watching, people watching with irritation, reading, people watching with thoughts of premeditated murder and eavesdropping on conversations of people who sound like they know what is going on. At least we were blessed by having interesting people to talk to, which did make things marginally tolerable.

Rumors circulated. One theory was bad weather at our destination. Another man claimed he saw a fire engine approach the plane to hose off the engines and cool them down (very reassuring). A third rumor was that the crew had overstepped the shift time limit and a new crew was being driven from Thimphu, an hour and a half away. Whatever, it kept delaying the flight further in half-hour increments.

I started chatting with an English couple. The husband complained hilariously about his job. "I don't know which it is I hate more, the company or just the idea of working." His wife complained hilariously about life in London.

At about 2:30, an announcement came. The plane now would leave at 5 P.M. and in the meantime, Druk Air would take us all to lunch. Three different-sized and labeled vans pulled up at the airport exit and we piled in for who knew where. I wondered to Mahrukh about walking past security and passport control where no one appeared to be in a position of authority.

Our van arrived at a dubious-looking hotel/restaurant and

we were told the restaurant was full. By the time we were finally seated a new theory for our delay had emerged. Because of canceled flights over the past few days, our flight was packed with people and baggage and therefore too heavy to lift off in the thin mountain air. We were waiting for the air to cool down (heat makes air thinner) before we could leave

After lunch we returned to the airport where Mahrukh struck up a conversation with a Druk Air employee, who confirmed that the delay was indeed something out of thin air. The temperature now was satisfactory, and we would be taking off at 5.

At about 5 they announced we would be taking off as soon as we all had tea and biscuits. "Why don't we just leave if everything is okay?" we asked each other, especially because half the sky had turned black and it was now raining fairly hard. As we were eating our snacks a new rumor began to circulate—that the temperature had dropped so much that we might be able to accommodate six standby passengers if it were to go down a little more. So we were going to wait until 6 o'clock to see.

Forgive me, but I had no sympathy for those standby passengers, whoever they were. For one thing, taking on more passengers implied a science and specificity to the weight/lift calculations that I didn't like. Can they really measure the incremental impact of one person on the plane's lift? And most of all, it was pouring rain and 6 o'clock was getting perilously close to sundown—witching hour for Druk Air (remember "daylight restricted?").

Well, something went right because we started boarding at 5:45, and the plane was indeed full. Then we got another nasty piece of information. Six hours earlier, we had seen the captain of our plane. He refused to fly in the prevailing conditions and walked out, to be replaced by a pilot from Thimphu.

Needless to say, we all held our breath as we took off (straight at the mountains) and were wondering about lift ratios and air density when at about 50 feet off the ground the pilot put the pedal to the metal.

We made our stop in Kathmandu and then made it to Delhi, missing our planned anniversary dinner but making our connection to Hong Kong. Upon landing (after dark) in Delhi we were informed that there would be no more Druk Air flights until the next morning, but, "please come back and see us again."

A Thousand Times, Non

by Eileen Mitchell

AFTER FIVE YEARS of friendship, you think you know someone. So when a friend suggested a vacation to Paris together,
it seemed like a great idea.

Baguettes and brie? Oui, oui!

Non, non!

She started with the weather. It was too windy. Too hot.
Too cold. Then, why had I selected *this* table to eat at because
there was a smoker two tables down? Why doesn't France, no,
make that the rest of the world, make smoking in restaurants
illegal anyway? What's wrong with these people? Damn foreigners.

Offering to treat was quickly rebuffed. She can pay her own
way, thank you very much. She doesn't need to rely on the
charity of others so I can put away my precious money and
where's that damn waiter? She thinks he's trying to rip her off
because her Vichyssoise Crème Glacee surely couldn't have
cost that much. Damn foreigners.

A drive to the countryside was no different. No, I couldn't
drive because she's the one who is the better driver and she's
never had an accident before. I have been rear-ended twice,
so where do I get off telling her to slow down even though she
just ran two consecutive red lights and is now blocking traffic and cars are honking but there isn't anyplace we can move.
Yes, Miriam, I believe flipping the bird *is* a universal symbol

because those people look mighty upset at your gesture. Serves them right. Damn foreigners.

And I come to truly regret that I won the coin toss and got the bed while she got the pullout. There were the nightly groans over the uncomfortable mattress with springs that would be forever imprinted on her back. When I offered to switch, she reminded me every single day, "No, not with your bad back. I couldn't do that do you, what kind of friend do you think I am?" I'm guessing one who favors mental torture as the preferred affliction of pain.

Hey, had I touched her map? She had left it on the end table and now it was on the coffee table and how could she expect to find anything in this dump of an apartment if I kept moving things around like that? Had I asked her permission to look at it anyway? Where were my manners? And speaking of manners, would I mind not using the toaster when she was asleep because it was unusually loud and yes, as a matter of fact, she *could* hear the bagel toasting, and excuse her if she's a late riser and doesn't get up till 9 A.M., I don't really have to eat breakfast in the morning, do I?

And so it went, for ten excruciating days. People and their damn dogs. Mothers and their damn crying babies. Men and their damn leers. Are they checking her out? Hey, why aren't they checking her out? Damn foreign men!

By the time we returned home, I was exhausted. Walking on eggshells is mighty tiresome. As we stood at the luggage carousal, all I could think about was getting as far away as possible. Then I spotted a tweed suitcase, wet with some goopy substance and ripped apart with its contents streaming out. She saw it too and muttered something about the poor sucker who owned that piece.

That would be moi.

But I was too browbeaten to get mad. And I'd survived. A torn suitcase was nothing.

And then she said, "Well, that was fun! How about Spain next year?"

Ay carumba.

My Tex-Mex Cowboy

by Renée Owen

When I first met Jake, he sold used rental cars and wore a pocket-pen protector stuffed full of ballpoint pens with his company's logo. His hair looked like it had been cut with sheep shears and he wore cowboy boots everywhere he went. I was sure I'd found a diamond in the rough, and spent many months polishing my gem. He soon became successfully self-employed and looked like a stud from the pages of *GQ* magazine. Well, sort of. He still wore his old cowboy boots, even in 95 degree Mexican heat. I, on the other hand, needed no polishing. I was a hot, twenty something Texan babe—big hair, push-up bra cleavage, skin-tight white jeans and 4-inch spiked "F. Me Pump" heels. I was made for romance.

Jake was one of my brighter stars in a long-running succession of serial monogamy—depressing except for the plenitude and the innocent hope that the next one would be It. Most were short-lived, as I or they would flee in terror at the first mention of the "C" word—commitment! But my romance with Jake had lasted a year. We decided to celebrate by taking a trip together—somewhere sunny and sexy. We finally settled on Puerto Vallarta. It was my first trip to Mexico.

We envisioned this as a romantic interlude from our busy lives. But getting to Mexico, by shuttle bus, plane and then taxi, ended up being a very long and tedious journey. By the time we arrived at our hotel, we were sweaty, hot and exhausted, sleep deprived, jet lagged and culture shocked. Surely it would be different once we checked in, had a swim and a stiff drink. We were, after all, from Texas.

We were greeted graciously by the hotel desk clerk, our passport to the oasis. "*Buenos dias Senora, Senor.*" But they had no trace of our prepaid reservations and no vacant rooms. Even in my delirious state, I was sure we'd be able to work something out. But Jake was, well, Jake. You can take the cowboy out of the barn, but you can't exactly take the barn out of the cowboy. I cringed with embarrassment and quickly walked away to avoid the scene that was brewing.

They eventually materialized a room for us. "But *Senor,* you must pay us for the room now, so sorry." Jake exploded. "You ass! Here's the prepaid receipt—can't you read?" Jake continued to refuse to pay for the room a second time. His face swelled, and he insisted that we take the first cab that could get us back to the airport. They dialed up a taxi, feeling more than ready to be rid of us. I was eventually able to rein in his foaming-at-the-mouth gallop. He began to relax after I agreed to charge our hotel stay on my credit card. I hoped our travel agent would work out the details later. Just a language problem, or some such silliness, I thought to myself.

Our room turned out to be fine, as those huge multiple-story hotels go. A Disney-Worldish swim-up bar, faux-tropical foliage and everything neat and tidy. Locals dressed as postcard Mexicans in full tourist-drag awaited our beck and call.

We rose early the next morning, eager to soak up some sun. Jake seemed bored until I paraded around the pool in my *minusculo* bikini, flirting with all the good-looking bartenders. He refused to leave my side after that and started turning on the charm. I noticed a group of matronly ladies nearby, giggling and staring hungrily at his bulging biceps. Maybe there was a chance for romance after all, I mused. After a long day at the pool, Jake suggested we dress up for dinner at the fancy hotel restaurant with the oh-so-beautiful sea view. After dinner, as we walked on the moonlit beach, I began feeling feverish and hot. Perhaps Jake's seduction tactics were working their spell on me, I thought.

An hour later, back at our room, chills began racking my fevered body. Cowboy Jake had every blanket in the hotel piled on top of me. I spent most of a sleepless night in the *bano*. Each time I threw up, Jake stood as far away from the bathroom as possible and yelled, "Darlin' ... are you all right?" Being too weak the next day to venture far, the very sight and smell of food left me gripping my bowels. I chose the wiser course, abstaining from most everything, including Jake.

A day or so passed in a heat-filled haze of sleep and alcohol. Jake insisted we partake of an "adventure." He'd planned it all while I was nursing myself back to health with sun and pina coladas. He raved that we would rent a jeep, spend the day exploring, then head south and east into the mountains to a rustic restaurant next to a waterfall for dinner. Now I knew what this was really about. It was the jeep. The rest of the plan was just an excuse for the cowboy to fulfill his fantasy of Marlboro man astride his mechanized horse. But I felt guilty as all get out for forcing a nursemaid role on this poor guy, and for having no energy to go anywhere or do anything (much less be romantic). So against my better judgment, I agreed.

It was a long hot day in the saddle, as Jake rented a manly jeep with no top. "Look sweetie, I scored the last convertible. Can you believe it?" No, I thought, hours later when my forearms broke out in a prickly heat rash from being exposed to the direct sun for hours. I gripped the rails tightly and hoped I'd survive John Wayne's day behind the wheel. He played chicken with the speeding taxi drivers, who rallied to his game by cursing us in Spanish, then nearly sending us off the seaside cliffs as they passed us on the narrow two-lane road. Not a minute too soon, it was finally time for our side-trip to the gorgeous restaurant.

Visions of jungle foliage surrounding a pristine waterfall played out in my heat-frenzied mind. But then there were a few wrong turns. Many actually, and no chance that John Wayne would stoop to ask for directions. "How'd we even understand them?" he'd shouted at me over the roar of the wind. I yelled back, "How about the ancient sign language for directions—you know, pointing?" He looked at me with malice and hit the gas hard, barely controlling the careening jeep.

It was dusk by the time we stumbled upon the restaurant's unlit sign off the main road, way, way out of town. The sign pointed up a dark and bumpy dirt road winding into the mountains. A very bad road, actually—rutted and washed out—perfect for a horse, not a jeep. Jake gripped the reins with glee and took off at a bruising pace, his hormone-driven energy silencing my whimpers and misgivings. We passed several thatch houses where locals stared out at us as if we were aliens. No *holas* or nods, just chilly stares. It got darker and darker as we wound up this road. I refused to continue pretending this dirt trail was a road, but Jake wouldn't listen to reason until he was forced to. I screamed out a warning that there was a herd of cows ahead. He wouldn't slow down.

The closer we got, the more it seemed as if the cows were hastening to block his way, if cows can hasten. The cowboy rudely blared his horn and flashed his lights, until several of the larger cows plopped themselves down across the path. They refused to budge and stared at us menacingly. A showdown ensued. "Move your fat asses, if you value your hide," he yelled as he edged the jeep closer to the cows. The beasts looked unconcerned at his antics and continued to stare, which infuriated him even more. He cursed, threatened and banged his fists, to no avail. In the end, he didn't really have the guts to run them over.

Jake drove down that mountain trail like there was no tomorrow. I feared there wouldn't be a tomorrow, at that speed in the dark. Recognizing that any effort to use reason was doomed to failure, I did what any upstanding Mexican woman might do under these circumstances—I prayed.

It was a long, silent meal in the hotel restaurant that night, in which I was still determined not to eat. "Suit yourself," he said as he wolfed down his steak and baked potato. The rest of the trip marked the beginning of a long and protracted ending for my (un)romance with the cowboy. But he never did give up that jeep. One day with it turned into many as he flashed his credit card without a thought. I think he may still be driving that jeep around Texas somewhere, on the long hot roads that stretch to nowhere. *Adios, amigo!*

Stars and a Stranger

by Nadine Michele Payn

NIGHT ARRIVES IMMEDIATELY after the sun disappears below the high horizon. Before I've gone more than a few hundred yards past the village center, I'm enveloped in a blackness that's total and soft, as if some night spirit has swathed me in a velvet shroud. No electricity, no flashlight, no moon to light the dusty path. I slow my pace, sliding my sandaled feet along the dirt ruts made by the yak carts. Then I glance upward and see the stars. Freed from the garish glare of civilization, they glow unabashedly. Not enough to illuminate my way back to the hotel but enough to inspire awe. Where do I end and the stars begin? I don't know, but here in a Himalayan valley along the Indus River, I relax and feel at peace.

Suddenly my hand brushes against a man walking in silence beside me. With a start I remember I'm not alone in a benign universe. I'm walking beside this man from Afghanistan I had met only two hours ago. I'm on a deserted road, the village of Leh shuttered behind me, the hotel whose name I've forgotten somewhere up ahead.

My heart pounds like a tabla drum as my vulnerability sinks in. The man seemed sweet enough in his jewelry shop, even gallant. But I wouldn't have accepted his offer to escort me to my hotel had I any idea that twilight didn't exist in Ladakh, India. I should have known that fact given this nation of brilliant colors and high contrasts, jewel-encrusted, silk-adorned wealth and dung-stinking, fly-swarming poverty. There are no pastels in India. Why shouldn't night follow day without the middle hues of dusk?

I pretend I'm dreaming and will wake up safe in day's reassuring light. My sandal strikes a sharp stone on the road and punctures my pretensions. Fear sears my insides. *This is real.*

I'm alone with stars and a stranger.

How did I let myself borrow trouble? It started when I signed up for a low-cost tour of Northern India that was going to places I had dreamed of and whose names had the rhythm of poetry: Khatmandu, Agra, Varanasi, Khajuraho, Jaipur, Srinagar, Ladakh. Ladakh was as close as you could get, geographically and spiritually, to Tibet.

The India itinerary was to travel by van from Srinagar, Kashmir, to Ladakh by way of the Himalaya. There were eight tourists including me and the tour leader, Raesh Gopandur. Only my fascination with India enabled me to endure traveling in close quarters for three weeks with people I didn't care for. In fairness, the tall podiatrist Bob and his quiet blond wife Millie were okay. They were intelligent and respectful of Indian culture. And I learned a lot about feet. Also along was a 60-something John Wayne double who was in fact named John. He was anything but heroic. John and his shorter buddy Frank had come to "do" India. They were bored just about everywhere but the Taj Mahal and the duty-free shops at Delhi airport. Stocky Josie, whose white straw hat was always clean and perfectly balanced on her short black hair, complained about the heat and insects. And Rhoda, who was tanned and muscled, routinely tossed her olive rucksack onto the best seat in the tour van, an unstuck window that offered air and view and was far from the rear axle's rough ride.

What I hated most about Josie and Rhoda, besides their

ignoring me and lack of awe for India, is that they met Elsie, the fourth single woman, at the pre-trip planning meeting I could not attend. Sizing Elsie up instantly, they colluded to pawn her off on me. I was only a nametag without a body then, so I understand that their move was an impersonal survival tactic. Thus, Josie and Rhoda shared a room, and I was paired in absentia with Elsie. I silently cursed them for their accurate instincts when I arrived jet lagged and headachy in my Delhi hotel room and discovered that Elsie had divided all bathroom objects in half, towels, washcloths, soaps, water glasses, matchbooks and toilet paper rolls. She had created an invisible Berlin Wall that I was forbidden to cross.

My timing was always rotten with her. I opened the curtains to let in the sun and enjoy a breathtaking view of Delhi from our 16-story hotel just when Elsie wanted to take an afternoon nap. I rattled the pages of my novel just as she decided to retire for the night. I turned on my long-awaited shower just when she wanted to brush her teeth. I ordered a pungent curry just as she concluded she couldn't tolerate the smell of lamb. She chastised me in her clipped Germanic accent when I rumpled the bathmat in our Lake Dal houseboat. When I saw her swimming alone late one afternoon in a stagnant pool whose green water I was about to risk my life entering, I nearly turned back. But I was hot, dusty and desperate for a dip. I camouflaged my chagrin with a cheery, "Hi Elsie, how's the water?" "How should I know?" barked Elsie, without a break in her backstroke. Stunned, I slid into the slime. Elsie flutter-kicked furiously to the shallow end of the pool and pointedly climbed out, leaving me alone with the growing swarm of mosquitoes.

That's when I'd had it.

Elsie's relentless provocations could only be blocked if I

paid a budget-breaking supplement for a single room. Ramesh was not happy with disharmony in the ranks, but neither did he want to exert himself to procure extra accommodations along our itinerary. I alternated between helpless supplicant and irate consumer. Finally I got my room. Elsie benefited from my abdication by not having to pay the extra tariff for solo occupancy. Yet, for the remainder of the voyage, her icy glares were the closest thing to air-conditioning in the 106-degree heat.

On a sun-filled Kashmiri morning a week into our trip, we were about to depart for Ladakh in a tarnished blue van. My throat was scratchy and my forehead feverish, though I realized these could be symptoms of stress. I asked Ramesh how long the van journey to Ladakh would take, wondering if I could handle it.

"Oh, not bad. About nine hours. We go through Zojila Pass and take a rest stop at Kargil. Then on past Lamarayu and down to Leh, the main town of Ladakh. It's a spectacular ride really."

It was imperative for me to get a good seat on the van. Bouncing over the rooftop of the world would not enhance my health. My luggage and I were beside the van uncharacteristically early, before the others showed up. I selected a right-side window seat in the first row behind the driver.

Soon Rhoda climbed into the van, ready to toss her rucksack like a shotput onto her target seat. She was astounded to see me there. With a blend of surprise and outrage, she hollered, "Nadine, you're sitting in my seat. That's my seat!"

"I don't see your name on it," I retorted, fed up with being amiable, and added, "It's not written anywhere that you get to have the best seat every time we ride."

"You have to give me that seat. I always sit there."

"Not this time. I'm not getting up."

In Rhoda's world of entitlement, it never occurred to her that I might put up a fight. But emboldened by my fever, I didn't budge. She stomped to a lumpy seat behind me, and I knew that war had been declared. "The enemy of my enemy is my friend," and now Elsie, whom Rhoda held in contempt, was to be her ally against me. I pressed my hot forehead against the cool windowpane and vowed to focus on what I came for: the privilege of visiting a remote and sacred region. As the other passengers settled themselves in the van, our driver jumped in and started the engine. It coughed, spluttered, then caught, and we lurched westward from Srinagar toward the snowcapped Himalaya.

The nine-hour ride turned into 40 hours during which we ate only one meal, our van broke down seven times, and we had to hitch a ride in another van while our driver went begging for a fan belt. My sore throat worsened, and when at last we arrived in our dimly lit hotel lobby, I was informed that a single room had not been reserved for me. I would have to bed with Elsie.

With great embarrassment I confess I had a temper tantrum directed at Ramesh for his negligence in this important matter. The entire tour group and hotel staff watched me in disapproving silence. So dedicated was Elsie to my misfortunes that even though she was about to become my fellow victim in Ramesh's mistake, she smirked triumphantly.

After a long and painful interval during which I was treated like a leper by the group, I was assigned a single room kept in reserve for visiting Indian VIPs. I regarded the brass key attached to a circle of rough wood as a finer treasure than any jewel bestowed by Moghul Emperor Shah Jahan on his beloved wife Mumtaz. Once inside my sanctuary, I fell onto my bed, and before I had time to dream, it was morning.

Because our arrival in Leh had been delayed by a day, and we were scheduled to fly to Delhi the following morning, Ramesh decided to compress two days of sights into one. We'd been on the go from 7 A.M. to 4 P.M., visiting three spectacular Buddhist monasteries, and now we had free time before dinner. I decided to forego a nap and wander into town. Needless to say, no one was interested in accompanying me. I grabbed my purse, key and camera and started down the dirt road just outside the hotel. I passed a swimming hole on my right and paused to watch slender children jump with glee into the dirty water. Their splashes and laughter followed me down the road as it curved to the left, sloped downhill and became the main and only street in the town of Leh.

I walked in fascination past small shops, stalls and clusters of women. Their unusual black stovepipe hats and garments contrasted with the colorful orange, red and yellow produce they were selling. The brown faces of the women were wizened and their teeth rotten. Their bursts of giggles punctured the thin mountain air. They hadn't sold much but were having a grand time. They grinned at me, delighted to be photographed. On my left I noticed a jewelry shop and made a mental note to stop in after I visited the open-air market at the end of the street. A young man observed my glance and beckoned me to come in. His manner was gracious rather than insistent, and I indicated smilingly I'd come by later.

The market, at the base of the dusty Himalaya, did not disappoint me, and in a joyful delirium I shot my last roll of film. There were many local families hunting for supplies, but, to my relief, I saw no one from my tour group. I was told that Leh was a stop on the fabled Silk Road, and soon I was lost in time. The orange sun dropped low in the sky, and my last loving shot was of two girls, about six years old, in bright cotton shirts balancing terra cotta urns on their heads. What the jugs contained I didn't know, but I imagined them filled with salt and spices in resplendent earth colors.

I returned to the storefronts and easily found the jewelry shop. The young man was waiting for me. He was quite handsome, now that I appraised him more carefully. He had shiny black hair, pale skin, large brown eyes, high cheekbones and an aquiline nose. He wore a long white shirt, lightly embroidered with shiny thread and looked to be in his early 20s. I longed to photograph him and rued the fact that I'd run out of film.

The shop was dark and narrow with a glass counter at the rear. As I looked at rings of silver with turquoise and coral stones and bangle bracelets and prayer wheels, the young man asked where I was from. I was pleased he hadn't immediately pegged me as an American, though, in spite of my sari, I clearly didn't hail from the Indian subcontinent. I told him I came from California and asked if he had grown up in Ladakh. "Oh no, I'm from Afghanistan," the stranger exclaimed with pride. My focus swung from the rings to his face, and the person became more important than the trinkets. My college boyfriend had joined the Peace Corps and was sent to Afghanistan. To us in those days, we thought the assignment was akin to exile in Siberia. Somewhere in a box at home I have a collection of two years of air mail letters from Kabul and Kandahar, and I had followed with interest the developments of the Soviet invasion in 1979. It was now 1986, and I knew about the *mujahedeen* and fierce fighting in rugged terrain.

"What's your name?" I asked the young man.

"Tarik. What is yours?" I told him and peppered him with questions. "Are you from Kabul? Did you learn English in school? Were you a mujahedeen? How did you get to India from Afghanistan?"

Tarik was patient with my exuberant interrogation.

"Yes, I am from Kabul. I learned English at school. My father was a shopkeeper. I was 13 when the Russians invaded. We hated them, but our family tried to go about our lives and stay out of it. Life got harder and harder. When I was 15, we took what belongings we could carry and got to the border, near Jalalabad. Then we walked through the mountain passes and reached Pakistan. The trip was very difficult. We were all cold, scared, tired and hungry. We had connections in India. My family is in Delhi now, and I'm here, trying to earn money so I can go to University."

Tarik was earnest as he talked, seemingly open and without guile. I was impressed with his family's escape and his own drive to better his life. I was delighted that fate brought me to a person whose life experience was so different from mine. Tarik exuded warmth and an equal curiosity about my life. As we continued our dialogue, I was amazed at how comfortable I felt—me, an ex-New Yorker, a psychologist, a woman on the down slope to 40—chatting cozily with this 20-year-old Muslim merchant. A mood filled the little shop like vapor from a genie's magic lamp, a softening of boundaries, a blurring of nationality, ethnicity, race, gender. We felt like old friends. My best chum in Berkeley would have remarked, "Obviously you knew each other in a past life."

A glance at my watch brought me back to this life and the fact that it was nearly dinner time. I returned to my original purpose: bringing home souvenirs. I narrowed down Tarik's many lovely wares to a silver ring, a stone-studded Buddhist prayer wheel and a tiny reliquary in hues of ivory and amber. I began the customary bargaining, and we settled on a fair price.

Tarik wrapped my purchases in paper with the care one would expect from Tiffany's and presented the packet to me with a flourish. Again I kicked myself for running out of film and losing the chance to photograph his noble face. I shook Tarik's hand, said my farewells and turned toward the doorway.

"Wait, Miss Nadine, it's time for me to close the shop. Might I be permitted to escort you to your hotel?" Tarik's request was so politely and quaintly put, I found it difficult to resist. An internal struggle between my paranoid and trusting sides resulted in consent. Tarik turned off the single dim light, locked the door to his shop, and we headed out. Within two minutes, as we strode past the last store, the curtain of night descended. I noticed all the shop lights were extinguished.

"Why is the electricity out?" I asked nervously. "It's dark everywhere."

"We don't need light any more," answered Tarik evenly.

I wasn't reassured, but I didn't challenge Tarik's pronouncement. We both became silent. I wondered if this was a comfortable silence between friends or an uneasy prelude to something sinister. But the stars commanded my attention and drew me from worry into reverie.

The accidental brush of Tarik's hand, skin on skin, subtle, seductive, brought me back to fear: I'm alone with stars and a stranger. Tarik was silent still. I attempted to calm myself with measured breathing. As in a parable, we arrived at a fork in the road. Tarik's voice startled me out of my morbid thoughts.

"Which way to your hotel?" he asked.

"To the right," I replied.

But everything changed in the night world, and I was no longer sure of my direction. We walked further; nothing seemed the same.

"What's the name of your hotel?"

I couldn't remember. I was there so briefly. But it would be on the key. I dug it out of my daypack. My hand clasped the cool brass, and I peered at the wooden tag. Even in the dark, we both realized—no name, not even a room number.

"Can you tell me names of the hotels in Leh?" I asked. "I might recognize it. There are only a few." Tarik claimed ignorance about hotels. How could this be when he runs a souvenir shop? Fear clutched me again.

I remembered the children and the pond. A marker. I told Tarik the pond would be on the left; it was close to the hotel. This bit of information failed to enlighten him. We walked on. No pond.

Soon we glimpsed shadows walking toward us. As they approached I saw they were men. "Oh, let's ask them if they know about hotels," I exclaimed excitedly. I felt Tarik's immediate tension; he grabbed my wrist hard.

"Be quiet. Don't say a word. I'll give a normal greeting. These types are trouble. They may have knives." He quickened his pace as we passed, still holding me firmly. His hand was sweaty now.

Tarik was afraid!

In that instant I knew with certainty that Tarik would not harm me. Yet my fear intensified because I knew also with certainty that Tarik was aware of the danger from others. This stranger was my friend after all, but he was a slender man of 20. He was unarmed and could not protect me.

I felt very alone.

We had to find the hotel. I didn't know if I was feeling Tarik's fear or my own. I wasn't sure if he feared harm to himself or the inevitable dishonor and guilt if something dire were to happen to me, a guest in his adopted land. I was afraid to ask. Suddenly I spotted the glow of electricity off to the right, through some trees and underbrush.

"Tarik, that might be the hotel!"

Tarik responded tensely, "Let's not risk walking along the road. We're better off cutting through these trees."

I let him lead me, still stunned at his sense of danger which was also mine. Striding as fast as we could for five long, heart-pounding minutes, we reached at last my hotel's illuminated entrance. Tarik released my hand, and we looked into each other's eyes with relief. In the delicious safety of return, my self-involvement ebbed. Insight arrived. Of course! Tarik must have lived in fear like this, and worse, throughout the many days and weeks of his family's escape from Afghanistan! Flooded with empathy, I wanted to hug him. So I did. He accepted my affection with neither embarrassment nor greed.

The invitation was now mine.

"Please, Tarik, you must come inside and have dinner with me. My group will be in the dining room now."

"Thank you, Miss Nadine, but I do not need to meet them. You are the one I am honored to escort."

"I think we share the honor of each other's company, Tarik. All the more reason for you to stay and eat. It's late. You must be hungry."

"No, I must go now. I wish you, *inshallah,* a safe flight to Delhi. Please enjoy your remaining days in India."

With those final words, Tarik kissed me softly on the lips, then slipped back into the night. Perhaps because he vanished so quickly, perhaps because I was too shaken to think clearly, I don't remember why, but Tarik and I did not exchange addresses. The stars of Ladakh still shine overhead, but I don't know what has become of this noble stranger in exile from a war-torn land.

Temblor at Tengboche

by E. Peabody Bradford

WHEN MY PEERS were burning their bras and trekking through the Himalaya in the '60s, I was getting married, buying a house in the Midwest and breeding. I often wondered what I missed. So when I was past 40 and my husband said one day, "On my 50th birthday, I plan to be trekking in the Himalaya," I thought, "I'm coming with you."

On his actual birthday, we weren't in the Himalaya. July is monsoon season in that part of the world. Instead, as a fore-taste of greater adventure, on the day he actually turned 50 I gave him a T-shirt that said "Aged to Perfection" on the front and we carried a champagne lunch to the top of Half Dome. It was 106 degrees in the Yosemite Valley and, in my hurried prepa-rations to get on the trail, I forgot to put on sunscreen. The champagne lunch contributed to an overlong nap—and a seri-ous sunburn. Perhaps this was the universe's way of warning me about the Himalaya, but I wasn't in any mood to listen.

By the end of the monsoon season that fall of 1989, the splendid results of my mothering were 15 and 16 years old—Aaron, a freshman, and Gabe, a sophomore, in high school. Their father was happy to have them with him for a month, so I felt completely at ease about a sojourn in the Orient begin-ning with two weeks hiking from Lukla to the base camp on Everest at Kala Patar.

Those first few days were glorious and beautiful. I'd prepared for this, not just by climbing Half Dome, but also by weekly hikes. Mornings we'd head downhill about a thousand feet and then in the afternoon make up that elevation and add another thousand. I was young and healthy. I hadn't *really* missed the sixties, I'd postponed them. The world was my oyster.

Each day at Everest was gradually steeper, but manageably so. On October 16 we entered the Sagarmatha National Park. Near the entrance there is an outhouse. Dark and forbidding when you first enter, once you're in position over the hole, if you glance to the side, a tiny window frames a perfect view of Everest.

Three days later, we were headed toward the monastery at Tengboche where we were planning to spend the night. It had been a long, steep afternoon and I was ready to be at our destination. We met a Western man coming toward us on the trail who greeted us saying, "Namaste. You are about ten minutes from the monastery and a cup of tea." I was instantly, if briefly, revived.

Perhaps two minutes later another man came abreast of us and said, "Hello. Do you know anything more about the earthquake in San Francisco?" It's funny how the word "more" was the one I latched onto. Anything *more*? His question was the first thing we'd heard about an earthquake at all. He told us there'd been a terrible earthquake, the city was in flames, thousands of people had been killed, the bridges had fallen, entire neighborhoods had crumbled. My children were there. My instinct was to run back down the mountain as fast as possible, or faster, until I got to a phone. The reality was that the nearest phone was in Kathmandu—two days walk and a plane flight away.

In a moment we were joined by other members of our

group, one of whom was from Oakland. His first words to me were, "There's no point getting upset. It won't change anything." I hid out in my tent until evening, when we'd been told we could hear a news broadcast on the radio some Japanese trekkers had brought so they could listen to the World Series. The newscast was in Japanese and, naturally, the person in our group who could translate was the man from Oakland who regarded me as nothing short of hysterical.

We all sat silently huddled around the radio for what seemed an hour while the newscaster spoke in Japanese. Our "translator" said not a word the entire time. Finally, when the newscast concluded and the radio was shut off, he turned to me and said, "You'll be happy to know that most of the damage and all of the deaths occurred in Oakland. "

The next morning when we got up, our colleague from Oakland had left to return home. While returning to Lukla and trying to get a flight to Kathmandu and the nearest phone remained an option, it was one made less palatable by my husband's determination to press on to Kala Patar, whether I went on or not. There was a radio at the Himalayan Rescue Station in the valley adjacent to the one that sheltered our next planned stop at Dingboche. The rescue station would certainly have news, and we might be able to patch through a telephone call home to be sure the children were safe.

Going to the rescue station meant hiking over a 500-foot ridge and then back down in addition to the elevation change from 12,700 feet to 14,300 feet already scheduled for the day, but I didn't feel I had a choice. We separated from the group we were traveling with at Pangboche and continued on under the protection of a guide named Chichima. Although she spoke little English, I knew she had children back in Lukla and must be sympathetic to my plight.

The day seemed so much colder and grayer than previous days. After several hours we arrived at the station and tumbled exhausted and frozen through the door. As we tried to catch our breath so we could ask all the questions that filled our minds, a man behind a desk said, "Oh, you're Americans. Can you tell us anything about the earthquake?" Their radio had been broken for months. If there was a disaster, they could jam the national radio station and have a helicopter sent, but, in spite of my conviction to the contrary, this didn't meet the criteria for such an intervention.

I stepped outside of the crowded, steamy hut, tears pouring out. I sat beside Chichima. Just then a woman brought her a glass of tea. Chichima nodded saying "my friend" toward each of us in turn—a limited but adequate introduction between her two friends. Then she took the glass of tea from her other friend, handed it to me and said again, "my friend."

The rest of the trip passed in something of a haze. There were memorable moments. Singing and dancing on the top of Kala Patar—17,700 feet above sea level and the highest I'd ever been outside of an airplane. Sliding in terror down steep trails when our head guide would say, "I know a shortcut." The market in Namche Bazaar. Having all of our yak porters quit and our head guide respond with his characteristic élan, "No problem." His children running down the road to meet him as we re-entered Lukla, the 3-year-old saying something over and over, which he finally translated for us: "Papa, will you kill a chicken?"

But my heart was always back in Kathmandu, a phone pressed to my ear, hearing my sons' voices. Finally, that day arrived. Always the thoughtful mother, I carefully calculated the time zones, knowing I could wait a few more hours to talk to them after all the waiting I'd already done. I didn't want to call in the middle of the night on a school day. Finally, I figured it to be 7:30 in San Francisco. They'd be up but wouldn't have left for school yet. I put the call through.

Aaron answered. I told him we'd heard about the earthquake, this was the first time we'd been near a phone and I was calling to make sure they were all right. "Sure, we're fine. We went by the house, it's fine. The dog's fine. Grandma's fine. We miss you. Everything's cool."

"Can I talk to Gabe?" I asked. "I was calling to make sure you were okay after the earthquake," I told him.

"Oh, yeah. That was last week." Gabe sounded annoyed. "We're fine."

Silence.

"I know it's been a while, but there were no phones where we were. This is the first chance I've had to call you."

"Mmmmph."

"Sweetie, you sound cross."

"Well, what do you expect?" he replied. "It's 3:30 in the morning!"

When It Rains …

by Donna Marchetti

I HAVE CONFRONTED venomous snakes in the Venezuelan jungle, slept with rats in a thatched hut on the island of Pohnpei (the same hut where I killed—sorry—a fist-sized spider) and flown through the edge of a typhoon near Guam. But I never expected one of my most miserable travel experiences to take place less than a hundred miles from my home.

I was writing a regional guidebook and scheduled a weekend to do research on a nearby Canadian island. The island is mostly farmland with a few B&Bs, a winery, museum and a couple of provincial parks. I could easily do my work in one day.

Though there is ferry service to the island, it was spring, and the service was limited. I couldn't get there and back in one weekend, so I bought a round-trip ticket for one of the six-seater planes that fly regularly from the mainland U.S. I could take my bike on the plane and have a way to get around the island.

As our plane approached my destination it began to sprinkle. By the time we landed, the sky was gushing. The airport, I discovered, was a landing strip not even remotely connected to a road. The pilot, who had been pleasantly chatty on the flight, quickly left my belongings in a dripping pile on the ground and was taxiing down the runway before I could even ask for directions.

I started off through the mud in a random direction, slipped and fell, and the bike fell on top of me. I got up and went on, my shoes making a sucking sound in the muck with each step. Eventually I came to a deep, wide ditch running with a river of brown water. A man working nearby saw me and took pity, ferrying my bike across on his shoulders, me slogging behind. Eventually we got to a road and he told me which way to go. I got to my B&B, sodden and mud-covered.

It's okay, I mused later over a glass of wine. It was over, and anyway, isn't that what travel's about—the unexpected? The next day, too, was fine. I pedaled around and did what I needed to do. It was the following day—the day I was supposed to leave—when the real problems began.

I checked out of my B&B and headed for the airstrip. Once again it began as a sprinkle. Then the sky opened up and rain came down in torrents. The temperature fell to 50 degrees. I had only T-shirts and a couple of summery dresses, and I was freezing. I remembered that the island winery sold sweatshirts, so I pedaled there through the rain. It was jammed with people who had come, I learned, for a bicycle race—hearty Canadians who don't let weather dampen their plans. I called the airport on the mainland from a pay phone at the winery. My plane was canceled—there was no visibility.

"Keep calling," they said.

"Want to race?" asked a fellow. "You can join us!" he urged. Too ill-humored to do something as much fun as a bike race in a monsoon, I declined.

I went to the museum and made small talk with the curator. Lots of it. A couple of hours later, when it became obvious the curator would really rather be curating than talking with me, I rode back to the winery.

"You should've raced," said the man who'd spoken to me

before. "You would've won the women's division. The rest of 'em chickened out."

The island had no store, no public buildings, not even a shelter at the ferry dock. I went back to the museum. I pleaded with my eyes: Please let me stay here. I'll sit in the corner and won't bother anyone. I promise. He wasn't buying it. I left. A phone booth was out front—the only one on the island. It had a roof. I hung out there for awhile. It seemed like a good idea to call the airport again. Still no planes in the air. It occurred to me that I probably wasn't going to get off the island that day and I'd better find a place to spend the night. I phoned my cozy B&B. Full. I tried another. Full. Slowly it dawned on me: It was the racers' fault. They had taken all the rooms. I finally found an unheated room with a bathroom down the hall.

I had dinner that night with a couple of Canadian customs officers who thought I looked lonely and invited me to join them. They regaled me with stories about the frenzied life of an island customs official ("Once I caught this guy trying to smuggle in a hamster ..."). I told them about my Pohnpeian spider.

The rain continued the next day, sheets that streamed down the windows and turned the ground to a soggy mess. I checked out of my room, hopeful that the planes would begin flying. I was permitted to stay and wait in a sitting room, huddled next to a space heater. The pay phone, the only phone I was allowed to use, was outside, uncovered, attached to a barn across a field. Every hour or so I would dash out to the barn to call the airport. I called my husband, who was visiting friends in Arizona.

"It's so *hot* here," he complained. "And so *sunny.*"

I went back to the sitting room and took notes for my guidebook until I ran out of paper, then looked around for something to do. I had finished reading the one book I'd brought to the island and the only books in the room were condensed novels. I hate condensed novels. On principle, I never read them. I read three that afternoon.

A friend with whom I share the longest-lasting relationship in my life was having her fortieth birthday party that night. It was a surprise party at a restaurant. I was supposed to be there. It became clear that I wouldn't. I waited until I knew they were all gathered then called the restaurant, rain pouring down my face.

"You're *where?*" she asked. "Oh well," she said after listening to my explanation, "at least it's not a typhoon."

There was a ferry leaving that evening. Though I would have to ride my bike a couple of miles on a busy road, presumably in the rain, to get from the mainland ferry dock to the airport, where my car was, I was desperate. I bought a ticket.

Passengers usually make the crossing on deck. But the torrential rain drove us all into the tiny forward cabin—50 or so people crammed into a space that would be intimate with 25. The boat pitched like a bronco, and every time it hit the bottom of a wave the portholes would be engulfed by angry green water and the cabin plunged into darkness. The kid next to me threw up. The couple on my other side began to pray, urgently, out loud. Someone—where do people leave their tact?—was telling shipwreck stories.

Two hours later we reached the mainland. The water was so high it covered the ramp entirely. I had to take off my shoes and socks and wade to shore in the mighty cold water. But we had made it. I was safe.

I would eventually be dry. Maybe even warm. My friend would forgive me. And I would never again underestimate the potential for travel angst in a nearby place.

Air Sickness

by Mark Cerulli

"YOU KNOW THE plane's been delayed, right?" the Air Afrique rep said as we finally advanced to the front of the passenger line, surrounded by mountains of suitcases, bulging cardboard boxes, and industrial-sized metal trunks. Uh, no, we had no idea. And, uh, no, there was no plane. Not that night. Instead, we flew to Senegal by way of the JFK Best Western Hotel in Jamaica, Queens. The revised departure time was 9 A.M. the following morning—not what my wife and I wanted, but at least we'd leave for Africa with a good night's sleep.

To unwind, we tried the hotel's lounge—a sad little place dominated by a dark wooden bar. The other passengers tossed down beers, smoked like chimneys, and laughed with each other, not disturbed in the least. Most of them were from various countries in West Africa with a smattering of Peace Corps types thrown in. Apparently this thing happens all the time and nobody seemed too concerned. I loosened up by watching a pudgy Mediterranean gentleman with a dyed comb-over put a move on a curvy woman holding a Liberian passport. He leaned towards her and whispered something in her ear. Without a word she grabbed her drink and cigarettes, and walked to the other side of the bar, leaving a tight smile frozen on the guy's face. *Smooth* ...

At 2:30 A.M. our room phone rang. I reached for it, bleary eyed. "This is Air Afrique ... an airline representative will be in the lobby at 11 A.M." Bang! They hung up in my ear. I started counting lost vacation days instead of sheep.

We did eventually leave that night—a full 22 hours after the scheduled departure time. Boarding by row numbers? Not here—instead there was an all-out rush towards the overwhelmed ticket taker and we were caught in a bottleneck. Once through, we thundered down the jetway towards the plane. Off to the side a young Senegalese tried to plead his way on board—he had a ticket, but no passport or other proof of ID. "You're taking an international flight and you *forgot* your passport?" an airline attendant asked him uncomprehendingly. Even in those heady, pre-9/11 days, this wasn't washing. Somehow everyone else made it onto the plane with no broken bones.

The next morning we landed in Dakar. The plane rolled to a stop and the pilot shut down the engines. As people rose and went for their bags, an irritated stewardess yelled (in French), "Sit down, the baggage people are on strike. We could be in here for hours." Like sheep, we all sat back down. As the sun rose outside, so did the temperature inside. A few passengers began grumbling angrily, then a handful moved towards the cockpit. "We gotta bust this motha ...... out!" yelled one large young man with dreadlocks. "Liberian," the passenger next to me said disapprovingly.

By now the cabin crew had disappeared. Eventually I noticed something rolling towards us. Slowly. *Very* slowly. A truck-mounted stairwell, which took a solid 20 minutes to make it to the doorway. After an eternity, the cabin attendant unlocked the cabin door and slid it open. White hot sunlight and the odor of jet fuel spilled in. We had made it—we were in Senegal! But our bags weren't, as we found out after several hours standing around, watching dumbfounded as the Air

Afrique baggage crew unloaded the flight's luggage virtually one at a time. (The strike, remember?)

"I'm sorry," the large Senegalese man who had sat next to me on the plane said, "this is no way for you to see my country." Occasionally the baggage handlers would turn on the conveyor belts, and they would clank around as a tease. A few exhausted passengers poked at the bags half-heartedly before giving up. I noticed a mailbag labeled "Swedish Embassy" sitting in a corner next to an ancient scale. After an older African woman suddenly began wailing hysterically—she had been at the airport for three days waiting for her bags—we decided to pack it in. Our bags showed up a day later. By then we had established a nodding acquaintance with the customs officers and they waved us through.

But all this was just a warm-up for the return flight. That was where Air Afrique pulled out all the stops. We were due to leave on a Sunday at 1:50 P.M. That date came and went with a phone call—my wife checking in with Air Afrique. "Oh la la, la la la laaaaah" Sandra moaned in French when they said there was no plane and no more info. She started to launch into a speech about playing with people's lives, but they hung up. So much for customer satisfaction.

Later that day we got word that the plane would be leaving at 6 A.M. Monday morning; check-in would begin at 2 A.M. By now we were so desperate to get back to our regularly scheduled lives that lining up for a flight in the middle of the night seemed entirely natural. (Especially after throwing a Hail Mary pass to Air France to buy our way onto their Sunday night flight. They *did* have two business-class seats Dakar to Paris and coach to New York. $2,500. "Let's dooo it," I yelled, whipping out my Amex card, feeling the same adrenaline rush you get when a Ticketmaster operator answers the exact moment

Springsteen tickets go on sale. Then they clarified—it was $2,500 *each*. Oh.)

Our local cab driver was afraid he'd oversleep, so he sacked-out in his taxi parked right outside our door. Senegal is definitely a car culture, but the cars are invariably ten to twenty years old. (Unless they're owned by a government minister or local high-roller in which case they're late model BMWs or Mercedes.) No taxi we rode in had air conditioning, most had their headliners hanging in tatters. Many sported dashboard stickers proclaiming "Allah is the one."

Whenever I buckled up, the cab driver would look at me as if I was some kind of pampered tourist wimp. The local highways are littered with the mangled corpses of cars, as if their owners were carted off or simply walked away. On a misguided trip to a game preserve in the south, we passed the three burnt and rusted sections of a tractor trailer. The accident must have been horrific as the pavement was still scorched.

On a trip of assorted miseries, our sojourn to the game park (whose exciting Internet homepage boasted prowling lions, elephants and other exotic creatures) was a new low. On the Discovery Channel, intrepid eco-tourists make nice with wildlife from late model Range Rovers. In the Nikola Koba Game Preserve, our gasping, rattling four-wheel drive diesel—which rolled off the assembly line sometime during the Eisenhower Administration—broadcast our approach yards before we ever got there. Over and over, we were treated to the ass end of various animals as they scampered off in search of peace and quiet. (When I asked our guide what the chances of seeing a lion were, he smiled softly and said, "I haven't seen a lion in three years.") I did emerge from the trip with one souvenir—the double-fanged bite of a vampire fly, which sent shooting pains up and down my arm. My paranoid New York mind went to work wondering what strange new toxins were now calling my bloodstream home.

At 2 A.M. we bolted out of bed and grabbed our packed bags. But not before one last call to Air Afrique. By now I had a hazy working knowledge of French—at least as it pertained to airline schedules. "Is the plane leaving on time?" Sandra asked. "Absolutely, we have already started the boarding process," came the confident reply. Whoopie! After rousing the driver and stuffing our luggage into the decrepit trunk, we were off. Our rolling deathtrap zipped through the empty roads towards Dakar's International Airport, visions of take-off and cocktails dancing in our heads.

In the ticketing area another good sign—the airline had set up a perimeter with ropes and small tables labeled "Securite." Each was manned by a guard who made the first of four passport checks. His partner carried what I thought was an emergency light wand in case the power went out. Instead he waved it over my passport and my wife's Green Card. (An infrared check for fakes.) At the ticket counter was where we were hit with the bad news—uh, the plane isn't here yet. *("But it's coming!")* Still, in a rush to do anything that would get us closer to a plane, we checked our bags, and re-re-confirmed our seats.

Days earlier we had visited the Air Afrique ticket office off Dakar's crumbling Plaza de l'Independence. (African airlines have a nasty habit of canceling paid reservations if not confirmed at least 72 hours in advance.) Somehow, my seat had vanished in spite of a "confirmed" reservation. The agent plonked on her ancient computer and found us two seats towards the rear of the plane.

After getting our passports stamped by a surprisingly kind Immigration Agent, we tried the door to the security check. Locked. A scowling customs guard shuffled over mumbling incoherently and motioned us away. The good guy immigration official poked his head out of his booth and asked his colleague what was going on. "Too early," came the reply. Not good. We stepped over sleeping passengers—Rome, Paris, South Africa, Ivory Coast—every flight was delayed. Only the coffee bar was open. An Italian tour group had taken it over under a cloud of bluish cigarette smoke. Apparently the words "lung" and "cancer" don't translate into Italian.

After an hour or so, Mr. Nice Immigration Agent wandered over and sat next to us. His colleagues and other passengers stared as he chatted with my wife in French. Like most Senegalese we encountered, he was exceedingly friendly. After he left a sleep-deprived South African passenger wandered over. "Excuse me, sir," he asked, staring at me with bloodshot eyes, his hair at odd angles from bed head, "did you find out anything?"

The hours dragged by. Slowly rumors began spreading—our plane was on its way. (Not true.) There was a coup attempt in neighboring Ivory Coast. (True!) At 4:15 A.M. I asked an Air Afrique staffer hurrying past for a heads up. "It's landing at 5:30," she said. (Not true.) Finally another rumor, one we had to act on—"They are boarding your flight," a smartly dressed African businessman told an older passenger nearby. We raced over to the security zone where the scowling agent had, reluctantly, opened the door. More pushing and shoving. Suddenly a collective sigh went up, and he switched off the X-ray machine—it had broken down. We shuffled over to the other side of the hall where another machine stood. Slowly we made our way through and into a small glass-fronted departure lounge. A group of Air Afrique ground personnel sat in a row, holding those strange light wands. They were sound asleep.

By now the rosy light of dawn was creeping in, illuminating a huge, white Air Afrique plane sitting on the tarmac right in front of us. It was there before we arrived, it would be there long after we left. It never moved. We had been had—our plane wasn't boarding. Not even close. Instead, the first flight out that morning was an Air Afrique flight to Abidjan—Ivory Coast's capital city—where a coup was in progress. That struck me as a pretty spunky move—not many airlines would risk a multimillion-dollar aircraft, not to mention the lives of their crew and passengers by flying into an unfolding military conflict, but that flight took off as scheduled. We would read later that gunfire broke out that morning in Abidjan and at least eight people were killed in a failed coup attempt. Coffee, tea or Kevlar?

Knowing local boarding procedures, we staked out floor space near our departure gate—the monitor curiously showing our original departure time throughout the day. Out on the runway beyond nothing moved—except for a line of uniformed troops who marched into the Arrivals gate with unsmiling faces and automatic weapons. The older African passenger standing next to me shook his head. "If there's trouble, the first thing they do is shut down the airport," he said, looking grim. I hadn't been to church in over a decade, but I re-introduced myself to the Almighty with the words, "Please God, no."

As the huge line behind us was processed through the X-ray machine, we found ourselves in the middle of a mob of teachers and students from Selma, Alabama. They had been in Africa for eight days. Their bags had never left the U.S. As the sun rose, the room became stiflingly hot. The airline staffers had at first manned the ticket desk, but then skedaddled when asked for information one too many times. A college kid tried to open the door to let in some air. Locked. An armed guard stood outside, staring in and smiling enthusiastically.

"I'm three months pregnant. I gotta have some water!" the tall African American schoolteacher standing next to me yelled. Her students unwrapped a pair of souvenir bongo drums and began pounding out a beat. *"No justice, no peace..."* the chant went up ... then, *"No plane, no peace!"* By now dozens of other people were clamoring for water, or any other cold beverage. Outside, the guard's smile vanished. As another hour crawled by, and more cries for water went up, an Air Afrique staffer made the mistake of walking in. He was besieged by pleas for liquids. He bolted. Then, miraculously, a small beverage cart was rolled in. "You go, there!" he screamed.

An inaudible boarding announcement foggily sounded and the Italian tour group was bused out to their plane. Another Air Afrique employee walked by. He must have been important as his frayed jacket had their logo stitched into the pocket. I nudged my wife, "Ask him!" I hissed. Sandra popped the question of the moment, "Where is the plane?" He answered in rapid-fire French, then split. I and other passengers looked at her expectantly. Well? "He said they were told to hold us here due to a snowstorm in New York. But they have just authorized us to fly."

Good news.

Unfortunately, not true.

There was no snowstorm, we would find out. But apparently there *was* a plane because several buses now pulled in front of the gates. There was no, "We invite passengers with small children or those needing a little more time to board." Instead the crowd surged towards the departure gate in an angry scrum. (The latest rumor was that the flight was oversold and there were not enough seats for everybody.)

"Somebody's in my seat, I'm gonna fight 'em for it," the schoolteacher confided to me.

She was at least six feet tall, broad-shouldered, and pregnant or not, I wouldn't want to tangle with her. "Um, just where are you sitting?" I casually inquired. Fortunately her seat was another ten rows back.

After a final security ritual where we had to identify our checked luggage, and one last passport check, it was onto a bus. Ours rolled a hundred feet, then stopped. The driver climbed off and we watched passengers screaming at baggage handlers and each other over their luggage. Finally a mild-mannered Senegalese man in a flowing Kente robe—a guy who had previously told one and all to stay calm—had had enough. He leaned out the window and began shouting furiously in Wolof, a strange-sounding language that resembles a series of "dunga dungas," followed by the teeth-sucking sound all Africans make when they are upset. The bus driver yelled back and for a moment it looked like he would be thrown off. But the bus finally moved in a big lazy circle towards a waiting jet—the same plane my wife had pointed out to me several hours earlier. I remembered it because I had never seen a passenger plane getting a tire changed before.

"*We invite our first class passengers to board at their leisure.*" Forget it! For once coach ruled and we shoved our way up the stairwell. The plane filled quickly, every seat taken. After an unintentionally funny safety video—highlighted by a vignette of a woman trying to sneak a smoke in a lavatory only to have the door yanked open by a furious Air Afrique steward aiming a fire extinguisher at her face—we were ready for the big moment. Instead we sat on the tarmac as a muzak version of Barry Manilow's "Even Now" played over and over and over. I giggled to myself—this had morphed way beyond a bad trip. Mind-numbing delays, rude service, sweltering heat, hungry vampire flies, all this I could handle with a reasonable degree of calm. But after the fifth consecutive play of "Even Now," I was starting to become unglued.

An hour dripped by and a garbled announcement in French wafted out . . . and we moved. We were taking off! I had never looked forward to going back to the office as much as I did right then. In minutes the rocky, arid Senegalese coast faded and something approximating cool air blasted down from the nozzles. We made it! I was rehearsing the words "Bloody Mary, please" when the pilot came on the PA. He welcomed us onboard and let us know that we were making an unscheduled "technical" stop in Sal. *Huh?* Sal—one of the Cape Verde Islands.

"The good news," he explained, " is we are taking off, the bad news is we have too much cargo, so we have to stop to refuel.")

Just 45 minutes later, we dropped down towards a windswept speck, rolling to a stop at a small, one-story airport. After another un-air-conditioned hour, we again sped down the runway and took off.

As the first of three movies played, a lone stewardess moved among the aisles serving water and juice. Where was the rest of the cabin staff? "Sleeping" we were told. Okayyy. . . . They did rouse themselves to serve a surprisingly tasty meal, but that bonus was offset by the fact that one lavatory was taped off as "Broken" and the others were filthy, and smelled like the Porta Potties after Woodstock '99.

We landed at JFK almost ten hours after we left Senegal, excuse me, *Sal.*

"We apologize for the delay and any inconvenience." the pilot declared as everyone staggered off the plane. "Thank you for your confidence in Air Afrique and we look forward to serving you again."

The 100,000 Lira Misunderstanding

by Priscilla Burgess

ON A MISTY April afternoon in Rome, two men were fighting on a cobbled street tucked away behind the Piazza Navona—and they were fighting over me.

I had just landed at Leonardo di Vinci Airport in Fiumi-cino, 22 miles from Rome, after a scary flight from San Francisco. I was tired and rattled and couldn't wait to get to my hotel. I disembarked and followed everyone else until, to my horror, I found myself outside the airport. The last time I was in Italy, Americans had to go through customs and get their passports stamped so I was sure I was going to be arrested for illegal entry and thrown into some ghastly Italian prison. Back inside, I found a couple *Caribinieri,* each wearing a beret with a spectacular spray of feathers. When I got their attention, I pounded my hand on my open passport.

"No stamp!" I said. "Dove get estampo?"

They laughed. "No necessary. Is okay, you go," they said, while waving me towards the exit.

I wasn't quite sure about this so I watched them over my shoulder as I headed back outside. They continued to wave and smile until the doors swished shut behind me.

By this time, the main crowd of passengers had vanished and there was only one taxi left in the arrivals zone. The driver, lounging against his cab, was tall, dark, around 30 years old, unbelievably buffed with gorgeous smoky-blue eyes. Yes, indeed, I'd be happy to take a ride in his taxi. He had a friend with him, and in not-bad English, he said, "My friend drive. I teach him to be taxi driver. Is okay?"

I shrugged and smiled. I really didn't care who drove as long as I got to the Raphael, a small hotel near the Piazza Navona, in one piece. In we all got and headed to Rome on the freeway, the blue-eyed guy and I chatting in broken English and French. He pointed out the UN building where I had a meeting the next day, the Coliseum, Roman ruins. He sympathized over schoolyard shootings, telling me he had two small children who were precious to him and whom he would protect at all costs. Nice guy, caring, involved with his family.

The streets transformed from wide boulevards to cobbled, medieval lanes. He was edgy and turned to guide his trainee through a maze of ancient narrow streets.

We finally arrived at the Raphael, or almost anyway. The blue-eyed hunk pointed up the narrow Largo di Febo and said, "One way. Car can't go." He rattled off fast Italian to his buddy, who trotted off with my luggage.

He asked for an astounding amount of money—200,000 lira—all those zeros and I hadn't bothered to figure out the exchange rate before I left home. I handed him two 100,000 lira notes (each 100,000 lira is about $60 as I found out later). He turned his back to me for a moment, then miming surprise, apologetically showed me two 10,000 lira notes. He handed them to me with one hand while pointing with the other to the 100,000 lira notes still in my wallet. I hesitantly pulled them out, not quite believing I'd made a mistake. The taxi driver plucked the cash from my hand.

Suddenly, from out of nowhere an elderly, white-haired man rushed up shouting, in American English, "He's a thief! Don't give him any more money!"

I stood on the street with my mouth agape as I watched this tall, slender gentleman in his late sixties come roaring up and snatch the money from the taxi driver, who showed his true colors by grabbing the money back while screaming in Italian at the new arrival. Large bills and small flew out of their hands, scattered on the ground, and they proceeded to the next stage: an actual fist fight, which I hadn't witnessed since elementary school. This fist fight was different from those I've seen on TV or in the movies. It wasn't choreographed. It reminded me of a kangaroo fight I'd seen on a National Geographic special—both men leaned back while they swiped at each other with their hands.

Paralyzed with disbelief, I watched the two men yell at each other in their native tongues while whacking away at the other's face. I thought it was tacky of the taxi driver to fight a man twice his age, but the new arrival was just as keen and I don't think he was thinking about his age at that particular moment. The gentleman's glasses flew off and the taxi-trainee, who had been delivering my suitcase a half-block up the street, returned, grabbed his friend—who scooped up the large bills—and dragged him to the car. The two of them sped off in a squeal of burning tires and shouts of, "You bastard! I'll get you for this!"

After a hasty introduction—his name was Peter—he crawled around on the ground picking up the small bills while I searched under parked cars trying to find his glasses. We were joined by an elderly, ovoid British gentleman who had been watching the spectacle with typical British *sangfroid*.

"Tried on me, too," he said. "Caught him at it."

This particular driver had pulled the same trick on both men. While the Brit didn't fall for it, Peter had. It was the same MO: drive around Rome until the meter was almost twice what it should be, then make sure that the taxi doesn't stop right in front of the hotel where the doorman could see what was happening, take the large bills, switch with smaller ones and show the sucker that she has made a mistake and collect yet another couple of large bills.

Peter, a retired professor of ancient Greek history, was on the warpath. He stormed into the lobby of the Raphael, where he, too, was staying, and shouted, "Call the police! This woman has just been robbed by a taxi driver." He'd had the sense to write down the license number, car model and color and the name of the taxi company. He shoved the paper under the nose of Tito, the desk clerk.

"No, no," soothed Tito, "No police—I tell manager."

The professor's adrenaline was up and his face was scratched. I urged him into the bar and ordered a carafe of *Frascati*, the only thanks he accepted from me. The waiter brought a linen napkin and a silver wine cooler full of ice for his reddening face.

The next day the professor parked himself in the small lobby at an antique table upon which sat the guests' computer and, by hand, wrote a three-page report for the police. I offered to type it into the computer but Peter was off on a journey of his own and refused my help. By then, all the guests knew what had happened because Peter spoke aloud as he wrote. With an entourage avidly watching, Peter delivered his letter directly into the hands of the hotel manager. The manager didn't want to call the police either, but he did call the taxi company. He told them that if they didn't fire the blue-eyed hunk and refund our money, they would never use the company again. That worked. Before I left Rome, I was presented with an envelope containing three 100,000 lira notes. By then the professor had moved on and out of my life.

In the long run, the money wouldn't have mattered, and I would have eventually forgotten about the incident. But every time I think about the elderly professor squaring off with the buffed Italian in an attempt to keep him from robbing me, I smile and shake my head in wonder.

From then on, I kept my eyes on the taxi drivers in each country I visited and insisted that we agree to a price before I got into the car. I figured it was unlikely that there would be another retired professor of ancient Greek history hanging out, waiting to rush to my rescue if I got in trouble—but I no longer discount the possibility.

Where Rattlesnakes Fear to Tread

by David Wright

OUR DESTINATION WAS Cabo Pulmo, a tiny village along the Sea of Cortez in Baja, California. The four of us—me, my girl-friend and her two young children, would fly to Cabo San Lucas, rent a car and then drive the last hour and half up a scenic Mexican highway to our little pearl on the peninsula. I envisioned an unspoiled paradise, even though I am a moun-tain person by nature and perhaps should have been warier.

Like a stick of butter onto a hot skillet, our plane landed on the newly poured concrete tarmac. After a slightly modi-fied rendition of Abbott and Costello's "Who's on First?" rou-tine with the car rental folks, they finally found the car we had reserved. The kids, ages 3 and 6, looked like adults with freak-ishly small heads as we pulled away from the car rental place. They were the right height for adults after all, seat belted and riding high above the luggage that wouldn't fit in the trunk. But we were in motion. I set the air conditioner over to the something that can only be found on the cold side of the Kelvin temperature scale and my girlfriend stabbed the gas pedal to the floor. Next stop, the grocery store.

Our cart quickly filled with rum, peanut butter, jelly, bread, more rum, Ramen noodles, instant potatoes, rum, beans and a few sodas. After some slight rearranging that mostly involved creating a crawl space for the kids near the roof of the car, we set out again for Cabo Pulmo. "Crap, I forgot something," my

girlfriend said and did a 180-degree turn. She emerged minutes later with two bags of ice and a Styrofoam cooler. "Ah,
cocktails." I said, smiling.

"No," she said, "they don't have electricity in Cabo Pulmo."

"They have running water, right?" I asked. She handed me
the cooler and the bags of ice and returned to the store. She
emerged with two gallons of water.

"Good thing you mentioned that, I almost forgot water
too."

The road to Cabo Pulmo from Cabo San Lucas is a two-
lane, sometimes blacktop highway dotted with burned-out
frames of former automobiles, meandering livestock, truck-
loads of workers and VW bugs filled with drunken tourists.
The speed limit is somewhere just under the speed of sound,
and this particular stretch of road was known for its high mor-
tality rate.

We eventually pulled into Cabo Pulmo. Livestock roamed
freely and ate piles of trash that littered the street. Dogs with
a wide variety of skin diseases roamed the streets looking for
handouts. The restaurants sold little food for lots of money
but still offered more of a bargain than the local bars, whose
world-famous margaritas were a fine blend of kerosene and
Kool-Aid. Residents were evenly split between rich white Americans who had bought vacation property and the locals.

In honor of our arrival, the ocean had spat up a rock wall
on the beach. We set up camp between the wall and the rows
of bushes that offered no protection from the sun. The sand
fleas held a small parade in demonstration against our
encroachment onto their turf as buzzards and pelicans flew
overhead looking at tomorrow's potential menu. While there
was still plenty of sand to get into every nook and cranny of
every single thing we owned, there wasn't enough sand to walk

on. Just a nice flat field of super-solar-heated rocks.

All of the wildlife, animal or plant, in Cabo Pulmo, burns, bites, cuts, stabs, chaffs, slices, stings or pricks. None of the wood is flammable, especially if you are trying to burn it in a fire to cook on. I was warned that the rattlesnakes weren't nearly as venomous or mean as the scorpions and spiders but I should still give them a wide berth.

On the second night of our stay, something landed in the bushes directly outside of our tent. My wife thought it was a pack of coyotes fighting over something dead. The kids thought it was two vultures ripping some smaller creature apart while it was still alive. I emerged from the tent, collected the biggest rocks I could find, and hurled them into the bushes along with every obscenity known to man. The next day I made my girl-friend take me to the local hardware store and I purchased an oak sledgehammer handle.

The beach where we camped is part of an official national park so we were fortunate to have "facilities." These consisted of a meandering trail through the cactus to a wooden box placed over a hole in the ground. The box, carefully unsanded and about 12 inches high, had thoughtfully been painted black. Small lizards ran out from underneath it upon approach; I nicknamed one of them "Stinky."

The locals embraced our wallets with open arms. Even though it is supposedly free to camp on the beach, we were immediately greeted by Pepe, a local entrepreneur. He told us the nightly camping fee was $2 and the money was used to maintain the bathroom and trash. I guess black paint is expensive down there. What he didn't have to tell us was that if we left our stuff unattended without paying, it would be taken as payment. We worked out a deal and paid him $20 for the 14 days we were there.

By the end of our two weeks, I had managed to sunburn at least 90 percent of my body, even through waterproof 1,000 SPF sun block. I also had an infection in both eyes and in both ears from some kind of irritant in the sea water. Despite all of the sand I had eaten, I had lost about ten pounds and even though I felt hungover every day, I had been unable to even get drunk. Our supply of ice would only last about a day and half before we had to get more and the idea of drinking warm rum in the hot sun always seemed less than inviting.

When we finally returned to the Estados Unidos, I found myself even more in love with my mountain home in Wyoming than before. The huge, motionless, granite tidal waves in the western sky were equal in size and mass to the weight that was now lifted from my shoulders.

I did end up marrying my girlfriend after the vacation. And the kids have forgiven me for the threats made while in Mexico, although they do eye me with apprehension every time I pick up the staple gun. One of the conditions of the marriage was that I get to pick the next vacation spot. Destination: Greenland.

D'Accord

by Julia Niebuhr Eulenberg

In Avignon, every evening ended the same way. My husband and I finished our unfashionably early dinner, wandered for a while, then turned back into the narrow street that led to our hotel and climbed the long stairway to our room. Once there, we adjusted the drapes, left the window open for air and got ready for bed. We were ready to turn out our lights long before the city beneath us was prepared to do so. This meant that not long after we had gone to sleep, we were wakened by the sounds of the restaurant next door as it closed up for the night.

Imagine Van Gogh's painting of the café on the terrace— wrought iron tables and chairs on a cobblestone street under starry skies—and you have the perfect image of the restaurant just below our open windows. Each night, aproned waiters dragged those tables and chairs across the rounded stones and placed them next to the exterior walls of the café. Metal scraped against stone until I was certain I'd counted every single cobblestone in the square. A moment of silence meant that the last chair and table were nestled up against all the others. But the waiters had not yet finished.

The silence was broken once more by the sounds of heavy metal chains pulled across the cobblestones and through the open tops of the wire chairs and around the pedestals of the tables. Marley's ghost could not have achieved better sound effects. Then, as quickly as it had begun, the job was finished. The waiters paused, lit cigarettes and exchanged adieus. The night grew silent.

So it went for the first four nights of our stay. On the fifth, we had just settled back onto our pillows and said goodnight when a whole new set of noises erupted. My eyes popped open. Sounds of passion—moans of pleasure, deep grunts, heavy breathing, a bed pounding against a wall—filtered through our window. I turned to my husband, and we laughed, a little embarrassed or perhaps wishing we had thought of it first. The sounds grew louder, escalated and then stopped. Apparently the couple's passion was spent. We settled back onto our pillows and hoped the other couple would do the same.

Once more, I drifted off to sleep, but it was not to be. A loud voice from the other side of our windows began to speak impassioned lines that might have come from one of the great operas. Deserted by his love, saddened, he poured out his soul. My own desire, after five minutes of this, was sufficient French to tell the poor man I felt his pain. Lacking that, I plumped up my pillows, sat up in bed and listened. Perhaps eavesdropping would improve my language skills since it was clear I wasn't going to be sleeping for some time. After what seemed an hour, I had learned words I hoped never to use. I wanted no tragic end to my great love. Eventually, his tears and emotion spent, he calmed down, with only a few hiccuping sobs left.

The last of those were drowned out by a burglar alarm. This would continue as background noise for the next two or three hours. On and off, so that we would let down our guard and relax, anticipating sleep. Then, on again—and off. Discussion down on the street failed to solve the problem. The police were summoned at last, but they were no more successful. There was, however, clearly no burglary.

The discussion continued, even after the owner of La Pharmacie arrived at the scene. *"D'accord,"* someone said. "It is perhaps an electrical short. Or something else." I sat up straighter in bed. Ah, I thought, my French is improving. I'm actually understanding what they're talking about. My husband started to say something. "Shhh," I whispered. "I'll tell you later."

"Alors." The policeman pronounced his opinion on the subject. No doubt he also shrugged his shoulders eloquently. "Go home. It will settle out later. Certainly by morning. Meantime, who knows?"

Oh, God, I thought. I didn't know if I could wait until later. I certainly wasn't prepared to wait until morning.

In the meantime, what was surely not the same burglar alarm began to ring out. Further away, but close enough to be penetrating. Luckily the policeman was still on the scene, and he went into action immediately.

"Attends! Attends!" This was followed by the sound of a shot, the gunning of an engine and tires squealing as a car roared off.

There was more discussion between the police and bystanders. How on earth, I wondered, could there be bystanders at 3 in the morning? Well, I took back my question. It was noisy enough by then—had been for hours—to be 3 in the afternoon. Why not bystanders?

And then, as if none of this had occurred, there was finally silence, and we slept.

The next morning, in very fractured French and with the aid of my small *Larousse*, I asked the landlord about the burglary and the sound of the shots. This too was vocabulary I thought I'd never need. The proprietor expressed the same thought.

"Non," he said in his very good French—slowly, patiently,

to be sure we understood. "This kind of thing happens in the big cities, not here. You have imagined it. Perhaps you heard wrong."

I looked at him skeptically. He tried again in his English, which corresponded in fluency to my French. We were locked in our own opinions of what had taken place during the night. For us, not one, but two burglar alarms—loud and unrelenting. For him, not a sound—"Surely, the dog, she would have barked, *n'est-ce pas?*"

I tried again. *"Attends!"* I said. "I am sure I heard someone cry out, '*Attends! Attends!*' and then 'Stop!' And we heard shots." I looked to my husband for confirmation. He nodded.

"Non," our hotelier was definite. "Not here. I didn't hear it."

We finished our breakfast quietly, keeping one eye on the huge dog that had not barked during the night but was quite prepared to snatch our croissants from the table. In front of the hotelier, my husband had been very supportive as I tried to tell my story. But outside the hotel, he shifted his backpack on his shoulders and said, "I told you so last night. All of it was probably just part of the Avignon Festival. Someone— maybe several someones—were just practicing."

I gave him a Gallic shrug of my own, and we set off on a day of exploring. By the end of the day, tired, we hoped there would be only the sounds of the restaurant's closing—and no further festival rehearsals. Our luck held.

The following morning at breakfast, a very sheepish proprietor came to our table, accompanied by his feckless dog. *"Lisez-vous francais?"* he asked. A fair question. Since it was obvious I didn't speak French very well, I might not read it either.

"Oui," I asserted.

"*D'accord,*" he said and handed me the weekly paper for Provence. "*La,*" he said and pointed to an article on page one. There had been, he confessed, a series of events on the evening in question—a broken burglar alarm at La Pharmacie around the corner, and across the street an attempted burglary at La Parfumerie. And, well, yes, it seemed bullets had been fired at the would-be burglars. I read on and began to laugh. "The escape car—a BMW. Wealthy thieves."

"*Oui,*" he said, and sighed.

I sensed his sorrow. Crime had come to Avignon, after all.

My husband and I went off to buy a copy of the paper. It made a perfect addition to our scrapbook and reinforced the new vocabulary skills I had begun to acquire.

After that, we slept very well. "*D'accord,*" as the French say, one can become accustomed to anything.

Playing Pool

by Judith Beck

As we traveled across North Africa and into Asia, it was turning out to be quite an unhoneymoon for my husband and me. We argued about where to go, where to stay, what to do and, especially, what to eat. Determined not to get whatever the local term was for dysentery, he viewed every morsel of food and drop of water as breeding grounds for gut-destroying bacteria. No matter where we went, he sought out Coca-Cola to drink (in his teens, he and his friends had stripped a dead mouse down to its skeleton by leaving it in a bottle of Coke for a few days, so he figured it would be sterile if drunk straight from the bottle) and deep-fried shrimp, believing no germ could survive dipping in a vat of boiling oil.

I, on the other hand, wanted to sample everything I possibly could. I scoffed at his timidity. I called him a wimp. What was the use of traveling all that distance if you weren't willing to experience the world? Biding his time and keeping track of the number of times I used the john, he gloated and hoarded the toilet paper he'd brought all the way from the suburbs of Philadelphia.

But things were perfectly calm for me as I wolfed down donkey heart grilled on skewers in Morocco, guzzled sweetened shaved ice in Istanbul and stuffed myself with stewed mutton in Pakistan.

Late one night, stomachs calm and well-regulated, we pulled

into Laurie's Hotel in Agra, India, an establishment that dated back to the days of the Raj. For once, both of us were enchanted with the idea of staying in a hotel. The service was bound to be more gracious and the accommodations quainter than in a modern hotel.

The porter helped us to our room, mentioning that Laurie's had a pool in the midst of its gardens. A very clean pool, he said, up to the *most* modern standards. It was swelteringly hot; we were tired and dusty, young, still marginally in love and in Agra. Agra is the site of the Taj Mahal, arguably the most romantic structure in the entire world, tomb of the favorite wife of a Shah who could build anything he wanted. How could we turn down swimming in a sequestered pool under a full tropical moon when the Taj was only a few steps away?

We slipped out of our room to the pool and waded in, the odor of jasmine redolent on the sultry air. I paddled around my husband; we kissed and more. It was a blissful experience until an uncanny sensation prickled my skin despite the body-temperature pool water. The heavy floral scents that surrounded us began to smell rancid, decaying. The gentle lapping of the water against the tiled sides of the pool began to take on an ominous portent. I pictured cobras slipping down from vines to swim sinuously in our direction, rabid pariah dogs salivating in the bushes. Despite the moon, it was pitch-dark in the depths of the garden.

I began to lobby for leaving the pool and heading back to our room. Importuning didn't work, but seduction did, though I was too frightened to really be in the mood. We retired to our dark room and our mosquito netting.

The morning arrived, bright, sunny and 90 degrees by 8 A.M. We got up for breakfast and a tour of the area in the daylight. The hotel was shabbier than we had expected, but not without charm. The gardens were run-down but perfectly harmless and ordinary in the morning sun. And the pool? By day, the pool was an unreal, psychedelic, nearly fluorescent green. The beautiful tiles on the walls disappeared under a slimy and viscid scrim of algae.

I began to giggle when I saw the expression on my husband's face. After all his care, he'd spent the evening sporting in the world's largest Petrie dish.

Following our itinerary, we left the next day for Bangladesh, flying out of New Delhi. In flight, my stomach began to percolate gently like a coffeepot on simmer. Judging by the pinched white skin around my husband's nostrils, I wasn't doing too badly.

Like a typhoon, the dysentery struck with full force in Dacca. We were both laid low. Neither of us could eat for days. We had no desire to sightsee. In a rare moment of agreement, we checked into the Intercontinental Hotel, the one place we could be sure to get a toilet that would keep flushing.

Had it not been for one thing, we would have had nothing left to squabble about. But that one thing kept us busy—disputing whose turn it was when we both raced to the john.

What a Nice Girl like Me
Was Doing in a Place like Africa

by Loretta Graziano Breuning

I WAS ALWAYS a good girl, not given to high-risk behaviors. Then I took off for the Central African Republic after finishing school in 1976. The United Nations assigned me to an economic planning project. But I had no work when I got there. In Central African Republic, it seems the economic plan is whatever the president decides to put in one pocket and pull out of the other. Anyone who questions that is fired or jailed, sometimes both.

You have a lot of free time when you're advisor to people who don't want your advice. Time to look for love. Time to apply for a transfer. Both of these came through for me in the same week.

The love object was a consultant from the World Trade Organization (then called GATT). In those days, GATT was not a four-letter word. It was an obscure treaty that graduate students wrote papers about. After all the research papers I'd written, the GATT guy visiting our project was a celebrity in my eyes. I offered to help the UN administrators host his visit.

He'd been sent from headquarters in Geneva, Switzerland, but was a native of Madagascar. He told me he was descended from the Indonesian boat people who sailed to Madagascar a thousand years ago. I escorted him by day and he escorted me by night.

It was just dinner, okay? And he was only in town for four days. But I have to admit that by the fourth night, I was smitten. Thinking back, I'm sure his principal charm was that he refused to speak English. I was living in French-speaking Africa, but my UN colleagues insisted on practicing their English on me. I was less assertive about practicing French. My new friend Dazs was willing to hear me out in French instead of switching languages the second I groped for a word.

As soon as he returned to Geneva, he sent me a telegram (yes, a telegram!) offering to buy me a ticket to visit him because he missed me. He had a wife back in Madagascar and I remember him teaching me the colloquial expression for what she can do if she doesn't like it: "She has only to shut herself up." *(Elle n'a qu'a se taire.)*

As luck would have it, the same week I also received a transfer from the United Nations to a different economic planning project, in Upper Volta (since re-named Burkina Faso, meaning "land of upright men"). Since I would be traveling from central Africa to west Africa, why not detour through Europe en route?

Taking vacation required permission from my supervisors at the United Nations as well as the Central African Republic Ministry of Planning. By the time both permissions came through, most flights out of the country were booked. It was September, and planes were full of aid-workers' kids going back to school in France. My only ticket out was on Aeroflot, the Russian airline. It had stopovers in Cairo and Moscow.

Yahoo! Free trips to two more countries. I was ready to go as soon as I completed the medical exit exam. This was routine for international staff, and I would not even remember it except for the blood test performed with the intimidating fat kind of needle. This re-usable needle was still vivid in my mind a few years later when AIDS was identified and traced back to Zaire, a stone's throw from where I was stuck.

Finally I boarded Aeroflot, the flagship airline of commu-
nism. Hot tea was served with lumps of sugar so hard they
didn't dissolve. I remember trying to console myself that their
sugar-processing technology could not possibly be a reflec-
tion on their aircraft technology.

Soon, the plane made an unscheduled landing. Hey, who's
to say the Soviet airline should abide by capitalist conventions
like rigid schedules? We were somewhere in northern Nige-
ria, taking on a hundred boys headed for scholarships at Patrice
Lumumba University in Moscow. Since I had an Ivy League
education, I knew chapter and verse about Patrice Lumumba,
CIA victim. (In fact, I had a command of every alleged CIA
assassination plot, not just those in the Congo, later Zaire, later
Congo.)

I had scheduled a two-day stay-over in Egypt. We landed
at midnight, and when I stepped out of the airport, I saw a
huge illuminated Exxon sign in Arabic script. This immersion
in the exotic thrilled me. If I had other feelings about being
alone in the Middle East at midnight, changing money and
asking a taxi driver for a hotel, I have blocked them out.

The hotel had bed bugs. I remember being awake the whole
night with insane itching. At dawn, I got up and started walking around Cairo. Newspapers for sale on the street had large
pictures of Mao Tse-tung. I couldn't read the Arabic headlines,
but clearly Mao had died.

By 6 A.M., I had stumbled across the breakfast buffet at the
Cairo Hilton. It was a good thing, because later I found it
impossible to eat. None of the restaurants I walked past had
any women in them. I bought some baklava and ate it while
walking the streets. I braved a restaurant before the dinner
hour, while it was still empty. I remember the owner standing
by my table to chat with me. He was very gentleman-like, but

at the same time it was one of those "Who are you with, little girl? Where are you staying?" conversations.

The next day I booked myself on a tour to Alexandria and a night tour of the Giza pyramids. I was befriended by a young man who was also traveling alone. By the end of the day, it seemed we had something in common. He told me he was Saudi, though he had introduced himself as Jordani. And I confessed that I was American, though I had introduced myself as British.

The next day I flew on to Moscow, carrying a kilo of exquisite Egyptian baklava under my arm. As I went through customs in the Soviet Union, a man with big boots and a machine gun ejected me from the line and sent me to a guarded holding area. My big-booted captors offered no explanation. The holding pen gradually filled up while I munched on baklava. Hours later we were herded to an airport restaurant. There I met an Indian woman en route to London who had a clue. Apparently, we all arrived in Moscow without a visa. That is effectively declaring yourself a spy.

After the meal, we were put on a bus under armed guard, driven a long distance to a hotel for suspected spies, and escorted to our rooms. Early in the morning, I was graciously awakened by a knock. I heard an attendant unlock my door. I stepped into the hallway in time to watch her unlocking other doors. Apparently we had all been locked in our rooms from the outside all night. Soon we were herded onto a bus back to the airport. There was no charge for this night on the town in Moscow—meals and accommodation for in-transit passengers provided courtesy of the Soviet people. There were obviously advantages to being a security risk.

Soon enough, the communist world was behind me and my true love lay ahead. Dazs escorted me through diplomatic

Geneva, which was quite a thrill for an international trade major. To my surprise, Geneva has a reputation for being a very quiet town. Drinking is the major activity. Most people have diplomatic access to tax-free alcohol.

Dazs, it turned out, was an alcoholic. Somehow that had escaped my notice during our dinners under the stars. But in his small Geneva apartment, the ubiquitous Scotch bottle could not be overlooked. Dazs was very sweet, and I felt no danger (except when he was driving). But because he was nice, I thought I might hide the bottle for him. It was the playful gesture of an innocent 23-year-old who had never encountered alcoholism.

Apparently I hid the bottle pretty well because he couldn't find it. He begged me for it. He begged in French! I remember the scene as if it were in a movie. I was so naïve that all I could think of was the pride of being able to have an argument in French. "If Madame Trottier from Oceanside Junior High could see me now...."

Dazs and I parted in Paris. I had a ticket from Paris to Ouagadougou (is your atlas handy?), and in the good old days, you could stop anywhere en route for free. I took it into my head to stop in Morocco, the Canary Islands and Senegal.

I was not the first girl to travel alone to Marrakesh, and in fact I had the brains to hook up with other girls en route. The most dangerous thing I did in Morocco was live on dried fruits and nuts. After several days' consumption, I found they had worms.

I got a bug in Morocco, but I didn't know it until later. My 6 A.M. departure from Casablanca was delayed, and by the time the flight took off I had shivered in the desert cold for hours. When I arrived in the Canary Islands, I had chills and a high fever. I passed out in a hotel room and didn't wake up until the next day. I struggled for the strength to find a doctor. I also struggled for the words to find a doctor, since Spanish was the language of the Islas Canarias.

The doctor diagnosed me with strep throat and prescribed—you will excuse my indelicacy—suppositories. I will never forget because they cured me instantaneously. I even saved one and carried it with me for years.

On the flight from the Canary Islands to Senegal, I survived another unscheduled stop—in Spanish Sahara. Your atlas may mention the civil war there at the time. But heck, when you need gas, you need gas.

Once in Dakar, Senegal, I took a cab driver's recommendation for a hotel. Euphemisms aside, the place was a whorehouse. I didn't figure it out until six months later, when I was in another whorehouse in Africa. Cut me some slack, here—the situation is more common than you might think. I could not afford the Western hotel chains, and I didn't know that local hotels are effectively "dual purpose." When you check in, there's a noisy scene going on in a saloon adjoining the lobby. You go to your spartan quarters and notice that the hotel seems empty. In the middle of the night, you hear lots of voices and door slamming. And in the morning, you sense that you are the only person in the hotel, again. When this happened to me on a later trip through Ghana, I finally put the pieces together. Believe me, I am not the first person this has happened to. I will bet you that somewhere in the world, an Italian Catholic girl with a Ph.D. in international trade is checking herself into a whorehouse right now.

If my daughter reads this story and gets any smart ideas, it'll kill me. Thank goodness she hated her French class.

Hong Kong Flush

by Cameron Burns

Editors' Note: Not every story that hits our desk is down and out. Occasionally writers such as Cameron Burns offer favorable accounts. Consider this one an intermission of sorts from the world of trouble travel.

HONG KONG is better known as a glittering, fast-paced commercial hub—Las Vegas meets Rodeo Drive or Times Square on steroids. But this city-state of seven million has two completely different faces: the dense, adrenaline-filled rush of pure urbanity; and the quiet, lush and totally compelling outdoors. Hong Kong, if you will, is really two places. The human and the non-human. The boxes—as I like to call the built environment—and the bush.

During a flight that circled around the northern perimeter of the Pacific Ocean, I read a few recent news clippings about Hong Kong. During the latter twentieth century, Hong Kong was in the news quite a bit because the colony was handed back to China after more than 150 years under British rule. Before the 1997 hand-over occurred, political analysts, journalists and much of the general public expected the proposed Sino-British Joint Declaration (which called for the Chinese government to employ a hands-off approach to ruling Hong Kong) to be nothing more than lip service. It was feared the people of Hong Kong were about to be muzzled, both socially and politically. Some businesses relocated to Singapore and other Pacific Rim cities, many Westerners moved out, and East Asia prepared for a jolt.

Of course, after a round of fireworks over Victoria Harbor on June 30, 1997, and some tearful speeches by Chris Patten, Hong Kong's last British governor, the expectations fueled by Tiananmen Square and the Chinese-Tibetan situation fizzled. The dire predictions about the Chinese rule did not come true and, from a historical perspective, were probably questionable to begin with. "Some of the worst fears about heavy-handed Chinese rule over Hong Kong have so far not come to pass," reported the *New York Times* on Jan. 17, 2001. "Just last weekend some 1,200 members of the Falun Gong sect (a group that practices a form of exercise, similar to Tai Chi), which has been heavily persecuted on the mainland, were allowed to hold a mass gathering in a concert hall owned by the Hong Kong government."

The British hand-over coincided loosely with the Asian financial crisis of the late 1990s. The day after Hong Kong went back under Chinese rule, Thailand devalued its currency, the *bhat*, causing—in part—the entire Eastern Hemisphere to grind into an economic slump. Hong Kong made headlines again, but mostly because it is the Western financial center for the Eastern world and its economy—like Tokyo's—was an icon of Asian prosperity. Hong Kong has never made headlines because of its outdoor activities. For the past 30 years, the city has been famous for Asia's top industrial trade hub, its dynamic, fast-paced retail life and great martial arts movies. People think of electronics, clothes, shoes and jewelry when the topic of Hong Kong comes up; not trail running, rock climbing and sea kayaking.

Luckily, for me I hadn't seen back-in-the-good-old-days

Hong Kong, before the Chinese takeover, and I wasn't a connoisseur of the art of shopping. I'd seen a photo of someone rock climbing on Kowloon Peak, and that's what I wanted to do—go rock climbing.

Ironically, when I started at the University of Colorado as an undergraduate in 1983, the first book I ever encountered in Norlin Library's Rare Books collection was a rock-climbing guide to Hong Kong (called, predictably enough, *Rock Climbs of Hong Kong*). If memory serves, it was a book dated to the mid-1950s. My closest companion of the period, Benny Bach, and I used to break up our long hours in the library with trips into Rare Books to examine and ponder this gem. Of course, the ancient pages of the tome couldn't handle much in the way of enthusiastic fondling, so after about three nights it was in tatters and we had to content ourselves with other rare books (like *An Historical Guide to Boulder County Irrigation Ditches: Vol IX*) lest studying get in the way of a pleasant evening out. *Rock Climbs of Hong Kong?* Was the author serious? Who knew?

The plane banked into its final turn, and we came rumbling down onto the runway. Out my window I could just make out the city's form: stacked vertical columns lit up like blockish Christmas trees spread across shimmering water. This looked like a fine city.

I caught a taxi into town and found my way to the Salisbury YMCA in the wonderfully named Tsim Sha Tsui area of Kowloon.

The Salisbury YMCA isn't really a YMCA—rather, it's a really posh hotel. I was shown to a room on the 12th floor. It was small but well-appointed with a stocked fridge, two single, neatly made beds and a desk with a comfortable chair. Everything was slightly smaller, slightly daintier than you'd find in an equivalent hotel in the States, but very clean, neat and appealing. Young Christian men in Asia must be regarded highly.

I dropped my bags, made a cup of tea (one of the benefits of visiting former British colonies) and headed out into the streets to find my old pal. Benny, never one to miss an interesting place, had flown in two days prior and was in a hotel just down the street. When I'd mentioned I was going to Hong Kong, he and his girlfriend, Angie Moquin, had traded in some frequent flier miles and decided to join me. I descended to Hankow Road, then wandered up to Peking Road, turned right toward Nathan Road and was pleasantly surprised to find myself looking at the infamous Chungking Mansions..

A rotten old concrete structure known for being something of a small city unto itself, Chunking Mansions is not a French country villa famous for its dim sum.. It's actually dozens of small hotels, some occupying a few rooms on each floor, some occupying whole floors. These hotels have names like Imperial Gardens Hotel and Chungking Boarding House, but the names do little to describe the physical form these hotels take. They are, simply, a collection of starkly lit, filthy box-shaped rooms with cheap cruddy furniture and generally very little in the way of windows or other access to air. One guidebook to Hong Kong calls Chungking Mansions "a high-rise dump," which sums it up rather accurately. I glanced back toward the Salisbury YMCA and thought of my room and smiled.

Benny was, of course, holed up in a building next door to the Chungking Mansions, which turned out to be its unofficial twin brother. We met on the street, then he led me up a tight stairway to a narrow hall with dozens of seedy-looking people going in all directions. He mentioned the name of the hotel as we squeezed past several young men in the hall. I could have sworn he said "fire hazard." We turned a corner, and Benny opened a door.

His room was about eight-by-ten feet, with an eight-foot ceiling. Its walls were completely finished with white bathroom tiles "so you can hose it down," Benny suggested. A large fluorescent light buzzed overhead. It reminded me of looking in the fridge at midnight. The entire room was filled with two large, rickety wooden beds that seemed bigger than the available space. How they were carried up the stairs and squeezed into such a small, confined space was an intriguing mystery until it was suggested they were built *insitu*.

Angie was lying on one of the beds studying a book about Hong Kong. She looked up when we arrived, her face a mixture of desperation and sadness. Benny pointed out the "bathroom" (and I use the term loosely here), a square space about the size of a phone booth. It was built into one wall, and a toilet sat in its center. Attached to the wall on the left side of the toilet was a sink. Above the sink was a showerhead. It was one of those arrangements where you can put your elbow on the sink, prop your head up in your palm and do your business while showering. "Yeah, and check this out," Benny said. One of the giant beds was crammed up so hard against the "bathroom" that you could stand on it, while peeing into the toilet. Benny did me the favor of demonstrating the stance but not the arc. I thought of my beloved Salisbury YMCA and felt warm and fuzzy.

We went out into the streets and wandered around for as long as possible before Benny and Angie eventually returned to the Kowloon Fire Hazard Inn and I to the Salisbury YMCA. The following morning, they moved in with me.

Once Benny and Angie were comfortably ensconced in the extra bed in Room 1202 of the Salisbury YMCA, we gathered our gear, and headed for the Tsim Sha Tsui MTR (Mass Transit Railway) station and worked our way onto a train for Central, the downtown part of Hong Kong. Not once, in 20 years of climbing, have I taken a bus or subway for a mountain experience, but as I quickly learned, Hong Kong is unique in every aspect—including its outdoors. At Central we switched trains and rode the subway out to Chai Wan, on the eastern side of Victoria Island. There, we caught a European-style double-decker bus and headed for a beach town called Shek-O, which is surrounded by brown granite domes popping up out of the water. The rock climbing at Shek-O, we soon learned, is superb. The orange-brown granite crags of Shek-O are some of the best I've ever touched. The rock is coarse but compact, just like California's Joshua Tree or Wyoming's Vedauwoo climbing areas.

Sea cliff climbing is rare in the Americas; decent oceanside cliffs simply don't exist. It is a much more European tradition, especially for the British, whose small but varied island is rimmed by a highly three-dimensional coast. Since Hong Kong has been British for so long, and it's geographically similar to the Mother Isle in terms of its rocky coast, it's no surprise that the coastline cliffs have been well developed for climbing. Several of the best crags are over the water, making for atmospheric and inspiring climbing.

Of course, after our day at Shek-O, it rained for two days. Benny, Angie and I had to be content with wandering around the city in a downpour while thumbing through the sodden pages of the 1994 edition of *Rock Climbs of Hong Kong,* bummed out that we were wasting so much time. Benny and Angie flew home a few days later, just when the weather was drying up, so I arranged to do things with Hong Kong locals with whom I'd been put in touch by the Hong Kong Tourist Association.

Over the remainder of my visit, I got to sea kayak for many miles through the clear blue waters around the Sai Kung Peninsula with local kayak guide Paul Etherington; climb at several crags, including the 600-foot tall cliffs on Kowloon Peak with Paul's brother in-law Guy Bigwood and his girlfriend Janet Cheung; and trail-run on Lantau Island's 3,000-foot Phoenix Peak (popular with peak-baggers). These are parts of Hong Kong most people—except a few diehard Westerners—don't ever see, or even have the desire to see. From my perspective, they are missing the best part of this strange little Chinese sub-nation. I've never been so impressed with a major city's great outdoors. Why would anyone want to squander time in Chungking Mansions or the Kowloon Fire Hazard Inn when there's so much to do outside?

To understand Hong Kong's vast outdoors, the city and its physical surroundings, you first need a little explanation. Hong Kong is not just one big city perched on the edge of Asia against the South China Sea. Hong Kong is, for all intents and purposes, a small, geographically diverse nation (the Hong Kong Special Administrative Region or SAR). This nation occupies a peninsula attached to mainland China, as well as an archipelago of some 235 islands of various sizes scattered around the peninsula. The total land area is about 400 square miles. The city part of Hong Kong—the part you already know about—lies mostly on two sides of Victoria Harbor on the southern edge of the archipelago.

More important than the physical layout of Hong Kong is the manner in which the built environment has evolved, or rather, not evolved. In Hong Kong, there are no suburbs. The built-up parts of Hong Kong are as built-up as any place on earth, with skyscrapers up to 50, 60, 70 stories and more. Meanwhile, you can step across a street and literally be in temperate jungle wilderness. There are no Western-style 35-acre ranchettes or sprawling subdivisions cluttering up the surface of the earth. It's all huge buildings (of little boxes) or wilderness. Even Hong Kong Island, a 30-square-mile island where downtown is located, is mostly natural land.

According to government figures, about 40 percent of Hong Kong's entire land area is formally set aside for conservation in 23 country and marine parks. Most of the rest of the land area of the Hong Kong SAR remains undeveloped too, and having seen a lot of it from many angles, I would venture to guess as much as 75 percent of the land remains in a natural state.

Biologically, Hong Kong is more diverse than all the Western U.S. states combined. Until almost a decade ago, Hong Kong's native flora and fauna was little documented. Then, in the early 1990s, the World Wide Fund for Nature helped fund a study that among other things revealed 210 types of seaweed, 175 types of fern, 1,900 flowering plants (including 120 orchid species), 2,000 moth species, 225 butterflies, 107 dragonflies, 96 freshwater fish species, 23 amphibians, 78 reptiles, 445 birds and 57 mammals (including civets and macaques). Not bad for a place regarded as Asia's biggest shopping mall.

Despite all this great outdoorsy stuff, Hong Kong is not famous for its rock climbing, sea kayaking and trail running. It is famous for Jackie Chan and knock-offs. Jackie Chan is an actor whose films have become phenomenally popular worldwide and who, hopefully, needs no introduction. Jackie Chan is my hero. He'll be your hero too, once you see one of his films. (I recently did a web search and found over a quarter-million web pages mentioning Jackie Chan—that's how cool he is.) It's no wonder that he's become a marketing tool for the Hong Kong government.

Meanwhile, knock-offs are brand name clothes and shoes that have been manufactured without consent of the brand owner. In other words, just as there are millions of Jackie Chan videos circling the globe, there are also millions of articles of fake clothing, shoes and accessories illegally labeled Nike, Adidas, Ralph Lauren, Tommy Hilfiger, Rolex, Coach, Louis Vuitton, The Gap, Eddie Bauer, WalMart and J.C. Penney.

The knock-off business is a worldwide game. In 1982, it was estimated that the illegal knock-off business cost the U.S. economy $5.5 billion in lost jobs and profits as well as law enforcement expenses. The estimate was revised in 1998 to $66 billion, and then to $200 billion in 1999. What it costs the entire world is a number I haven't found. But it's Hong Kong that has been at the center of the knock-off industry for many years, not because counterfeit products are necessarily made in the City of Life but because Hong Kong is a major business hub for the region.

Sitting close to mainland China, Taiwan, Vietnam, Thailand and other poor Southeast Asian nations where the stuff is made, Hong Kong is a town filled with agents, business managers and manufacturing subcontractors of big name footwear and clothing apparel. Most are conducting legitimate trade and are overseeing the manufacturing of their goods. But others are doing less than honorable work, organizing the manufacture and shipping of questionable products with million-dollar labels on them.

And still others are spies. The clothing, footwear and accessories industries are so big they have their own spies working diligently to catch and prosecute counterfeiters. They roam the back alleys, factories and ports of Southeast Asia looking for fake shoes, clothes, purses and belts. The counterfeit industry is so big in Southeast Asia that dozens of law firms from around the globe have branches there dealing—in many cases—primarily with knock-offs.

One law firm in Bangkok, Tilleke & Gibbins, has done so much work with knocked-off goods that they've actually created a museum dedicated to these artifacts. And this is an amazing thing. I'll quote from Tilleke & Gibbins excellent web page: "The Tilleke & Gibbins Museum of Counterfeit Goods was established in 1989 at the firm's Bangkok, Thailand, office. However, long before that time, the firm had already in hand the main prerequisites to start a museum in the form of a large volume of counterfeit and pirated goods accumulated over the years from raids conducted on behalf of the firm's clients. The goods, which were used as evidence in court, were then stashed away in boxes, taking up valuable storage space and serving no purpose whatsoever. With the collection growing rapidly, it became apparent that a way should be found which would take advantage of the counterfeit goods and turn them from the liability they were posing to a useful purpose."

Tilleke & Gibbins's then senior partner David Lyman realized that his firm's rip-off collection might "prove useful as educational tools if properly displayed and accessible for public viewing" and a museum was born. The museum started out with about 100 items separated into several areas: clothing, leather goods, electronics and toiletries. "However, with new items gathered on a continuing basis from raids overseen by the firm, plus samples of the genuine goods which the firm obtains, the collection has rapidly grown. At present, the museum has approximately fifteen hundred pieces of infringing trademark and copyrighted goods, making it the largest one of its kind in Thailand."

From a quick look at the museum (visible online at www.tginfo.com/museum/museum.htm), it's clear that Tilleke &

Gibbins's lawyers aren't messing around. If you look in the section called "Edible Products," there is a picture of a box of Mrs. Fields Cookies. Sitting next to it is a similar box with a very similar design, except the words say Denis' Cookies, not Mrs. Fields Cookies. To the left and below the cookie infraction are two bars of chocolate. The upper bar is good old Toblerone, that great Swiss stuff that breaks off in the triangular chunks and is the single best gift to have on hand when disembarking a plane from Europe. Below the bar of Toblerone is a similarly shaped bar of something called Tamborine.

"These counterfeit packagings of edible products differ only slightly from the genuine packagings," states the photo caption. "At a glance, many nonregular consumers would mistake the counterfeit version for the original. As for the goods themselves, one can never tell if they meet health and safety standards."

Like I said, these lawyers aren't messing around. Obviously, there has been an infraction of some kind of copyrighted packaging and name recognition thing—Denis and the folks at Tamborine Chocolate Co. have trodden on sacred ground. But let's look at the bigger picture. Who doesn't love traveling to foreign lands and seeing stuff like bars of Tamborine Chocolate and Denis' Cookies? I mean, sure, they're ripping off the designs and the names, but these lawyers seem to fail to realize the entertainment value here is greater than any cookie or bar of chocolate. Who hasn't giggled at an Adidas T-shirt on a poor Mexican farmer, or chuckled with glee over an L.A. Lakers jersey in the African countryside? I've had the opportunity to do both and found the experiences incredibly rewarding.

Heck, I've never bought Mrs. Fields Cookies, but I sure would buy myself a box of Denis' Cookies if the opportunity arose simply because they are Denis' Cookies. (Perhaps Mrs.

Fields would be wise to rip off Denis and start calling her product Mrs. Denis Fields Cookies, but I digress.)

The night after climbing at Shek-O, Benny, Angie and I wandered the Temple Street night market for many hours (even my Salisbury YMCA room, we decided, was cramped). Here, in block after block of closed-off streets filled with stalls and vendors and all sorts of bright lights, it's possible to buy anything. I bought silk shirts, underwear and robes, all with interesting names and logos. The underwear had "Rock Star" on the label, the shirts were made by a company that put no label in the product, and the robes had a Chinese character. The 20 silk ties I purchased all had South Park and Warner Bros. characters on them, undoubtedly sans permission from the owners of the images. The best was a vest with the label Versanni, which I can only imagine was meant to be a Versace knock-off. Heck, who can fault the Chinese factory workers making the stuff. Versanni, Versace, it must all read the same to them. Ironically, four months after I had wandered down from rock climbing on Kowloon Peak, through the Tung Choi Street neighborhood in Hong Kong's Mong Kok neighborhood, customs officers seized $1.3 million worth of counterfeit goods.

"In the first case, Customs officers of Trade Descriptions Investigation Division in an anti-counterfeiting operation seized about 4,300 garments and 1,300 counterfeit leather goods," said a news statement. "In another case, Customs officers at Lok Ma Chau Control Point seized 9,802 pairs of shoes, all bearing false origin labels, worth about $1.06 million, from an incoming lorry. Among the seizure, 810 pairs were counterfeit shoes."

So what happens to counterfeit goods? When knock-off artists are busted, often the company they work for and the local police insist on destroying the goods, usually by burning them. In early 2000, the athletic shoe company New Balance helped police nab counterfeiters in Indonesia, who had manufactured some 160,000 pairs of knock-off shoes.

"The shoes, called New Basket, Dallas Star and One Star, which infringed upon both New Balance and Converse trademarks, were burned publicly at the police headquarters in West Java," stated a May 9, 2000, New Balance press release. "This event represented the largest seizure/destruction of counterfeit footwear in Asia to date."

Certainly, the knock-off trade is a truly massive industry. But you've got to wonder whether destroying all these counterfeit shoes is such a great idea. Aren't they still wearable, regardless of the label on the side? And the amount of resources gobbled up when more than a hundred thousand pairs of shoes are burned must be huge. Certainly the carbon emissions generated through the destruction of these illegal goods (by burning them) must be sizable, and the resources and energy required to re-manufacture 160,000 pairs of shoes can't be good for Mother Earth either.

One has to wonder whether New Balance's marketing plan wouldn't have been better aided if the company (and law enforcement officials) had simply seized the shoes, then sent them to charities.

Walking around in my running shoes, I found it strange that the local Chinese residents seem to have little interest in any outdoor activities. When I went hiking on the peaks above the Choi Hung neighborhood I had the place to myself. When rock climbing—on any of Hong Kong's cliffs—there was no one else around. When I went sea kayaking for two full days around Sai Kung Paul I saw a few fishermen but certainly no other kayakers; and when trail running on Lantau it was just the birds and me.

The Japanese and Koreans are nutty about skiing and running and climbing. Japan boasts the biggest indoor ski slopes on earth, and last time I was big-walling on El Capitan in Yosemite Valley, there were several Korean teams slaving away. But the Chinese of Hong Kong seem uninterested. Taiwan, I was told, is similar. A large island covered with some of Asia's most beautiful outdoors, it boasts great hiking, climbing, camping, kayaking ... whatever you like. There, I know of a man — a friend of a friend — who owns an outdoor equipment shop. He has no competition, yet sales are so poor he has trouble staying in business.

That's not to say Southeastern Asia's people are backward or uninspired — to the contrary. I found Hong Kong's Chinese some of the most polite, considerate, hard-working and orderly folks on earth. In fact, they are — in almost every way — far in advance of us Westerners. Their streets are spotless, their society is immaculately ordered and their technological innovations seem constantly ahead.

So, maybe that's what makes Hong Kong unique. The built, human, urban side of Hong Kong, is amazing — outdistancing most Western urban areas in terms of civility and functionality by leaps and bounds. Yet, on the other hand, Hong Kong's pristine, rugged, untrammeled outdoors are among the finest. It's a combination that's hard to fathom, yet easy to experience. Step off a subway, and within a few steps you can be hiking; hop out a taxi door and you can be next to a seriously good cragging cliff; get off the bus and across the street you squeeze into a sea kayak. It's a great mix, easily worth shaking up your senses and every preconceived notion you've ever had about Hong Kong. After all, Hong Kong is really two places. The human, and the nonhuman.

In Hong Kong there's life inside the box, so to speak, and life out of the box. I liked both.

French Fried

by Brian Abrahams

Only peril can bring the French together. One can't impose unity out of the blue on a country that has 265 different kinds of cheese.
—*Charles de Gaulle*

THE FRENCH do everything more beautifully and elegantly than anyone else, and unfortunately they know it.

In keeping with their love of aesthetics, no one is allowed to walk on their wonderful green spaces. Strictly lookee, no touchee (amazing what 150 hours of French lessons can do, huh?). However, *you* try to keep a toddler off a gorgeous empty expanse.

We were with my 2-year-old son and another couple in the Tuileries, the decorative gardens next to the Louvre in Paris. A royal palace used to be there, but in a fit of the anti-establishment fever that overcomes the French regularly, they burned it down. Some wigged dude's loss is our gain because the Tuileries are beautiful, full of statues, fountains and French babes wearing black. Posted signs in French warn passersby not to go on the lawns, but my son didn't parlez vous and made a beeline for one of them. From the edge of the grass I was calling in a stage whisper, "Coby, you get back here, right now! *Right now!*" He wouldn't listen, of course.

A narrow, muddy drainage groove ran across the lawn, and he started digging his foot in it. I called again, but he was in full toddler mode. I hurried across the grass trying to step as lightly as possible. I finally reached Coby and swept him up in my arms angrily. The French can be so intimidating (and don't they love it) that I couldn't bear to have my feet on their grass. So I hurried back across the lawn trying to fit my steps into the drainage groove as I went so I didn't damage a single green blade. Big mistake. I tripped and went flying, my son sailing out of my arms. I landed in the mud and grass, pulling muscles in my neck and hurting my arm and wrist. My son landed on his face and had the first bloody nose of his life. For a kid who rarely cries in pain he screamed. Lots of Frenchies were looking, and I was mortified.

When we had all calmed down and bucked up with some Roquefort, we decided to continue with our plans for the day. Inside the Louvre was the Paris Antiques Biennial, a once every two years opportunity to see wares of the top antiques dealers in the world. I was muddy and because of the fall was in a lot of pain. The best position to minimize it was to hold my arm awkwardly to one side and tilt my head slightly to the left. I decided to gamely proceed, so we all went into the Louvre to see the show and maybe pick up a few French knickknacks for the ol' mantle.

I was doing my best to try and not look like a complete freak show. Needless to say none of the other patrons or exhibitors at the show were muddy with one arm hanging uselessly. My wife was pushing our son in the stroller. (He was, of course, totally recovered, and the incident already forgotten.) One wheel on the stroller was spinning wildly in all the wrong directions. These strollers have to be designed on purpose for the wheels to so consistently become deliriously insane. As a Type A, rather than have my wife actually stop the stroller for few seconds I decided to use one foot to fix it while the stroller was still moving. The problem was that the mud from the Tuileries had dried to a thin film on the bottom of my shoes. So when I threw one leg forward to kick the stroller wheel into submission, my other foot went smoothly out from under me and I did a triple axel onto my spine and shoulder blade onto the cold marble floor. The wind was knocked out of me, and I wrenched my back. I heard some kind of hue and cry in French, but before too many people could rush over I did my best to jump up and act like nothing had happened.

Now I was in really serious pain. My neck, wrist and arm from before, plus my back and shoulder blade. The only way to minimize the pain was to keep the limp arm dangling in front of my belly, hunch my right shoulder, tilt my head slightly to the left and bend a little forward. Plus I was muddy.

We were less than a mile or so from Notre Dame in case they ordered me into the bell tower, but I was determined to see this antiques show. Far from a flea market with a bunch of rickety card tables set up displaying used Barbies and *Green Acres* matching salt and pepper shakers, the Paris Biennial is *tres* chic. We're talking Ramses II and the Tang Dynasty, one of those "If you have to ask, you can't afford it" deals. Most of the patrons were in suits and dresses, providing a vivid contrast to my "muddy American hunchback in jeans" look. As I hinked and limped through the show I got more bad looks from the elegant Parisians. To make matters more stressful, this was probably the worst place on the entire planet to take an active toddler. Every time he got more than a few feet from one of us, I pictured years in a French prison, unable to pay for the rare Shlong Dynasty jade bidet that had been broken by my son.

Suddenly I came upon an alcove where there seemed to be a little buzz. I looked up and there standing in front of me was

Jacques Chirac, the president of France. Here I was, hunch-backed and twisted, my face contorted in pain, standing just a few feet away from Le Man. In America you can't get within a football field of the president without a body cavity search. In Paris I was close enough for their leader to see the dirt pattern on my jeans. He did have security, and one of them was staring me down with a cold, angry look. Couldn't they afford Ray-Bans? I pretended to be examining a vase, and when I looked up he was still watching me. Ah, they were all probably forgeries anyway. I gave my wife the "Let's get out of this overpriced Popsicle stand" look and we left for the hotel, where a hot bath gave me back some of my range of movement, although none of my dignity or pride.

A Synagogue in Kabul

by Jake Greenberg

"So where are you going on your next trip?" my mother asked.

"Afghanistan, India and Nepal," I replied. It was a hot, humid July night in 1976.

My father had passed away that week, and we were observing the Jewish mourning ritual of "sitting Shiva." I assumed my mother was making idle conversation, until sometime later when she said, "I thought about your trip and would like to join you." I couldn't believe my ears. My parents' idea of an exotic adventure was staying at the Caribe Hilton Hotel in San Juan, Puerto Rico. I explained that India, Afghanistan and Nepal were primitive countries and travel under the best of conditions would be difficult. Mom remained steadfast. She wanted to get away from Scarsdale, New York, and that was as far away as she could imagine being for the Jewish High Holy days. Besides we could stop off in Israel for a few days. I could see that this was one debate that I was not going to win with a 67-year-old recently widowed mother.

She insisted we stay at five-star hotels at her expense. This would be a novel experience. A $5 a night hotel was a splurge for me. We landed in Tel Aviv's Ben Gurion Airport, where I was stopped at passport control when Israeli agents noticed that I had Egypt, Morocco, Turkey, Jordan and Syria stamped but none from Israel. I spent the next two hours explaining to them that I imported oriental carpets. Reluctantly, they let me pass through and we taxied to Jerusalem, where I booked us into the American Colony Hotel, a former sultan's palace with 20-foot ceilings, oriental rugs and marble floors At 5 A.M. we were awakened by the first call to Moslem prayer. "You couldn't have booked us into the King David Hotel on the Jewish side?" my mother asked plaintively. This was going to be a long, long trip.

After three days in Israel we flew to Tehran, where we were scheduled to spend two hours and then board our Ariana Afghan Airways flight to Kabul. Hour after hour passed with no flight in sight. We sat on wooden benches, and our only refreshment options were vodka, caviar, pistachios and Coca-Cola. Every now and then a group of Iranians would leer at my mother.

Finally after 14 hours in the airport we boarded our flight for Kabul. The Kabul Intercontinental Hotel looked as if it should be in Paris with elegant rooms and public spaces. On the other hand the streets of Kabul were dirty and dusty. My mother chose the hotel over the streets after a ten-minute tour of the downtown. I explored the carpet stalls on Chicken Street.

When I returned to our room, my mother was out cold on the bed with a sheet over her. She remained in this state for three days. A hotel doctor examined her and shrugged his shoulders when asked his medical opinion. I was in a state of near panic, facing the prospect of taking my mother home in a body bag. Finally, the next morning she stirred and opened her eyes. "How are you feeling, Mother?" I asked. She smiled and said, "I think tomorrow is Yom Kippur. Find out if there is a synagogue in Kabul we can go to."

The synagogue in Kabul was an experience I will never forget. It was as if we had gone back 500 years in time. The small building looked like it had been carved out of ancient rock. Inside the dimly lit room were about a dozen benches. Fewer then 20 people were inside, most of them as ancient as the building. I realize now that this group probably comprised the total Jewish population of Kabul. I sat in one of the front rows, and my mother sat in back with the other women in keeping with the Orthodox custom of segregating the sexes. I understood very little of the service. However, there was something moving about praying halfway around the world with people who shared a common bond. And, I had something to pray and say thanks for, with the safe and healthy return of my mother.

The Ruins of Copán

by Thomas O. Sloane

"RELAX FOR A WHILE. Sleep if you like," Al suggested. We had just boarded his bus. "By sunrise we'll be at San Pedro Sula, partway up the mountain, where we'll stop for a break."

A pleasant-looking young Honduran who spoke almost accentless English, Al was to be our guide for the day. After his announcement, he sat down near our driver in one of those forward-facing seats designed for tour guides aboard luxury buses (we had been assured many times that this was indeed to be a *luxury* tour, worth the money) and turned off his microphone. A large TV set, its screen easily visible by all passengers, hung over the front windshield, just above Al's chair. The TV was off. In fact, it was never to come on. The air conditioning was also off. There was no need for either just then, since the passengers were still drowsy and the air was cool in the early summer pre-dawn of Puerto Cortés.

Three buses were gathered on the dock alongside our cruise ship, the *Regent Sea*. Two were full—the third, ours, was almost full—their motors humming in preparation for our departure into the Honduran interior. We were going to visit Copán, site of some of the most famous ruins along the Maya Route. Promptly at 3:45 A.M. the buses departed, their interiors darkened.

Barbara and I seemed to be the only two passengers with reading lights on. We were still poring over guidebooks and weren't sleepy anyway. Retired teachers and long-time students of European culture, we were experienced travelers, mainly in Europe of the Frommer do-it-yourself type. This was our first trip to Central America, our first cruise, our first luxury trip. Because we had read that certain Mayan ruins were nearly inaccessible, we thought a little splurge might be worth it. Aboard ship, though, we quickly discovered that many of the cruise line's luxury features were a dud. The Vegas-style entertainment was boring, and the midnight banquets were for gluttons only. So we'd fallen into the habit of retiring early.

As our bus moved up the mountain, we continued to read while most of the others slept. Of course at that dreary hour there was little to be seen outside. "Darkness visible" was the phrase that popped into my head as I glanced up. The phrase was to prove curiously prophetic.

By the time we reached San Pedro Sula, Barbara and I had read enough. A sparkling, clear day had dawned. The other passengers started rousing themselves. After a brief stop at the Copantl Hotel, we resumed our trip, and Al began a narrative of Honduran history. The views from the bus then—ours was the last of the three to leave the Copantl—were lovely: the mountains and valleys deep green, with misty fogs rising slowly toward a bright blue sky. Al had earlier said that we would eventually climb to 3,000 feet.

"Hmm," I murmured, "we climb over twice that high when we drive from the Bay Area to Tahoe."

"Yeah, but," Barbara said, pointing to a thin red line that on our map stretched from San Pedro Sula to Copán, "this is not Route 80." Whatever it was, it was better than the route our guidebooks had described, the one most non-splurging visitors take, overland from Guatemala to Copán. We were traveling in an air-conditioned bus with plush seats. And we were on a paved road. Well, mostly paved. There were large patches of cracked and worn concrete. Several sections were marked off for repair, forcing detours over baseball-size gravel on a route that wound around sharply and ascended steeply. As the morning progressed, the bus bumped and hummed along and climbed steadily. With the sun blazing, we surmised that the heat was climbing too. Just then the air conditioning began a curiously strained whir.

Almost immediately, the whir was joined by some troubling noises from the motor and curious rumblings beneath our feet. Then the motor stopped.. Al and the driver conferred in rapid Spanish. Mysteriously the motor began again. But no sooner had Al resumed his narrative than the noises, the whirring and the rumblings also resumed, and again the motor stopped. This time the conference between Al and the driver was in urgent if muffled Spanish. "What the hell?" asked a bald man, seated near us with his wife. Another nearby passenger, an attractive woman apparently traveling alone, leaned forward to try to hear what Al and the driver were saying. Across the aisle from us, a sturdily built middle-aged woman, with her equally sturdily built husband, began grumbling loudly in some foreign tongue that itself rumbled. Most of us were simply perplexed, though a little fear surely began to creep in as we saw the other two buses climb well ahead of us and disappear around a turn. Stalled and abandoned, we were alone in a wilderness that just moments ago was only a lovely deep green background to Al's history lesson.

"Our bus is losing power," said Al, "and, uh, well, help is not available." He said this with that wonderful Hispanic shrug in which the shoulders come up almost even with the ears and the hands are splayed outward, a gesture that can speak volumes. For miles now our three buses had seemed to be the only vehicles on the road. Even the road repair crews were curiously absent. Cell phones, I should add, were several years in the future, since this was 1994. "It's an hour to Copán," Al continued, "by bus. We are going to try to make it with the air conditioning off to conserve power. Sorry."

The restarted motor didn't exactly hum. It sounded, rather, like a rudely awakened jungle beast. Decidedly unluxurious, but functioning. Heat gradually filled our space. The bald man and I struggled to open windows. Climate-controlled luxury buses are not designed to have any apertures that are easily opened by passengers. Though the heat was defeating us all, it had apparently not affected the motor's power. "What little it has left," I muttered. Al's tactic seemed to be working. We continued our climb with no more stalls. "Just about 20 minutes," he said, turning toward us in his seat. His words were less spoken than chattered out, as the bus began a shuddering ascent over another rocky construction-zone detour, this one on a particularly steep incline. Just as Al completed his message and turned forward in his seat, the large television set slipped its mooring and came crashing down, hitting his left arm and landing in the aisle.

The bald man—a doctor, it turned out—rushed forward. Al signaled the driver to continue and tried to reassure the passengers with dismissive gestures. But several of the overheated, perplexed and at least vaguely fearful passengers hurried forward to help. Notable exceptions were the sturdily built lady and her husband, who remained stationary and audibly disgusted. "Please return to your seats," the doctor advised. "We'll get help for Al when we reach Copán." Al glanced back, with at least a faint affirming smile, and tried to wave with his good arm.

"There's a laceration with minor bleeding on his forearm,"

the doctor said to me quietly upon returning to our seats, "but a very suspicious bruise on his upper arm, in the middle of the humerus. I wouldn't be surprised if the arm were broken. Though how in the hell we're to find out, I don't know. I gave him some Motrin, but I've never seen a more stoic guy. Machismo, perhaps." The doctor's wife looked distressed and wilted, like the rest of us.

In about 20 minutes we arrived at Copán. The doctor accompanied Al to a medical station that, he said, seemed less well equipped than those in children's day camps. Not much aid was available for the motor either, little more than the puzzled expressions of assorted tour bus drivers and guides who peered under the hood and shrugged.

We needed a new guide. Copán offered Spanish-speakers, but most of us had only a tacqueria fluency. One of the available guides, whose remarkable face with its sloping forehead and aquiline nose seemed straight off a Mayan glyph, spoke at least minimal English. And Lorraine, the attractive woman who had strained forward to hear the conference between Al and our driver, said she had spent three years in Peru two decades ago and thought her memory of the language might suffice for translations. So several of us chipped in and hired our Mayan look-alike for two hours. The results proved more than satisfactory. Lorraine's translations at times won the smiling approval of our new guide, who charmed us with his affability. And because our tour was somewhat self-propelled, many of our individual interests, in art, architecture, paleontology, engineering, sports, whatever, were actually catered to. Not surprisingly, some chose not to accompany Lorraine and our Mayan guide, the sturdily built couple prominent among them. These passengers, out of disgust, despair or perhaps believing we had achieved the ultimate in catastrophe for the day, angrily struck out on their own.

The ruins of Copán are extraordinary. This eighth-century city had become the artistic heart of Mayan civilization, and many of its ancient artifacts are still *in situ*. A millennium after its curious abandonment, it was reclaimed from the jungle. Several of its glyphs, stelae and monuments, like the great Hieroglyphic Stairway with its more than 1,250 blocks, have been roofed by archaeologists to prevent damage to their exterior surfaces by exposure to the elements. Barbara left behind a little of herself at this splendid site when she tripped and scraped her shin on stones ascending from the Great Plaza. Fortunately, a towellette and bandage were all she required, though her leg bled profusely at first and she still has the scar.

By the time we returned to the bus, the heat had become ever more intense. The dissident group, our grumbling neighbors among them, were already munching their lunches in the shade, their faces wearing the looks of people drafting letters of complaint. Al, his arm in a sling, was there, assisting with the distribution of box lunches and smiling wanly. Any concern that we had for his condition was immediately countered by his concern for us, "How was the guide?" he asked. We assured him we had a splendid tour, thanks not only to our hired embodiment of a Mayan glyph but also to Lorraine's sharp linguistic memory.

"Ready for the return trip?"

Barbara quickly forgot her aching shin in the presence of Al's apparent cheerfulness.

Again with no air conditioning and with a black hole where the TV had been, we started our grinding descent, box lunches on our laps. The low gear did not bother us much, though it may have bothered the other buses behind us now as a precaution. All seemed to be okay again as we headed back to the

Regent Sea in time for its scheduled departure at 3:30 P.M.

Then came the flat tire.

Replacing a tire on a bus is not an easy or rapid task, particularly when the bus is stopped on a steep and winding Honduran road. The other two buses stopped and allowed us to stand in their air-conditioned aisles and cool off for about half an hour while three drivers and two able-bodied tour guides removed the damaged tire and put the spare in place. Then, saying they were worried about notifying the ship, the guides loaded the other two buses and left. Sure thing. I wouldn't want to be behind this doomed crate either. We were abandoned again, though not exactly marooned. Not at first.

We resumed our descent. What little water we had, including what we had begged from passengers on the other buses, was rapidly used up. By mid-afternoon the heat had become as visible as the morning darkness had been. Dry inside, drenched outside, we reached San Pedro Sula and the Copantl Hotel ten minutes after the ship was scheduled to depart from its dock, which was still two hours distant. Al, his voice weak, stayed with us long enough to phone the ship from the Copantl and to relay to us the news that the *Regent Sea* would be there "whenever we arrive." Our so-called companion buses had apparently already reached the ship, and their passengers had conveyed news of our disastrous journey.

"Good Lord, I'm dry," I moaned as the hotel's cool air swept over us. "I'll drink anything that's cold, except of course the water." But by the time Barbara and I reached the bar, thoroughly cold drinks were in short supply. The hotel had been prepared, but too bad, *senor*, two busloads of tourists had, not long ago, put a drain on the hotel's cache. Our Cokes were tepid. When the bartender offered to spike them up with a few ice cubes, we eagerly and gratefully accepted.

We drained our glasses and felt we were ready for what should be no more than an easy coast to the coast, to Puerto Cortés and our awaiting ship, refreshed and almost relaxed. To hell with the heat. Juan, sent from Al's agency to accompany us to the ship, was now in the tour guide's seat—a large man with a worried look, perhaps the result, we thought, of this quick assignment. He began by assuring us that Al was receiving medical attention and that his arm was indeed broken but he's doing fine. Before long, the real reason for Juan's worried look began to materialize. Just beyond Baracoa, less than half an hour from the coast, we hit stalled traffic, dozens of trucks, cars, and buses, many of them with their motors idling. Up ahead we saw a line of men with machine guns guarding a bridge over a small drainage creek.

"They've taken the road," Juan announced, sighing as if his fears had been confirmed. Relaxed but jaded, I was ready to believe the worst. A rebel army, I had no doubt. This is it, I thought. I would die in a Honduran uprising.

Well, not exactly. The guys who would normally be at work repairing the road to Copán were striking for higher pay and were trying to close the highway by restricting vehicular traffic across the bridge. Foot traffic, *si;* cars, *no.* Juan's hurried telephone call to the ship from a neighboring shop (it was then past 5) produced a promise that a bus would be waiting on the other side of the bridge to take us to the *Regent Sea.* To get there, we'd have to hoof it through the heavily armed picket line. Most of us greeted the news with relief, but not the sturdily built woman. As we disembarked and approached the armed strikers to begin our half-mile walk across the bridge, she flapped her arms at them in disgust. "Lady," I began, seeing no need to provoke armed men even if they were only striking concrete workers. Then I caught a hot look in her eyes and stopped my reprimand. Meanwhile, the doctor's wife, wilting alongside us and looking pale and skittish, moaned succinctly, "Oh dear."

"This is the way the tour ends," Barbara added, cutting her eyes toward the doctor's wife and beyond toward the ragged, unsmiling, ominous line of men, "with a whimper. As well as a bang?" We hurried across the bridge, eager to leave our ailing and doomed bus behind, equally eager to avoid the strikers and downright anxious to dissociate ourselves from the grumblers.

The waiting bus, surely the best that could be provided on short notice, may not have been luxurious, but it ran. Its tires seemed sturdy. There were benches instead of seats. The back window had been broken out, and a few side windows were missing. These let the air in, though they let none of the odor of small animal detritus out. Nonetheless we made it, all the way back to the blessed sight of the waiting ship. We thanked Juan, everyone except the grumblers, that is, as we shambled away from the bus and proceeded up the dock.

It was then well after 6, almost three hours after the ship's scheduled departure, and the first call to dinner was being announced. Ah, dinner, we thought, a settled, civilized and luxurious contrast to the day's events, a good ending after all. Home is the hunter, home from the hill.

"Do you," Barbara began as we walked down the passageway to our stateroom for a wash-up, "have a rather strange rumbling here?" She placed her hands on her midsection.

"Yes, as a matter of fact, I do. . . . Oh my God, the ice cubes!"

This Won't Hurt a Bit

by Kellie Schmitt

IT WAS TIME to leave Peru. The Inca Trail had been breath-taking and the little town of Cuzco charming, but we had reached that point—the one where you are tired of wearing crusty clothes, carting around your toothpaste and turning all night on a lumpy mattress.

At 9:45 A.M., I sat up in bed and threw off the heavy blanket. "What time is it? What time is the flight?" I asked Nikki, my traveling companion.

Eight o'clock had come and gone without a peep from the plastic alarm clock. Staying in a hostel, we didn't have the luxury of a telephone, much less a wake-up call.

"We can still make it. Grab the stuff, I'll find a cab," Nikki said, twisting her foot into a sneaker.

Our flight from Peru to Bolivia and back to Argentina was set to leave at 11. If everything went well we could still make it, I assured myself as I grabbed T-shirts off the floor and stuffed everything into our hiker's backpacks. Fifteen minutes later, we were standing in the main square of Cuzco, trying to get the attention of a cab driver who seemed content cruising around and talking out the window at a leisurely tropical pace. The early morning sun was piercing, and we shifted our backpacks uncomfortably.

Finally he saw us, and we were back on schedule, at least our revised one. From the cab window, I looked at kids playing football in the square, the stone church and then the mountains fade into a dark green background. Soon I would be back in Buenos Aires, where I was studying for the semester. The teachers had been lenient about missing classes, but we both knew the grace period was running out. We had skipped more than ten classes, and counting. An internship commitment also loomed over my head. They had told me in the beginning that long vacations were discouraged.

The taxi ride took ten minutes, dropping us off at 10:16. Giving each other a triumphant look, we entered the Cuzco airport.

No one else was in line in the one-room check-in area. We hurried to the front and set our tickets and passports on the counter. A woman with hair in a tightly knotted bun did not smile as I gushed out details of our near mishap. I had hoped to elicit some sort of laughter or a sympathetic smile, but her lips remained pursed.

"Now, I need your airport tax fee, $30 each."

I had heard of an airport tax fee in some countries but hadn't thought ahead in my sleeping-in stupor. The taxi ride had just about cleaned us out, leaving us well short of the $60 required.

"Do you take credit cards?" I asked.

"No."

"Is there an ATM in the airport?"

"The nearest one is in downtown Cuzco."

I waited at the airport while Nikki hailed a cab back. She would have to pay the driver with some of the money she withdrew at the ATM. I waited near the counter, fidgeting with my bags.

"Everything else is set, right? We are all ticketed so that we can hand over the money and board?"

She looked up from the computer with an annoyed glance. "Well, you do have your health cards, yes?"

"What kind of health cards?" I felt my blood pressure rising.

"The ones that certify you have had a measles shot."

There had been a measles outbreak in Bolivia. In order to enter the country, you needed to prove you would not be susceptible to the illness.

"What? Look, I am sure we've had our shots. We are from the U.S. It's required there."

"We need proof. You can go to Lima and try to contact someone at the U.S. Embassy to get your certification."

Lima was a plane flight away.

"Or," she said, "there is a room right in the back. You can get your shots there."

Nikki rushed into the airport, her hair falling in her face, flushed from the race to get the cash. It was now 10:51, nine minutes until our flight left. I pulled her over to the side, trying to recount the news about the shots, but it came out jumbled and disoriented.

"I don't understand. What is this? I have never heard of this before."

Before she could fully process a thought, two tall Peruvian guards came up to us. They were armed. The guards said something quickly in Spanish and escorted us to the room the airport clerk had mentioned. I glanced at Nikki nervously. Our decision had been made for us. They would wait outside while we got our shots.

A woman in a pink smock pulled back a curtain. Behind it was a small room with a bed and counter with medical supplies. She began pulling out the needles from a rusty drawer.

"Can we have some privacy?" I said, motioning to the

guards waiting outside. I looked over at the woman as she began preparing the shots. I felt a sick churning in my stomach. I was sure of one thing: Nikki and I did not want to get an injection we didn't need in a tiny room in the back of a one-room Peruvian airport.

Were the needles clean? How many times had they been used? What happened if you got a shot for something you were already immune to? I could just imagine Nikki and I returning to Argentina covered with measles. Not that I was completely sure what they looked like. Were they closer to chicken pox or mumps?

The nurse held up the sharp, silver enemy and motioned to the table. It looked as if it would collapse if I were to sit on it. I felt panicky as the adrenaline pumped. And I cried.

"*Senora,* I promise you we have had these shots. Is there any way at all we could avoid getting them again?"

She looked at me, her face showing a hint of interest, but clearly my tears weren't the best method. Still, her wavering gave me hope. There was another option. It seemed absurd. Being a student doesn't allow you to throw around money but considering the value of the dollar in Peru, we might have a little leverage.

I turned to Nikki, asking her in English how much she had withdrawn from the ATM. We had $40 after the airport tax.

"I have some money with me, how much would it take? I can give it to you now."

"*Cinco soles,*" she said without pausing, her eyes averting ours.

Without a word, I opened my wallet and handed over the five *soles,* the equivalent of $1.50. I was afraid of breathing too loudly, moving too quickly, anything that could tip the fragile equilibrium of her decision. She pulled us into the corner of the room and whispered the instructions. If anyone asked us, the shots were on our upper arm. And they hurt. She took a little paper square from a drawer and scribbled a signature on it. The card had a cartoon-like picture of a doctor and his patient, who was sitting eagerly on a table, beaming at a man with a stethoscope.

Nikki looked at her watch as we dashed out the door and back to the ticketing line. It was 11:08. Before we could say a word to the woman at the counter, a thundering airplane passed overhead.

"Was that...?"

She nodded without a trace of pity.

The next flight was three days later. By the time our cab arrived back at the hostel I had started to develop a case of sun poisoning. During the four-day Inca Trail hike, I had forgotten to spread sunscreen on my back, which now was blistering up. I wish I could say the extra time in Peru was wonderful and that I saw more of the landscape and people. Instead, I spent the next few days commuting between the communal bathroom and the same lumpy bed. From the soiled look of the hostel bathroom, my experience wasn't uncommon.

Nikki hung out with a Polish-Australian we had met on the Inca Trail. He had seemed like a fun, outgoing guy. By the third day, he wasn't much fun. His excessive inquisitiveness and constant chatter motivated her to drag me out of my sick bed to join them for dinner—despite the fact that I couldn't eat.

When the day of our flight arrived, we happily marched up to the ticket counter two hours before our flight. With complete confidence and a touch of satisfaction, we handed over the little paper squares with the cartoon doctors, our ticket out of town. We were no longer stuck in Peru.

Prison, Anyone?

by Karen van der Zee

WE'RE OFF TO JAIL, a bush prison somewhere in Uganda, not exactly our intended vacation destination. Our passports—two American, one Norwegian and one Dutch (mine)—have been confiscated. Back in Kenya, where we live, no one will miss us for weeks.

Ordered to follow the police car, we're in a rented Peugeot, the rear window shattered. With a convoy of 15 trucks from the Congo behind us on the narrow road running through the protected game reserve, there is no escape possible. Besides, the policeman in charge is armed and dangerous, not to mention drunk out of his skull.

How did I find myself in this bizarre situation? I could have been home in Holland in my mother's house drinking tea and eating cookies. But no, I had to follow my heart and come out to Africa to be with my beloved American, who is a Peace Corps volunteer in Kenya. And then I married him, which led me to accompany him and a couple of friends on a camping trip to the game parks of Uganda.

What kind of place will this jail be, out there in a bush village in deepest Uganda? I think of this as we follow the car in front, like lambs to the slaughter. I think of being separated from the others in a cell by myself, of rats and repulsive food and malaria. I have a well-developed imagination.

"It will be an international incident," says Norwegian Lillian hopefully. "Three Western nations involved."

If they ever find us, I answer in silence, the words too terrifying to speak out loud.

I squeeze my husband's hand. We've been married six months and maybe we'll never sleep in each other's arms again.

We should not have come here, knowing what we know, but we are young and stupid. We began our trip a couple of days before in Nairobi. The news on the radio that morning was not good. In Uganda someone had tried to shoot President Obote, and the country was in a state of emergency with roadblocks everywhere and heavy security at the borders.

Nothing to do with Americans and Europeans, we all agree. Purely an internal thing. Why call off our trip? Nobody's going to be interested in us.

We ride the train to Kisumu and cross Lake Victoria by boat. On the other side we rent a car, load it with our camping gear and some food and off we go, direction Kampala. Slowly. Roadblocks everywhere. Long lines. Lots of waiting. The police and soldiers are not interested in us, as expected. None of them search our car for weapons or suspicious persons.

In Kampala the roads are clogged, but once we are out of the city, things ease up a bit. The scenery is spectacular, lush green hills, terraced and cultivated with a variety of crops. This place is beautiful. Coming here was a good decision. We had nothing to fear.

We stop for lunch at a rustic eatery in a small village and order the local grub: *matoke,* a starchy food made from boiled plantain. People are friendly, interested. We laugh, we chat.

Moving on, we drive down a narrow road through a wooded area when out of nowhere appears a cute little boy. We've not seen a sign of life for miles, no villages, no people, no roadblocks. We wave. Suddenly a rock hits the back window, shattering the glass into a thousand pieces that go flying into the car. The cute little boy, running, disappears in the trees.

We are not hurt, but our hearts are pounding. We expected dangerous wildlife but never considered that a little boy would try to harm us. Finally, we reach open country, a game reserve. A sign warns us we are in a protected area and we may not leave the road to cruise across the reserve in search of game.

After stopping to clean up the broken glass, we pause for something to eat. I take a knife from the food box to cut up some bread. All of a sudden, we have company.

A long line of trucks is winding its way toward us, a police car in front escorting the convoy.

The police car stops. All the trucks stop. They hail from the Congo, hence the Ugandan escort. A huge, fat policeman rolls out of the car and comes barreling toward us.

The armed policeman attacks us with a barrage of words. He claims we are trespassing, breaking the law, committing a crime by being in the reserve. We politely point out that only the back wheels of our car are in the reserve, that our window is broken and that we, being responsible people, wish to keep the road glass-free for other vehicles in this remote area.

In the meantime, more than a dozen Congolese truck drivers have decided a little entertainment is welcome after spending hours on the road. They've leaped from their trucks and have formed a circle around us to watch the spectacle.

The officer is not interested in our story. With his mean little eyes, he has all the charm of a wart hog.

He demands to see our passports and makes a great pretense of inspecting them, then starts in again and gives us hell for breaking the law while the Congolese truck drivers stand by and watch, mesmerized.

Then we notice something else. Another African, a young, handsome man in civilian clothes, has emerged from the police car and is now standing unobtrusively near us. "Don't say anything," he says quietly. "Stay calm."

The policeman looks at me, stops his tirade for a moment, his beady eyes focused on the bread knife in my hand.

If the man was mad before, he is now livid. He demands to know what I think I am doing with that weapon in my hand. Am I going to kill the president?

"This is a *bread* knife. I was going to cut bread." I should have followed the advice of the other man, but the cop's stupidity is hard to swallow.

"Shut up," my husband hisses in my ear.

The officer, drunk, sweating and swaying, is now beside himself, seized by the idea that we are out to kill the president and that it is his duty to save Uganda from the likes of us. He shouts that we're all going to jail and waves our passports in the air with one hand and his gun with the other. The truck drivers are loving it.

"Get in your car! Follow me!" the officer shouts at us. "I'm taking you to prison!" He staggers off to his own car, followed by the handsome young man who has said nothing to the policeman. Wimp, I think.

We do as we are told, kept hostage by the man's gun and inebriated mind.

The road through the reserve seems endless, desolate, leading us deeper into danger and despair. No villages, no people, not even any elephants.

Then we reach a junction, the first one we've come across, and the police car stops. We stop. The convoy of trucks behind us stops.

Out comes the handsome man in civilian clothes, striding

toward us, passports in hand.

"Please," he says as he hands them back through the open window, "please, accept my sincere apologies for this incident. You are guests in my country and this was an appalling incident." He goes on to apologize effusively, in perfect British English, his embarrassment acute. He tells us he once spent time in England and was treated with friendliness and respect and wishes we could have been granted the same treatment in his country, but alas.

Through all this, the plastered officer of the law does not make an appearance. It occurs to me that our hero was unable to do anything earlier because making the drunk lose face in front of his audience would have been counterproductive. Alone in the car with him the official had obviously succeeded with his diplomatic skills.

Our hero goes on to suggest we get rid of the knife. These are bad times, he says, and people are nervous about the attempted assassination of President Obote. Why take risks? He then points to the left. "This road will take you to Queen Elizabeth Game Park," he tells us. "Please have a wonderful time and don't let this incident ruin your opinion of our country."

A Bridge over Troubling Waters

by Carole Dickerson

A SAILBOAT TRIP on Puget Sound can certainly be an exciting vacation with wind, sunshine and sea as far as you can see. No house painting on our time off! My husband arranged to borrow a large, snazzy sailboat from another newsman and his lawyer partner, who moored it in West Seattle. The owners accompanied us several times to show us exactly how everything should work, including us, and to assure them that we were capable of taking their boat. We were cautioned that sailing was work and serious business. Sailing meant paying attention to wind flukes and mastering several kinds of sails. A pesky sail called the jib in the forward part seems to pull the boat and needs to be put up and taken down whenever Captain Bligh orders. There are also cranks to add needed muscle in getting sails to move, and other shiny hardware. The lines (called "sheets") control the sails. (Real sailors would *never* refer to ropes that hold everything together on a sailboat as anything other than "sheets.")

Our nearly adult children were along on the trip so we had plenty of hands on board for navigation and help in bringing the boat around—the technique of making the boat head in a different direction so that you don't get the sail caught in a tree, for example.

From Seattle's Elliot Bay we headed for Port Townsend, located at the tip of Washington State's side of the Strait of Juan de Fuca. The strait is as big and unpredictable as any ocean. The only real difference is that land is a little easier to reach.

The afternoon sun was getting lower in the horizon as my husband, The Captain, pored over charts while our oldest son, Geoff, got the feel of the helm. My main job was to handle the jib. All seemed well until it appeared that there was more than one way to sail into Port Townsend Harbor. A shortcut was possible by going south around a small island, saving at least an hour it appeared, and also getting out of the wind that was blowing so hard we had to shout at each other to be heard.

"Carole!" Mike yelled as he took over the helm to head the ship south of Marrowstone Island. "Check the documents on board for the mast height."

This important sailboat was "documented," which means it had specifications, in writing, about how long, wide and deep the sailboat was as well as specifications for the head and galley. These documents were stored in the galley table drawer.

Okay, I thought, I can do this. Many attempts at the helm had proved me worthless, but by gum, I could read. Charts, charts, charts. Lots of interesting information about how long the boat was, how many sails and their size, the galley and number of square feet, but I could find nothing at all about the mast. Must not be important how tall the mast was, I concluded.

"Carole!" This time I heard a special urgency in Mike's voice. "Where is the document that tells the height of the mast?"

"There is no document that tells the mast height," I answered. "How about the head dimensions?" I muttered to myself. I could find every square inch documented about the boat but nothing at all about the mast. I wondered why he even cared about the mast height. Maybe this was just one of his keeping-me-busy projects.

Geoff took back the helm position so Mike could look for the documenting of the mast height himself.

"We have to go under a bridge, and I want to make sure the mast will go under the bridge," Mike said.

This did seem reasonable since sailing on water moved by tides affects the distance between the top of the mast and the bridge we planned to pass under. Figuring the tide was easy from tide charts; the question was would there be space enough from the mast top to clear the bridge?

With this in mind, we began entering a narrowing channel with the bridge in view. When sailing in a confined area, sailors must resort to using the motor since control is a major consideration. By now Mike also became convinced that indeed there was no documentation on board to tell us the height of the mast.

"How about eyeballing it?" I suggested. Mike is 6 feet tall. If he'd stand next to the mast I figured I could make a pretty good guess as to how many of him would reach the top of the mast. It looked like about three of his height could make it under the bridge. At this point, we noticed that there were a number of people lining both sides of this passage watching our progress. Why were those people there? I wondered. Do they know something we don't?

"We can't make it!" Mike said urgently. "We'll have to turn back."

There are no brakes on a sailboat. To turn around or slow down, the boat motor is put into reverse. This action causes the boat to ever so slowly turn sideways in an effort to make a U-type turn to head in the opposite direction.

Suddenly, we and the sailboat moved sideways between cement pillars holding up the bridge. Ask any of us aboard just how much room we had between the mast and the bridge and you'll get a different answer. Looked to me like about four inches, but then I've never been great on measuring distances, especially looking up. All of us held our breath as we passed cleanly to the other side of the bridge and listened to cheers from the folks on the banks of the channel.

It was several months before we had the courage and opportunity to relay this story to the owner of the boat. I got to the part about looking for the documentation of the mast when the owner said, "It won't make it!"

But it did, and all concerned are grateful to the god of tides and any other sailor deity for making it happen.

The Norman Bates Airport Motel

by Brian Abrahams

I HAD A COMMAND performance to visit the out-laws in Phoenix and then had to fly immediately to Atlanta for a conference. Because it was expensive to fly the Chicago-Phoenix-Atlanta Triangle, I had to fly two roundtrips from Chicago, one to Phoenix and then right back out of Midway to Atlanta.

The trouble started when my travel agent issued me a paper ticket instead of an e-ticket. It got worse when she sent the ticket to the wrong address the day before I was leaving for Phoenix. I had the Fedex letter rerouted to Phoenix but that was worsened when Fedex lost it. So in Phoenix the travel agent switched me to an e-ticket.

I flew from Phoenix to Chicago with a 90-minute layover, time enough to get dinner. First, the airline took a full hour to deliver my bag to the luggage carrier. The whole flight from Phoenix was only 2 hours 50 minutes. So I had only 30 minutes to get checked-in for Atlanta and board. However, when I got to the counter they said I wasn't e-ticketed and had to pay $200 for a new ticket. They wouldn't budge and by the time all the paperwork was finished I had only ten minutes to catch my Atlanta flight. Midway was using its new building for check-in and its old building for departure so the distance to the gate wasn't short. I asked them several times to advise the gate that I was coming, but they wouldn't respond. So I sprinted to the gate and arrived with three minutes to spare.

I was dripping sweat, but I would make Atlanta. The agent took my ticket, I boarded and aside from someone being assigned to the same seat as me, I had an uneventful flight.

The flight attendant then made the usual landing announcements because "the pilot is preparing our initial descent into Pittsburgh." I smiled and said to the woman next to me, "She means Atlanta."

"No, this is a flight to Pittsburgh," the woman said.

"WHAT? Are you serious?" She nodded. "This was supposed to be a flight to Atlanta. I have to be in Atlanta." In my agitation I must have gotten loud because everyone within several rows had all turned to look at me. Some began to murmur to each other. Now I knew why someone had the same seat assignment I did.

As I found out later, my flight to Atlanta was delayed an hour and 15 minutes. The airline then cleared the gate so it could board a Pittsburgh-bound flight. Not being at the gate, I missed the announcements. And the gate agent looked right at my ticket, read it and boarded me anyway. I went through the correct gate at the correct time, but got on the wrong plane to the wrong city.

On landing I called the 24-hour number of the travel agent and found that all the flights to Chicago or Atlanta were gone for the night. Now it was 9:30 Sunday night, my bag was in Atlanta where my conference was well under way, I was in the Pittsburgh airport, which was shutting down, and I had nowhere to go. The airline agreed to put me up for the night and send me out on the first flight to Atlanta, which would be at 6 A.M.

The airport hotel they sent me to was a 15-minute ride and in the middle of pitch-black nowhere. It wasn't a national chain and was seedy and just this side of scary. Sort of like if

Norman Bates and his mother had opened an airport motel. There were strange people hanging around the front desk. The guy put me in a room in a strange little corridor right off the lobby. It was a ground floor room with a sliding glass door. The door had one of those poles that was supposed to keep it from sliding open from the outside, but the pole had been installed wrong and didn't block the door. With a casual glance it looked secure, but in fact wasn't. There were high bushes planted just outside the door, which obscured the view through all that glass. The curtains were torn and the room smelled.

To make the bus to make my flight I had to set a wake-up call for 4:30 A.M.—2:30 A.M. Phoenix time, where my body clock was set. The picture on the 12-inch TV was terrible, so I just lay in bed and my mind began to work. And things weren't adding up too well.

It was after midnight in the middle of nowhere, no way to just hail a cab and get out. But what if I was just being paranoid? Naaah.

I dragged the desk in front of the main door. That would at least delay an intruder's entry. There wasn't much I could do about the glass door. So I leaned and piled every other piece of furniture in the room against it. Chairs, the folding metal luggage rack, drawers from the bureau, I didn't care. If someone came through, there would be enough noise to give me a chance to at least wake up and defend myself. As I balanced a lamp on top of the pile I thought of the marble, linen and polished wood of my empty room at the Ritz-Carlton in Atlanta.

I put my open pocketknife on the floor next to the bed and left the lights on. Eventually, sometime close to 2 A.M., I must have drifted off to sleep. At 4 I bolted awake from a loud noise in the hallway. Thirty minutes later was my wake-up call. I showered, put on the clothes I had flown in the previous day, and with a robust 2½ hours sleep flew to Atlanta. My bag was waiting and I went to the Ritz. I wasn't one of the more attractive people in the lobby, wrinkled, unshaven and uncombed after my shower.

I changed in my room and went to my conference. Late in the day, I had a one-hour window to take a quick nap. I went up to my room and my message light was on. It was a voice-mail from the Director of Security. I called him back and after sitting on hold for a long time was informed that there were 12 noise complaints against me and that if there was one more I would be physically escorted from the hotel. I protested that I had been in a conference all day and it must have been another room. Every complaint from the prior night was carefully documented. While I was barricaded into my room in Pittsburgh.

That settled, I finally lay down for a nap. Just as I started to drift off the headboard in the room next to me began to methodically thump against the wall where my headboard rested. The people next to me were having sex. Excellent sex. That finally stopped and as I drifted off again, the maids in the hall began to shovel ice into buckets to put in each room for the turndown. They laughed, they chatted in Spanish. Finally, my hour window was over, no nap. That night I fell into bed exhausted and decided to sleep in a little the next morning.

Thump thump thump thump. I looked over at the clock. 6:50 A.M. My neighbors were wide awake. But at least we had one thing in common. I, too, was getting screwed.

That afternoon the conference ended and I flew home to Chicago. As we landed in the dark, I could see an ambulance racing across the airport grounds. The plane came to a halt and the pilot informed us that because of a medical emergency at our gate we would have to wait on the tarmac. This turned into a full hour wait. The flight from Atlanta was only an hour and 45 minutes. I came home late that night and fell into bed. The next morning my wife and I and our two boys raced out of the house to make a parent-teacher conference. One of the tires was flat on our only car. At least I wasn't in Pittsburgh.

Things That Go Boomp in the Night

by Eric Steiner

IF THIS HAD HAPPENED in Albania or Burma, it would merely have been local color. In fact, it would be disappointing to travel all the way to an exotic destination without encountering major deviations from the game plan. But this was Belgium, a well-oiled tourist machine accustomed to providing culture and comfort in equal measure.

Brussels is Belgium's political and commercial hub. I went there to meet some colleagues, all very routine. I arrived by train the evening before. It was a short walk to my hotel. "La Coupole" was old, but clean and centrally located, just right for my one-night stay.

I'm not exactly sure when World War III broke out. There was loud crashing, followed by the smell of dust. I felt stuff landing on me, I tasted gritty bits of plaster. I saw little beyond shapes and blurred motion.

Time passed. Maybe all of ten seconds. The turbulence in my brain receded just a little. I was groggy, but so far—undamaged. Surprise: the lamp on my nightstand worked. Now to check off the items from the traveler's mantra: Passport-Wallet-Tickets, Passport-Wallet-Tickets.

They were on the dresser on the far side of the room. Problem: there was no longer another side of the room. Where it used to be—along with the bathroom and my suitcase—was a gaping void, and a mess of splintered timbers, mortar, twisted wires and broken glass.

I'm a San Franciscan, and my first thought was, "This is the Big One." But I was a long way from the San Andreas Fault, and it just didn't feel like an earthquake. What it turned out to be was much more prosaic—part of the outside wall of the building had collapsed, because of a sink hole.

The place was in shambles but nobody was seriously hurt. Four rooms were affected. We huddled in a little group in the lobby in various states of undress. The night clerk, the fire department and assorted functionaries comforted us, twittering their concern. Apologies and glasses of cognac were offered and accepted. Within a few hours new, and presumably more durable, accommodations were found for us.

When I returned to the hotel, after meeting my colleagues the following morning, repairs were already under way. There were more apologies, and even better, my belongings had been found, only slightly the worse for wear. My suitcase bears a wonderful array of dings and scratches from the incident, bestowing character and status, much like those colorful luggage labels that used to adorn old steamer trunks.

Cliff Hanger

by Jean Sigler

I MADE THE FIRST hiking trip of my life—to the bottom of the Grand Canyon at age 54.

I now own a backpack that could accommodate all the needs of a healthy toddler for two weeks, a trekking pole that would make a sherpa jealous. I have soap-on-a-rope, Chapstick-on-a-rope, a really cute little flashlight-on-a-rope, a combination whistle, mirror, compass and secret compartment for your Ibuprofen-on-a-rope. I have $200 hiking boots, heavy socks, medium socks, sock liners and the entire line of Dr. Scholl's blister treatments. I have glove warmers and crampons, hats for warmth, hats for shade and a hat just to cover my hair, which always looks completely dorky from wearing the other hats.

And I have 14 layers of fleece, wicking polypropylene and breathable nylon.

For those of you who know about this hike, we are talking about anywhere from three to ten hours of either being propelled by the weight of your gear as gravity drags you down the pit or the reverse on the return trip.

Traveling light is nonnegotiable. It is also very difficult for those, like me, who are a tiny bit past middle age. By then, in addition to clothes, you also need make-up and toilette items, hair-do enhancers, a curling iron, hair dryer, hormone pills, blood pressure pills, cholesterol pills, antihistamine pills, antacid pills, more Ibuprofen, camera, journal, guidebooks, mini bottle of wine and oh yes, food and water.

On the first round of packing, my Camelback Trans Alp Daypack weighed 117 pounds. It slipped on easily, but I immediately fell over backwards. Until one of my fellow travelers freed me, I was only able to flail my legs in the air like a turtle upended on its shell. My thought was to dispense with the heaviest thing first—the water. After all it was cold outside and how thirsty could you get when you're cold? Then my eye caught sight of the tag for my backpack and one of the most effective advertising slogans I have ever seen: "Hydrate or Die." I tell you, it made me want to buy another Trans Alp backpack just to fill a second bladder with water.

Obviously, something else had to go. I bit the bullet and left the hair dryer, camera, airline wine and journal behind. I figured I had the hats, my girlfriend had 12 rolls of film and her camera, there was wine at the ranch, the hormones would help me to remember my deep thoughts and hiking hints, and I could fill-in the journal when I returned to civilization.

We all packed most of the clothes and laid out a few layers for the morning. When we woke up, the weather channel said it was 4 degrees. I unpacked all of my clothes and put on every last layer, also my gloves and glove warmers, Chapstick, crampons, two pairs of socks and all of my hats. Despite our carefully chosen apparel we were plenty cold by the time we hiked to the trailhead and started down the South Kaibab Trail, a 5,000-foot vertical descent to the Colorado River and Phantom Ranch.

The road to hell, as it turns out, is not paved with good intentions but with mule droppings (not to mention drippings). In the winter these naturally occurring phenomena freeze into ice covered, boulder-sized hazards. With each step, the unwary hiker runs the risk of slipping on one of these Donkey Death Traps and plunging to a sure and certain demise—or at the very least absolutely ruining her brand new Patagonia breathable, wicking fleece pullover.

We completed the downhill trek in 6 hours and 15 minutes and were met at the canteen by fellow hikers, who all greeted us with a, "Hi, I think we passed you on the trail!" If I could have unclenched the fist locked permanently around my telescoping trekking pole, I would have decked one of them. Instead, we enjoyed our wine and went to the cabin for a nice nap before dinner.

Cabin is a term that means many things to many people. To me, it represents curling up on a big couch in front of a roaring fire with a glass of wine after a nice hot shower. To the operators of Phantom Ranch it means two sets of bunk beds, cold water sink, toilet, ice-cold concrete floor and a mirror. There was a fireplace at some point, but it was bricked over.

I fell into the bottom bunk. If I had had to jump out of the top bunk, the by-now granite muscles in my legs would have hit that cold concrete and shattered. I took a brief nap and limped over to the community shower, which had plenty of hot water but no heat.

The good thing about hiking is that you're required to consume double your normal calorie intake. The dinner of stew, cornbread, salad and chocolate cake was not only appealing but guilt-free. As we ate, I took an instant dislike to the young couple at our table who made it down the hill in half our time. We were all sound asleep by 8 P.M.

We took off the next day to hike to Ribbon Falls six miles away. The very young man at our table the previous night said if he were to repeat the hike again, he would have worn a coat. I had enough apparel with me to clothe the faculty of a medium-size college, and this guy had worn a T-shirt! He was starting to get on my nerves.

We hiked all day, finding cairns, fording streams, entering and leaving canyons and replacing Dr. Scholl's products. We ate a hearty meal and fell into bed for a short night's rest.

This left only the trip back up, a ten-mile trek on the Bright Angel Trail. Believe it or not, the hike up was much easier than down. For one thing, it was longer, which made for relatively gradual gains in altitude and gentler switchbacks. Also, it didn't seem that the mule teams used this trail, or if they did, the animals were seriously constipated.

It took us eight hours to ascend to the trailhead. We could have made it in less time, but there does not seem to be any way to coordinate the bladder, nutrition and layering/unlayering needs of four menopausal women. We stopped about every 8.5 minutes while someone scampered into the bushes, took a picture, ate some trail mix or layered up/down to accommodate her hormonally challenged internal thermostat.

We reached the rim around 3 and spent the rest of the afternoon showering, napping and packing again for the trip home and our group spent the evening celebrating by doubling our wine intake to two glasses. We slept 11 hours.

By the following day I knew the Grand Canyon was the source of some profound truths. The universe is vast and I am insignificant. And shit happens.

RVs Aren't Us

by Joyce Evans

MY EX-HUSBAND AND I, our friends, and combined four children, rented a Winnebago for a tour of Death Valley, California.

Our trip started in Larkspur, California, at Motor Home Mayhem with a fridge full of homemade casseroles, beer, sodas and several quarts of juice. My job was to load the fridge, but unfortunately, I didn't know that the door had to be secured with a pin attached to the side. Five minutes into the trip, my ex-husband made the first left turn out of our neighborhood and ran over a curb. The fridge door flew open, and the whole weekend's worth of food smashed on to the floor. Glass from the casserole dish pierced the beer cans and sent spray over the walls and ceiling.

We were in heavy morning commute traffic, unable to stop. The first time my ex-husband hit the brakes for a light, a wave of prune and orange juice rushed from the front of the motor home, clear to the bedroom in the back. There was no way to stop the momentum of the mess. My boys jumped onto the kitchen table and yelled "hang ten" every time the wave went back and forth.

We had hoped to make 300 miles that day but ended up in a Co-op market parking lot in Berkeley trying to regroup and clean up.

There we noticed we had also ripped off the little step under the only exit door when we hit the curb. As a result we spent the entire weekend jumping down several feet to the ground, and shoved each other back inside at night like members of the Ringling Brothers Circus.

Our children learned to walk along the walls of the motor home like Spiderman to avoid touching the carpet we couldn't seem to dry out. Going to the bathroom was also a challenge. You had to leave the door open while on the pot or your legs would be crushed. As a result bathroom breaks were banned at mealtime.

Returning the motor home was difficult. We parked under a tree near our home to unload our clothes and left the skylight up in an attempt to dry out the carpet. When we pulled away, we ripped the skylight off as cleanly as the steps below and limped back to the rental place with a cardboard box containing the wreckage. By the time we paid for all the damages, we could have bought the entire motor home and used it as a second unit.

Too Close for Comfort

by Jillian Shanebrook

I WAS IN NEW YORK doing editorial work for a teen magazine when the good news arrived. An international advertising agency had seen my modeling and, according to my agent, wanted me to represent their cosmetic and shampoo clients. She told me I would be flying out within the week.

The following day, my agent called again. The ad agency was putting the beauty product promotion on hold to front burner another intriguing campaign. The PSP Group, a fashion, travel and real estate conglomerate had recently completed a luxury apartment complex in Indonesia, and was promoting sales by offering an all-expense-paid trip to Paris for one lucky buyer. This is where I came in—the winner of the Paris trip would be traveling with me.

The campaign would culminate with a launch party and ceremony televised across Indonesia. Afterward the winner and I would jet off to Paris (along with a couple of "chaperones"). My role sounded a tiny bit bizarre, but probably enjoyable. My agent also reminded me that in addition to Paris sightseeing, I would receive incredible exposure and publicity.

PSP wanted to start the campaign immediately and needed a glamorous picture. I had a choice: my head shot already on hand, or I could go to Jakarta for a photo shoot within two days. Hmm.... Guess I'll go to Jakarta.

I arrived in the late afternoon. An agency driver took me

to the hotel, and as we drove through Jakarta, I could see hordes of soldiers and groups of people marching and protesting. Elections were due in ten days, and the situation was tense.

I felt more secure when we reached the luxurious Hotel Ibis, owned by my sponsors PSP. Late that night I met up with a Singaporean girlfriend of mine who lived in Jakarta. She suggested we unwind at a disco in the back streets of Glodok Plaza.

We danced a while and soon two Indonesian girls approached us to ask for my autograph. I obliged, and then they asked if they could give me a kiss. Why not? The first girl planted a kiss on my cheek, as I had expected, but the other girl smooched me right on my lips. I was very surprised and confused. Was this an Indonesian custom? The two girls grinned and the bolder one slipped me a card with her phone number. Then both of them walked off into the crowd.

Angela started to laugh, and as I turned towards her, I noticed that everyone on the dance floor was staring at our little spectacle. Larger spectacles awaited, it turns out. The next afternoon I went to the offices of *Dewi*, a hip new magazine for young women, and returned to my hotel—and reached safety—just in time. From my windows I saw mobs of angry and frantic people running through the streets, throwing bottles and smashing store windows. Fires burned throughout the city. I was safe, but two days later there was a new problem.

While I was visiting a producer at his office, his secretary buzzed him urgently. He listened briefly, and with a look of alarm told me rioters were approaching the building. We needed to leave immediately.

I fled with the entire office staff by a side exit. Once we were on the street, I could see a huge shouting mob about a block away. A lone taxi was driving by. I stopped it and several of us jumped in (the rest of the staff were rushing to their own cars). Before the taxi was able to drive away, some of the rioters reached us and started beating on the trunk with their fists. The taxi driver slowly accelerated. We finally broke free and made it to the highway. I had been around crowds of excited fans before, but I didn't think these folks wanted my autograph.

I woke up the next day glad I was leaving that night. Downstairs at breakfast, however, Dutch businessmen friends reported rumors that rioters had formed a barricade on the road to the airport, now closed indefinitely.

I immediately called Singapore Airlines to find out if the airport was open and if my flight was still scheduled to leave. They said yes and yes—but for some reason they could not find my reservation on their computer. The next available seat was several weeks away because hordes of people were fleeing to Singapore until the elections were over. I pleaded over the phone to reinstate my reservation but they were unyielding. My only recourse was to come down in person to their office— a lengthy drive away—and make my case. Since I was scheduled for my cover shoot that morning, I called my assistant back in the States, who said she would phone Singapore Airlines in New York about my reservation.

Towards the end of the shoot, my assistant called to say she had straightened everything out and I had a new reservation. I cooed my gratitude into the phone and managed to get to the airport without encountering any rioting crowds or barricades.

The ad campaign, it turns out, was a big success, and the apartments sold out ahead of schedule. But months of turmoil, only a tiny portion of which I had witnessed, made my modeling role seem very trivial by comparison.

I've Got a Headache

by Lacy David

WHEN OUR PLANE took off from Lima, Peru, which is at sea level, and landed an hour later at 10,000 feet, the guidebook suggested we should take a nap to get used to the altitude. But our hiking group was late for the open-air market in Cusco, so we were rushed aboard a square-wheeled bus that groaned us up a bumpy dirt road called the Pan-American Highway. Altogether, we climbed 13,000 feet. And I got a monster headache.

Altitude sickness is common in the Andes. And the usual treatment is cocoa tea. But it didn't work for me, so I asked to see a doctor. The HMO in Cusco was a little backed up with bloated goats, but I finally found an Aztec medicine man who did a little dance, shook a few rattles and prescribed chicken soup. I didn't know I had family in Peru!

When the chicken soup didn't work, a donkey delivered me to the airport, where I boarded a plane home to LAX. Seeing on my passport that I had been to Peru and back in just three days, the customs people whipped open my luggage, convinced they'd find narcotics in my mascara wand or sewn into the seams of my No Nonsense pantyhose.

Relieved to be at zero altitude, where my headache quickly disappeared, I joked with the customs officers. "Hey, you guys really insult me. I'm an entrepreneur. If I were going to smuggle drugs, I'd fill up a whole 747!"

I guess they didn't share my sense of humor because seconds later all of my body cavities were being strip-searched. Too bad I missed Machu Pichu, but hey, that's cool. I'll catch it at an IMAX, somewhere at sea level.

The Magic of Polaroid

by Judith Beck

As part of the all-inclusive fee for our trip to China, we'd been promised first-class accommodations in Guangzhou at the White Swan Hotel, then under construction. A group of medical personnel on a tax-deductible "educational" tour of the wonders of acupuncture, moxibustion and intravenous herbs, we were middle-aged, well-off and spoiled.

But when we arrived, there was no room at the White Swan Inn. Another group had checked in two hours before us. "No problem!" our tour guides cried cheerily. "They'll just find us alternate accommodations."

They booked us into the local YMCA. Instead of rooms overlooking the Pearl River, we had small cells holding two single cots apiece, cots with bare, striped mattresses. We stood around while staff scrambled to find linens and pillows. I held my bag, uncertain whether to put it down on the dirty floor.

The room I shared with a talkative nurse from Texas had a small window overlooking the narrow street. The bare plaster walls were covered in splotches of uncertain origin as well as chips, graffiti and scratch marks that looked as if prisoners had tried to claw their way to freedom. It was a grim and uncertain place to spend our first night in this vast land so newly opened to the Western world.

The bathroom was worse. Toilet stalls without doors, sinks without water or with permanently dripping faucets to torture those unlucky enough to have a room nearby, rust-stained bowls and a permanently wet floor no one would set foot on while wearing dress shoes. (This was the ladies' accommodation.) Showers were out of the question. For our entry visit to Guangzhou, we were going to be dirty doctors.

I was up early, raring to get away from the musty smell of the room. I slung both cameras about my neck—the Ricoh I was using to capture images to process at home and the Polaroid I'd brought to give out instant photo gratification to the locals. It didn't matter to me that the guides told us not to give out photos (or the balloons, needles and can openers I'd brought as gifts and bribes). I didn't care if I spoiled the Chinese. I couldn't bear the idea that people had no mementos of their families—even mementos that would fade with time. Besides, gift photos were a wonderful way to persuade people to pose for scenes I wanted to snap.

Heading around a corner, down an alley, I found myself in the midst of a farmer's market. Heaps of cabbage, celery and other produce were being picked over by a throng of people, all of whom stopped to stare at me.

A good rule for photographers: go for the kids. An adorable baby, held by a woman near a dusty pile of greens, looked at me wide-eyed. I snapped her with the Polaroid. The mother, and a few of the men beside her, scowled. I waved them over. A crowd was soon looking down at what appeared to be a failed attempt at photo taking. They snickered and pointed. Miming "wait," I held up my hand.

Moments later the sniggering turned to gasps of pleasure as a perfect likeness of the baby appeared. The gasps of pleasure turned to shocked disbelief and rapid tonal murmuring in Cantonese as I handed the Polaroid to the mother. She smiled, fondled it, then tried to give it back, but I refused to take it. Then I got off two or three shots of the alley, the open doors of the houses and the busy shoppers.

Another baby, in the arms of a father or grandfather—someone without teeth, anyway—quickly appeared from one of the homes. I took another Polaroid and waved it as the child's image slowly appeared through the magic of chemistry. More people gathered around.

It was time to teach them some American. "Polaroid!" I said, smiling so broadly I was afraid my face would crack. "Polaroid!" I pointed at the cardboard image.

There was more discussion I didn't understand and then someone yelled out, "Polaroid!"

"Yes!" I yelled, thrusting the photo high and turning it over to the baby's dad.

"Polaroid!" the surging crowd chanted happily back.

A few young men around me tried to cop a picture.

"Uh-uh." I shook my head and pointed to the kid. "Babies and little children only!"

They got the point. Out of nowhere, toddlers and infants were dragged before me. I clicked away with both cameras as the horde chanted "Polaroid, Polaroid," grinned and clapped me on the back.

Our love fest lasted until the camera ran out of film. A universal gesture indicating empty caused a momentary spell of sadness to wash over everyone not holding a precious white square, but a wave of geniality swept me along out of the alley onto the street where the YMCA stood.

"Where were you?" several of my fellow travelers asked. "You always seem to have such interesting adventures."

"Around the corner at a farmer's market" was all I said as they started out.

They were back within minutes, furious. As soon as they'd

rounded the corner, a horde of locals surrounded them, demanding "Polaroid! Polaroid! Polaroid!" Only the crowd's honesty allowed them to escape with their cameras. "You think you're so damn funny," they fumed. All I could do was grin.

We returned to Guangzhou after a two-week excursion. This time, as promised, we were booked into the White Swan, which, alas, had no friendly farmer's market around the corner. Instead, rats scurried in the acoustic-tiled ceilings and came down at night to gnaw on the sesame candy given to us on the train. It wasn't a real Chinese experience like the YMCA, where the rats had left our food alone!

Why Oh Why Oh Why Oh
Did I Ever Leave Wyoming

by Amy Forkner

THE WYOMING HIGHWAYS looked endless and uninviting on the morning of May 30, 1999. The sun was just an orange pretense in the vast, cloudless sky, the wind had yet to emerge from the folds of its starry blanket, and I, eight weeks pregnant, had already seen the urine-stained rims of three rest stop toilets.

My 18-month-old son, Jake, was zoned in his car seat with strawberry Pop Tart smeared in his fine blond hair. My mother dozed in the seat next to me. Her gray hair was thrown together in a narrow clip at the base of her neck, and her glasses were halfway down her nose. I sipped at my cappuccino.

"Drink." Jake had his fatty little hands stretched forward as he eyed my coffee.

"Be careful," I said as I handed it to him.

He took a sip of the cooled drink, tilting the cup at a 90-degree angle to his face. Then the lid popped off.

"Grab it," I shouted as I swerved to the right.

"Watch the road." My mom awoke from her slumber and these were the first words from her mouth?

"He just dumped it everywhere."

"You shouldn't be drinking the caffeine anyway."

I tightened my grasp on the steering wheel. The last thing I needed at 6:00 in the morning was a lecture about the caffeine I desperately needed. "There's a rest stop up ahead. We'll stop there and clean it up."

"This will make what? Three in an hour?"

"Four. Four rest stops, Mom." Yes, there was animosity in my voice. She had not been the one puking her caffeine-free guts out.

"How do you think the guys are doing?"

The guys -- my husband, Albert, and my stepfather, Jack --- were somewhere behind us driving the ancient Ryder truck filled with everything I owned, from the china I never used to the toilet paper.

We rented it from an eighteen-year-old counter boy with a trout tattoo on his forearm and a silver earring in his tongue. "Make sure we get a new one," I told him.

"Sure thing," he said as he scanned my credit card.

"We're moving all the way to North Dakota. Grand Forks, which is in the northeast section, in case you didn't know. I think it's something like a thousand miles from Cheyenne. I would hate to get halfway there and have something happen to the truck."

He blew a bubble with his watermelon-scented chewing gum. "Sure thing," he said again.

The truck was made in 1979 and had nearly 200,000 miles on it.

"How do I think they're doing?" I asked as I looked into my rearview mirror. There was nothing behind us except miles of pavement and a barren prairie with a few scattered cattle. "I'm not sure they're going to make it." As I said it, I felt another wave of nausea.

"There's the rest stop."

"Just in time."

We were supposed to meet Albert and Jack at a little diner in New Castle called the Fountain. After my second pancake and third cup of coffee, the cell phone rang.

My mom answered and talked for a few minutes in a series of brief, exclamatory phrases. "You're kidding! Really? So now what? You're kidding! All right."

She hung up and sipped her coffee like it was an after-dinner brandy.

"What?" I asked, annoyed I even had to ask.

"The truck."

"Broke down?"

She nodded and took another drink.

"I'm not surprised."

"They're waiting for the tow truck."

"Tow truck? From where? Cheyenne is four hours away."

"Rapid City."

"Even better." Now it was my turn to take a drink. I looked at Jake, who played in the syrup like it was finger paint, and let out a quick breath. "I thought we'd at least get to South Dakota before this happened."

"They'll have to unload the truck and reload everything onto another one."

"It will take them all day."

"Probably."

"You should have seen the engineering involved in loading that truck, and they had four other people helping."

"I think we should go ahead without them."

"I think we should go back."

My mom raised her eyebrows.

"I don't want to move anyway. We could try to get our house back, move everything back into it in a few days, and forget this whole mess."

"What about his job?"

"He could get it back."

"No, in North Dakota."

"This is a sign, you know. I haven't had any peace about moving to North Dakota, and this is just the beginning of what's to come."

It was then that Jake reached across the table for the glass of orange juice. In slow motion he lifted it from the table with his syrup-coated hands. It slid from his grasp and fell on its side in one smooth motion.

As the juice ran down the tablecloth onto my white T-shirt, I couldn't help but think, *I should have just stayed home.*

That thought stayed with me as we resumed our trip, as the highways blended together like the wheat fields we passed by. It stayed with me into the night as we slept on a leaky air mattress on the floor of my new second-story apartment. Some time after midnight the window air conditioner stopped working. I opened the windows and finally the scent of the rotten onions and potatoes we found in the kitchen drawer faded, but the thought never did.

Jack and Albert arrived late the next day in a new Ryder truck that they had moved our things into.

"How do you like the apartment?" Albert asked when he came in tired and dreary from the long journey.

I wanted to be positive, but as I look around all I could do was cry.

I've never smiled brighter than the day I left North Dakota only ten months later when Albert transferred to another job. I knew I would always remember it as a rainy potato field farmed by Scandinavians, but I would not miss it.

"Adios, North Dakota," I said as we drove into Wyoming.

As I looked out into the hills and folds of the countryside, I caught a glimpse of myself in the window. There was a smile plastered on my freckled face and for the first time in nine months, I felt like it might stay there. My two boys were sound asleep in their car seats, the sun was high in the bright blue sky, and the evergreens of Wyoming were there to welcome us across the border. Professional movers had my things, and the broken-down Ryder truck was a distant memory.

"Any regrets?" asked my husband.

"Yes. I wish we never would have moved there."

"Just look at it like an adventure."

"Or an abyss. I think we just lost nine months of our lives."

He slowed the car down and pointed to the side of the road. "See the deer?" There was a fawn and a doe camouflaged in the layers of trees and brush. The doe looked up as we passed by.

"Didn't see that in North Dakota," I said, awed by the beauty of the game, the lighting of the sun peering through the trees, the roundness of the hills we drove.

"You never saw it before North Dakota either."

"What?"

"You don't know what you've got until it's gone."

"That's a very cliché thing to say."

He shrugged his shoulders and I turned to look out the window again. We reached a clearing in the trees and from the ridge I could see the new green of spring grass emerge from the winter brown. The meadow colors shimmered in the sunlight, the hills tumbled on top of one another like a disheveled blanket.

It was the most beautiful landscape I would ever see. I felt like Dorothy from the *Wizard of Oz* and almost clicked the heels of my grass-stained tennis shoes.

A Late Arrival

by Ralph Bolton

Our friends were shocked when we told them that we were
planning to visit Turkey in March 1999. At the time when we
first thought of visiting this land where Christianity began,
nothing out of the ordinary was happening in that part of the
world.

Even so, people would look at us with a funny expression
and ask, "Whatever possessed you to want to go to Turkey?"

Actually, we had visited Istanbul and Ephesus a few years
earlier and found the people friendly and the land rich with
historical significance. Istanbul is a great city with an extraordinary past and we were eager for a more extended visit.
The anxiety of friends and family would not intimidate us.
What did they know? Our family and friends wondered why
we just couldn't take a nice vacation in Hawaii or go to Florida
and see our many friends. We wanted an adventure.

A few months prior to our date of departure, a civil war
erupted between two ethnic groups near Turkey. In early March
as the fighting worsened, NATO declared war on the Serbs.
With the help of aircraft from the United States, NATO began
to bomb the city of Kosovo.

As soon as the news broke about the fighting, our telephone began to ring. "Are you guys still planning to go to
Turkey?" "Are you nuts?" "Have you lost your mind?" "Is your
life insurance paid?" I calmly explained that the daily brief-

ings from the State Department did not indicate a "warning" against travel in Turkey, only a "caution."

Our children reluctantly drove us to the airport for our flight to Istanbul. We arrived at New York's Kennedy Airport with plenty of time to change terminals and check-in with Turkish Airlines. Our plane was parked at the gate when we arrived. The TV monitor indicated a slight delay in boarding.

The pilots and crew were all seated in the departure lounge waiting with us. I managed to talk to one of the pilots and he indicated that the airline was changing its flight plan. As it turned out, the original flight plan was over Kosovo where fighting was going on. We were finally allowed to board our new Airbus 340 almost two hours late and settled in for the overnight flight to Istanbul.

The flight was delightful. Wonderful service, good food and best of all, we were able to get a few hours sleep. When we awoke it was almost dawn and our plane was well into the new flight plan, which took us over Belgrade, Yugoslavia. Looking at the ground from 35,000 feet, I could see flashes of light that appeared to be lightning, which seemed odd since I couldn't see any thunder clouds. We learned the next day that the NATO air forces were bombing Belgrade at the same time we were flying directly over the city.

Touchdown in Istanbul was as light as a feather. We paid for our visas, cleared customs and retrieved our luggage with no delays. As we were loading our suitcases onto a pushcart, we heard our names announced over the loudspeaker. Our tour host was waiting just outside the front entrance of the customs area. This was clearly going to be another fine trip to Turkey.

We happily introduced ourselves and got into a new Ford van for the short trip to the Marmara Hotel. Istanbul is a bustling, modern city of over ten million people with a storied past. As we drove toward our hotel, I noticed an ancient wall and arched gateways and imagined the Crusaders storming the walls of Constantinople, as this city was once named. I also noticed that the streets were designed for three lanes of traffic. This didn't deter Turkish drivers from squeezing into traffic four cars abreast, nor from cutting off all oncoming vehicles by making a left turn from the far right lane. Even more amazing was the sight of a herd of animals in the middle of the city. We found out later that they were being purchased for sacrifice.

As we crossed the bridge leading from the old part of the city, our tour host pointed out a tall building on a hill in the distance. This was the Marmara Hotel, a beautiful modern building at least 40 stories high. Although we had sped through the city at up to 70 miles per hour, traffic slowed as we approached our hotel. Suddenly, our van came to a halt. Soldiers and police carrying submachine guns and dressed for battle surrounded us. A policeman came up to our van and motioned us to turn around with his machine gun. The driver rolled down the window and said something in Turkish that sounded like "Americans to the Marmara." With that the policeman pointed his gun through the window and began screaming and waving his arms in every direction.

Our driver did not get the message and continued to argue. We cringed. Perhaps we should have listened to our family and friends.

Finally, our driver turned onto a side street away from the hotel. Slipping through alleyways barely wide enough for a pair of donkeys, he circumvented the barricades.

At the Marmara, we were met by hotel security and required to pass through a metal detector. Our host got into a heated conversation with staff in the hotel lobby. There had been a problem, he explained nonchalantly.

"Some woman fanatic that appeared pregnant to everyone just blew herself up in front of the hotel. They were still taking the injured away when we arrived, that's why they made us turn around."

Every newspaper in Turkey had pictures of this gruesome suicide on the front page the next morning. The suicide bomber carried seven bombs under her robes. The next day our guide instructed us to always cross the street and run if we spotted a pregnant woman. It was entirely possible this innocent-looking mother-to-be might not be carrying a baby.

Flight of Fancy

by Inette Dishler

MY DREAM VACATION came in the summer of 1990. I had always wanted to ride in a hot air balloon and decided that I had to do it right—either in the south of France or the Napa Valley. Given my budget at the time, Napa won out. My first California trip started in Monterey, driving the coast down to Big Sur and up to San Francisco, then on to Napa. As soon as we arrived I called around and booked a flight for the next morning.

My partner was very nervous because she has a fear of heights and was only doing this for me. The pilot reassured her that ballooning is completely safe, and in 17 years he had never had an accident. Our balloon had six passengers, a pilot and all the tanks. The peaceful take-off was incredible. We floated over wineries and estates surrounded by mountains. We even saw a double rainbow, which made me nervous as rainbows usually indicate a storm. Not to worry, said the reassuring pilot. The storm was hours off in the distance and he liked the "texture" in the air.

After 45 minutes of heavenly floating, things suddenly shifted. We were caught in a wind shear and whipped around 180 degrees and because the pilot had started our descent our balloon was caught in a downdraft. Suddenly searching for a new landing spot in the opposite direction, all he had time to say was, "Bend your knees, it's going to be a rough one." I followed his instructions but when we hit the ground, hard and at an angle, I went flying through the air, along with my shoes and camera bag, and landed with a hard thump. When I looked up, the balloon was gone. I found out later it kept bouncing 1200 feet through a hayfield, until the ropes finally got caught in a chain link fence just before crashing into someone's house.

I knew not to try to move. An ICU nurse who happened to see the crash from her kitchen window rushed out and took my vital signs. The balloon chase team was right behind her and radioed for an ambulance. I was taken to the ER in excruciating pain. Three balloons crashed that day, with 17 people hurt, ten requiring overnight care in a hospital. I was the most seriously injured with a fractured pelvis and sacrum in seven places. Instead of enjoying Napa, I spent the next 12 days in a hospital there.

My partner was also injured when the balloon bounced down the field and was taken to another hospital. We each spent several hours trying to find out what had happened to each other. An orderly was finally able to tell me where she was. She had to have two surgeries on her hand and wrist. After five days, she was given a pass to come and see me for a couple hours, and she was released three days later. She returned to the B&B where we had been staying, and stayed gratis at the vacant owner's house until we could return home.

Twelve days after the accident, my partner had to fly back to Florida to begin a new job. Unwilling to remain in California by myself, I convinced my doctor to let me go. He didn't know how I would be able to sit for such a long flight but I was determined to leave. I was drugged for the flight, transferred by ambulance to San Francisco and wheeled by a gurney onto the plane. I was met by an ambulance and admitted into a local hospital for a few more days. After three months of therapy at home I learned to walk again and slowly resumed normal life. But to this day, hearing that familiar whoosh of the gas jets or seeing a colorful balloon takes me back to the Napa Valley and my dream vacation.

Working with a Chain Gang

by Stefan Sharkansky

ONE MONDAY IN MARCH 2002 we took our four-month-old son David on his first car trip to Lake Tahoe. David's Grandma joined us in Vacaville. On Tuesday I skied, while Irene and Grandma entertained David in the casino. A snowstorm was expected on Wednesday. The plan was to leave that morning before the storm hit and to be home by 5:30 to meet our daughter Olivia returning from an overnight school trip. The drive home normally takes four hours and we absolutely had to beat the storm. My BMW M-3's owner's manual warns that the tires won't take chains, so we can't drive in snow. Over dinner I told the ladies we should leave first thing in the morning, "no later than 9:30 or 10."

I awaken at 7:30 to a squealing David. Outside there are storm clouds. I pack my suitcase. Irene nurses David and goes back to sleep. We leave the hotel at 9:59. (Note to self: Next time we need to leave "first thing in the morning," don't say "9:30 or 10.") At the junction of U.S. 50 and California 89 there is a "Chains Required" sign, but it's only drizzling, so I convince myself it doesn't apply to us.

A few miles outside of town, some men in yellow astronaut suits are installing chains on a row of cars. Chains would be required after all.

At the second gas station we visit, the blue-shirted man confirms that no cables or chains will fit my tires. He sends us to the nearest auto parts store to buy something called a "Spikes Spider."

At the second auto parts store we visit, another blue-shirted man is all excited.

"We don't normally carry the Spikes Spiders, but I ordered a set by mistake."

But he didn't order the mounting brackets. He makes some phone calls. Nearly an hour later he reports he'll have the brackets on the 22nd.

"Of March?" I ask. Today was the 6th.

"Yes."

"When is the storm supposed to clear?"

"Not until late tomorrow."

"What are my options other than waiting out the storm?"

"I don't think you have any."

We can't stay another night; we go sit in a café to think. Grandma is desperate to get home because of a doctor's appointment Thursday morning. She's even willing to take the overnight bus to Vacaville, but Irene talks her out of it. Irene phones the mothers of Olivia's classmates until she finds one who can pick Olivia up at 5:30. I reminisce about Chompers the Cat, who hasn't been fed in 24 hours.

The road conditions hotline says nothing about chains on I-80. From I-80, it would be a straight shot to Vacaville and San Francisco. A straight shot, that is, if we manage to cross the Donner Summit. The Donner Summit is named after a group of pioneers who tried to cross the Sierra Nevada but were stranded in the snow in 1847. Half the Donner party died; some survived by eating their comrades' remains. The snow and rain have stopped, the sun is almost shining again. We decide to try I-80. We get back in the car around noon. The drive toward I-80 around the west shore of the lake is storm-free, and we're confident we'll be home by evening. It starts to snow as we reach the diaper-pin curves of Emerald Bay, where the two-lane road dangles hundreds of feet above the lake, without so much as a tissue paper guardrail to prevent a chainless automobile from sliding off the slippery pavement like a hockey puck into the freezing lake below.

"Wow," Grandma says. "Look at how steep that is."

We stop at a hardware store to see if they sell Spikes Spiders. They don't. The red-shirted man advises me to try I-80 anyway, and "in the worst case, they'll just send you back. But don't come here again, because we can't help you."

I call around Reno, 35 miles in the wrong direction, searching for Spikes Spiders. One store promises they have both the Spikes Spiders *and* the mounting brackets.

First we try I-80 west toward home, until we get to the enormous light board that says "Chains Required."

We reach the auto parts store in Reno around 3. The Spiders and brackets cost $330. The saleslady explains that the mounting brackets have to be installed on the wheel hubs only once. The Spider attaches to the mounting bracket and fits around the tire like a giant claw. To illustrate, she makes a claw with her two-inch fingernails. I open the box and see dozens if not thousands of little screws, bolts, nuts, washers, barbells, boomerangs, halos, anvils, horseshoes, curlicues and other assorted pieces of metal for which I have neither the tools nor the patience to assemble.

"How long is this supposed to take to install?" I ask, crestfallen.

"The tire store down the street will put them on for you."

I pay the tire store $33 for the installation and ask for a demonstration on attaching the Spiders. The green-suited mechanic shows how easy it is. Just grip the Spider around the tire, attach the coverplate to the hub and turn the handle.

"And how do you get the spikes to grab the part of the tire nearest the ground?" I ask.

He looks at me for a moment and says: "[Idiot] you probably want to jack up the wheel a bit first [you clueless BMW snob who comes to Lake Tahoe in the winter without arranging chains first. Ha ha ha.]"

I make room for the Spiders in my lunchbox of a trunk by moving some of the suitcases to the back seat, hoping they won't shift and crush the baby.

We get back on the highway. The weather is clear again. A sign says "San Francisco 199 miles," which means we should be home by 10. Grandma is still worried she won't make it to tomorrow's doctor appointment, so Irene spends dozens of dollars calling the doctor's office to tell the receptionist that Grandma may or may not make it to the appointment. In the mountains outside the city it starts to rain.

The rain turns to sleet as we ascend toward the summit. It's 5 P.M. and getting dark. I have to scrunch down to see out the windshield. Irene suggests we spend the night in Truckee. I agree. Grandma says nothing. David continues to suck on the stuffed bunny Grandma gave him, whom we've named Charlie.

We take rooms in a hotel that looks like a saloon in a spaghetti western. I notice another guest's belongings on the bed, and my reward for alerting the hotel staff is to be transferred to a room with a smaller bed for the same price. On our night table lie some earplugs with a card:

Since we're in the heart of the historic railroad town of Truckee, you might hear the rumble and whistle of one of our trains. These disposable earplugs can soften those sounds when you go down for a nap or the night. Sweet dreams.

Grandma's room is on the cold and noisy street side of the

hotel. They offer her a quiet interior room instead, but she declines, not wanting to cause any trouble.

Irene calls Olivia's friend's mother to thank her for hosting the school-night sleepover and also talks to Olivia. "I'm so mad that you went to Lake Tahoe without me," Olivia says. "I'm glad you're stuck. That's your punishment."

Grandma prefers to relax in her room with David while Irene and I go out to dinner. David cries the entire time.

At 11:30 P.M. Grandma wakes up to the noise and flashing red lights of the town snowplow.

The alarm clock rings at 6:15, Irene having pulled the pin the night before without knowing what time the alarm was set for. Grandma has been awake since 11:30. Even though she wore the earplugs and wrapped pillows and blankets around her head, she still heard the trains and the snowplow all night long.

My car is encrusted with four inches of snow, and the plow has blocked the car's exit with two feet of snow and ice. I brush off the car's windows and borrow a shovel. Irene looks out the window of the hotel breakfast room, holding David, and points to Daddy digging the family car out of the snow.

I finish clearing a path and drive to a gas station to fill the tank and install the Spiders. Once I jack up the car, the fitting of the Spider takes only a few seconds.

Equipped for the snow at last, I drive out towards the hotel, only to get stuck in the gas station's driveway. The manager, the mechanic and another customer push me out. The mechanic looks at my Ultimate Driving Machine and says: "Promise me that as soon as you get home you're going to sell this piece of shit and buy a real car."

The family gets back in and we head onto the Interstate. We can't exceed 30 mph on account of the Spikes, which also inflict unpleasant vibrations. Fortunately, all of the other cars are also going 30 mph. Along the shoulder a row of truck dri-vers are installing chains on their rigs.

We approach the California Agricultural Inspection Sta-tion. The traffic is backed up in a long line. A Highway Patrol vehicle is on the left shoulder.

As we reach the inspector's booth, the cars are still backed up beyond the station. The inspector explains that two big rigs are jackknifed ahead. I turn off the ignition.

"You know," Grandma says optimistically, "this is an expe-rience."

I add philosophically, "Getting kicked in the face is also an experience."

Grandma and Irene leave the car to go to the ladies room.

By the time we start moving again, it's just after 10 A.M., 24 hours since we left our hotel 40 miles to the southeast. Chom-pers the Cat hasn't been fed in two days.

It snows as we reach Donner Summit. Traffic is still at 30 mph. The mountain vistas are spectacular, but nobody's in the mood to stop at the lookout point.

The storm has increased to a total whiteout. I slow to 5 mph. The whiteout clears after only a couple of minutes. The car hits a bump and starts to fishtail, nearly sliding into some other cars. I grew up in Wisconsin but never actually drove in serious snow. I remember hearing that one must always "steer in the direction of the skid." Now that I have to apply this wis-dom, I'm not sure whether this means the direction that the front wheels or the rear wheels are skidding. So I try steering in both directions, but it doesn't seem to matter as the car whips from side to side and then straightens out on its own.

We take a break three hours (22 miles) out of Truckee. The man at the next urinal complains, "It took me forever to get here."

"This is the worst driving of my entire life," I agree.

"I can't believe they made me use chains," he continues. "Where I come from, they only require chains when there's real snow."

At the end of the snow zone, I get out of the car in freezing rain, jack up the rear and remove the Spikes Spiders. I stuff them into the trunk, where they drip their filthy, greasy, melting snow all over the baby supplies. The descent out of the mountains into the Sacramento Valley is obscured by heavy rain, poor visibility and the constant danger of hydroplaning.

After we leave Grandma's house in Vacaville, David starts to cry.

We arrive home at 4 P.M. Chompers is alive and still has food in his bowl.

Epilogue:

Grandma was reportedly telling her other children she had a "horrible trip." Irene has no desire to return to Lake Tahoe. I enjoyed my one ski-day of the year and am eager to go back, preferably by air. David is still fond of Charlie the Bunny.

Grenada Mon Amour

by Lee Arnold

AFTER BEING TOSSED back and forth for centuries between French and British rulers, Grenada, a Caribbean Island smaller than Philadelphia, finally achieved independence on February 7, 1974. Nine years, eight months and twelve days later, Grenada's socialist Prime Minister Maurice Bishop and ten of his cabinet ministers were assassinated at Fort George, the French-built fortress overlooking the capitol. Six days later, American troops invaded the island. In less than a month, the second-smallest nation in the Western hemisphere was declared liberated.

I wanted to know what Grenadians had to say about their liberation. I wanted to see the ruins of the insane asylum that was accidentally bombed by American forces. I wanted to see the work Cuban crews had begun on the airport runway, a project that caused President Reagan sleepless nights.

Grenada may seem like a tropical paradise, but the island's history does not read like a love-in. The peaceful Siboney Indians came to Grenada from South America in the first century. They were followed 600 years later by the equally peaceful Arawaks. Next were the war-like Carib Indians, who wiped out most of the Arawaks, enslaving the survivors. They remained powerful in Grenada and the other Caribbean islands until the Europeans came.

The French bought Grenada from the Caribs in 1650 for a

few sharp objects, glass beads and two bottles of brandy. When the Carib chief realized that he'd been swindled, he vowed to drive the French from Grenada. They attacked French settlements, but Paris sent in more armed force and wiped out most of the civilian Carib population. The French troops drove 800 Carib warriors to the tip of the island, who chose to plunge to their deaths off the cliff rather than deal with the French. That point is now known as Carib's Leap.

Grenada passed from French to British hands, back to France and then eventually back to Britain in 1783. During the nineteenth century, the country began to play an important role in the spice trade. In 1840 sugar plantation overseers from Grenada were brought to Malaysia to tend nutmeg plantations. In 1843 they returned home with small nutmeg trees and began their own plantations. Then, in 1851 disease wiped out the Far Eastern nutmeg plantations, driving the prices skyward. Grenadians planted more trees and by 1881 (it takes 30 years for a tree to mature) they exported their first crop.

Today the entire island smells of nutmeg and a host of other spices and flowers.

On my first heavenly afternoon in Grenada I flagged down a minibus in Grand Anse and headed north five miles to the capital, St. George's. Here I visited the fort where Bishop and his cabinet colleagues were killed. Next I walked up to the hillside cemetery where I noticed another sweet smell that I recalled from my youth. I looked up and noticed about ten teenagers sitting on tombs, passing something between them that did not smell like nutmeg.

Later I stopped at an art gallery run by a woman from London. We spoke about the heat, her divorce, animals, her work with a budding AIDS organization, and (yes) Grenadian art. After visiting with several other locals, I returned to my room, looked in the mirror and saw that part of a paper napkin I had used to dry my face on this humid afternoon had stuck to my face.

I hired a guide and took a horse ride in the mountains and sugarcane fields outside St. Paul's, a village a few miles northeast of St. George's. The guide, known as The Horseman, told me about what it was like during The Invasion. He and his family hid in the bush. He lost three horses to bullets, although he did not think it was intentional, just friendly-fire casualties. We rode to the bay where there had been a big battle between the Marines and the Grenadian and Cuban forces in the hills. He said that you could still find dead bodies in those thick forests.

Back in Grand Anse I thought I would do a little shopping and have lunch. Nothing too remarkable about that plan; it only involved crossing the main road. In Grenada many things cross the road: chickens, goats, cows. The only problem was that people here drive on the wrong side of the road. I looked left, took a step out onto the pavement and found myself in the path of a speeding minibus coming from the right. Luckily the bus was blaring reggae music and no one could hear me screaming hysterically as I jumped back into the grass, only seconds before I would have become another American friendly-fire casualty.

St. George's University School of Medicine has two campuses in Grenada: a main campus at True Blue near the airport and a branch in Grand Anse, about equidistant between the airport and St. George's. Decked out in shorts, T-shirt, and a backpack, I looked like the average medical student. At the True Blue, campus security did not try to stop me or check for my nonexistent student I.D. I asked at the Chancellor's Office about a memorial at the Grand Anse campus. They said it would not be finished until the twenty fifth anniversary of The Invasion.

Heading back into town I asked every Grenadian I met about The Invasion. Most described it as a necessary evil. One told me he watched the battle of the airport from his house high in the hills above St. George's. I saw the bombed-out headquarters of Maurice Bishop. It had been a hotel before Bishop took it over. Still in ruins, it is slated to be a hotel again. I saw the powerful radio station that the Cubans had built. The Americans bombed it too—only the now-defunct tower remains. The airport runway that the Cubans began was later completed by the Americans.

A popular prime minister had been killed by a bunch of thugs, and the U.S. restored order. The fact that the whole episode also wiped out Bishop's socialist direction appeared to be incidental. At Point Salines International Airport is a monument dedicated by Reagan to The Invasion troops.

The Grenadians are happy as clams (or perhaps conches is a better word) about the American invasion which they refer to as The Intervention. The Americans are seen as liberators who freed their island from chaos. The medical school not only survived but also has expanded into a full-fledged arts and sciences university. Those medical students who were turned down at Harvard or Northwestern are having the last laugh, attending class in shorts every day while their counterparts wade through slush in February.

I walked back to the airport to learn that my flight to Puerto Rico had been delayed. There is nothing like waiting at an open-air airport in oppressive heat and sweltering humidity. After a five-hour delay the staff finally conceded that there were mechanical problems with the inbound aircraft from Puerto Rico. The flight had been canceled. Mañana would have to be good enough for me.

South of the Border, Down Mordida Way

by Jake Greenberg

THIS WAS GOING to be our best Mexican vacation ever. In past trips, we had toured the ancient Mayan temples of the Yucatan, dove in Cozumel and luxuriated at Las Brisas in Acapulco, but this trip promised to be even better.

We flew into Mexico City and caught the first plane to Oaxaca to explore the ruins at Monte Alban, shop colorful native markets and feast on local cuisine. Hard as it was to leave, we flew to the seaside village of Puerto Escondido to stay at our friend Robin Cleaver's Santa Fe Hotel. Our room had a panoramic view of the sea, and we walked on beaches of the finest, whitest sand. After a week of being total lounge lizards we decided that we had to move on and see more of colonial Mexico.

By bus, taxi and air, we found ourselves back in the Mexico City Airport. We had been to Mexico City several times without incident. Still, there were so many stories of crime that we decided the airport was as much of Mexico City as we wanted to see. The best bargain was a Volkswagen Beetle for $59 a day. "Highway robbery," we said but decided that we were tired of being beholden to bus schedules. I plunked down my credit card, signed an incomprehensible rental contract, took a map and headed out to take on the Mexican roads. With my wife as my co-pilot, we drove out of the airport along the Periferico, the highway that skirts the city. "What could be better?"

my wife exclaimed. "A beautiful sunny day, cruising along on our way to Taxco, the silver city."

Up ahead I spotted a policeman who waved me over with one hand, holding a sandwich with the other. How nice I thought, taking time from his lunch. He probably sensed we were tourists, unsure of our way and would provide guidance.

"Driver's license and passport," he barked. It dawned on me that he was not part of the Mexico City Welcome Wagon. "Excuse me, officer," I said. "What have I done wrong?" He answered in a machine gun burst of Spanish. Although I have been to Mexico nine times, my Spanish was mostly limited to phrases involving bathrooms and restaurants. And nowhere in his diatribe did I hear mention of toilettes or tortillas.

We had a definite language problem, and tempers on both sides were escalating. He, furious that I did not seem to understand one word of what he was growling, and I, angry that he had no reason to pull us over. Meanwhile, his two police buddies were eating their sandwiches, seemingly oblivious as to what was going on.

Now we were shouting at each other. This was probably not the brightest thing I could do as he had a large gun in his holster and our passports in his hand. I guess this was what they call a Mexican standoff. At this point I thought maybe I should offer him a bribe. No, to offer a cop a bribe would be really dangerous.

The policeman, sensing that this verbal exchange was going nowhere, decided on a visual presentation. He opened his flack jacket, pulled out a clip of bullets and put them in our glove compartment. Thank God my wife had the presence of mind to throw them out the window where they landed at his feet. Outraged, he ordered me out of the car while he pondered his next move.

I found myself going from pissed to panicked. I started to remember tales of Mexico City's notorious La Cumberi prison, considered to be one of the world's worst penal hellholes where some prisoners are never heard from. *Ever.*

The cop obviously sensed my fear and decided I was now in a better bargaining mood. I shuffled back into the car thinking, if only I knew what he wanted from us. And then I heard the magic word, one of the select few in my Spanish vocabulary, *mordida,* "the bite." He wants a bribe! My wife thought she heard *morte,* and her French vocabulary kicked in. She was certain he meant death and that he was going to kill us there and then.

I took out my wallet and a big grin came over the cop's face. After a little old-fashioned bargaining, with my hands shaking in the process, we agreed on a $20 settlement, and he smiled and waved us on. We drove off relieved but still very shaken.

Our first reaction was to say, "To hell with Mexico. Let's turn around, go back to the airport and take the next flight home." Calmer heads prevailed, and we decided to go on to the town of Cuernevaca and spend the night there. We found a beautiful hotel and checked in.

Several margaritas later, we sat down next to a group of English-speaking local Mexican yuppies armed with cell phones. They talked about their great jobs in Mexico City, BMWs and European travels. I hesitated to tell them about our encounter with the police, but another margarita loosened my tongue. I started by saying, "You're not going to believe what just happened to us" and then recounted the day's events.

"Oh," they said, "that happens every day. In Mexico City, they give the police a gun, a badge and $100 a month and tell them to go out and make a living. In Mexico City being a policeman is a freelance occupation. They pull us over because our cars are expensive. So we always have a $20 bill ready to hand them."

At least I didn't overtip. Knowing what was going on, we would keep $20 at the ready. After three days in colonial Taxco, it was back to Mexico City and home. As we neared the airport, I looked into my rearview mirror and saw a motorcycle cop following me. He flashed his lights and motioned me to pull over. Here we go again, I thought.

"Why did you pull me over?" I asked. Fortunately, he spoke some English and told me that I did not yield the right of way to a car entering the highway. This was pure Mexican bull bleep, but I figured it was the best he could come up with on the spot. He then informed us that if we wanted to make our flight we should pay our ticket to him, or we could go to the courthouse and tell it to the judge. I handed him a crisp $20 bill and he gave us a smile and a *"Vaya con Dios."*

Turtle Tales

by Donna Feuerstein

An adventurous vacation by the sea has always been my favorite getaway. For our family, collecting seashells has allowed us to preserve memories of time spent at the ocean. Every now and then my oldest son takes out the box where we keep them and gently spills the shells out onto the floor. He marvels at the smooth surface and rough edges of each piece, tracing the intricate patterns with his fingertips, then returns the shells to the box as grains of sand spill from hidden crevices.

Our most recent shoreline expedition was a two-mile drive we frequently make from our home to the water's edge of the Wisconsin River. While a warm summer day in the Midwest can't compare to a week on the Gulf of Mexico, we acquired our most precious shell along the riverbank, and created a memory that will last forever ... or at least until we have the carpet replaced in our minivan.

It was a perfect afternoon. I packed the cooler with cheese (this is Wisconsin, after all), crackers and beverages. My husband loaded the van with beach towels, sand toys and our two boys (7 and 3). We drove to the river, unpacked and walked out across the squeaky sandbar. The boys splashed in the shallow pools of water close by, and I spread out our belongings for a comfy stay. Once settled, I laid back on the hot sand, and my husband gathered the boys for a little exploring.

I watched the three of them slowly disappear down a stretch

of sand at the water's edge, their eyes down, searching for something precious. Usually they return with hands and pockets filled with snail shells, interesting stones and sun-bleached fish bones.

Today was different. They ran back towards me arms waving, voices shouting. "Mom, Mom, look what we found!" My oldest son beamed with excitement as he bobbled a bucket sloshing with river water. "What, what?" I asked, feeling his enthusiasm. But before he got any closer, I caught a whiff of something horrifically foul. "It's a big turtle."

My husband came from behind with little brother fast on his heels. "My God, it stinks!" I tried to laugh, but choked instead. "It's not moving either," I added. "It's dead, Mom!" My youngest spoke knowingly, seriously. He looked down at their discovery, his tummy protruding with each breath.

It seems the poor creature died days earlier, and as luck would have it, the kids came upon the rotting remains. Intrigued by the turtle's shell, the boys convinced their father to take it home. "I'll clean it, don't worry," my husband said reassuringly. I believe the first mistake was filling the bucket with river water in the hopes it would reduce the smell of the car ride home.

I'm sure the second mistake (I won't say who made this decision) was designating our 7-year-old to hold the bucket between his knees for the short drive. The whole thing went sour with the right turn onto our street, where skinny legs and a heavy bucket became separated. The smell of death poured out onto the floor of our recently new vehicle.

As if it were on fire, we all lunged from the car when we reached the driveway, trying to escape the putrid odor. I corralled my hysterical sons into the house, looked back at my husband angrily and barked out orders. "Use the old towels, the shop vac is in the basement, don't expect me to help, and do you realize how incredibly." I didn't finish, for fear of what I might say next.

I have never considered myself squeamish. I majored in animal science and experienced docking pig tails, castrating bull calves and even found myself up to my shoulder inside a cow. But when I saw my husband scraping the turtle from its shell, I almost lost it.

Neighbors were peeking out their windows trying to discover where the rank smell was coming from. I overheard my husband mumble something about this not being his finest hour. I hid in the house and hung my head.

After what I considered to be a fair amount of time for one to skin a turtle, I headed back out to finish my lecture. I was sure we would be voted out of the neighborhood. I found my husband still scratching at the empty shell, much like you carve a pumpkin. "Aren't you finished?" I said and grimaced. A huge, I'm-not-as-bad-as-you-think-I-am grin spread across his face. "I am done with our turtle," he replied. It seems our neighbor had a deceased pet turtle stored in their freezer, awaiting taxidermy services. My husband offered to do the job, and they accepted. "So, now I'm working on their turtle."

Several days passed, and I had almost forgotten about the trip to the river. Then I spied something hanging from our oldest boy's tree house. He had tied the turtle shell to a branch for safekeeping (mostly to keep it out of the hands and/or mouth of his 3-year-old brother). I slipped into my sandals and walked through the dew-covered grass out to the backyard. Reaching up, I untied the shell to get a better look. It was beautiful. I traced the intricate patterns with the tips of my fingers. This really was a small miracle of nature. I was grateful that my husband was actively, though sometimes a bit too enthusiastically, passing on this appreciation to our sons. I smiled as I hung the shell back in place as a few tiny grains of river sand sprinkled my palms. You don't have to travel far to find adventure.

Let 'er Blow!

by Candy Hisert

IN SPRING 1982 a volcano erupted in southern Mexico, smothering the city of Villahermosa with smoke and ash and causing major damage. I am responsible for that disaster. In March that year, my husband and I had signed up for a tour of the Yucatan, and as an afterthought we added two days to see the ruins at Palenque. We planned to fly to Villahermosa and rent a car, which we viewed with some trepidation since we were both nervous about driving in Mexico. As it turned out, the agency lost our rent-a-car reservation, delaying our trip to the ruins by half a day, and our drive to Palenque landed us in the middle of a major bicycle race.

But those were the least of our problems. Our flight from Merida to Villahermosa was delayed for several hours, and we arrived late at our hotel. They had not lost our reservation, but our room was dirty, and the bed was unmade and crawling with ants. Not very calmly, I asked the hotel to remedy this situation while we went down to dinner. When we returned, the room was marginally cleaner; and the ants were gone. The entire room (including our pillows) had been sprayed with DDT. There was not another room available in the entire hotel because it was full of traveling salesmen and oil crews, both of whom celebrated loudly all night long. We tried to clear out the room by opening a window and the door, but only succeeded in welcoming hordes of mosquitoes that stung us all night long. We had to wait until 10 A.M. for the rental car and then had to drive slowly out to the ruins to avoid hitting the bicycle racers. Palenque was great but because of all of the delays we had limited time here.

We drove back to Villahermosa and returned to our room to discover that it was not made up and that the toilet was broken.

Rather than eat another terrible meal in the hotel, we walked miles in the heat and intense humidity looking for a restaurant. We finally found one, which served a slightly improved version of the hotel's cuisine for approximately half the price. It was the high point of our stay in Villahermosa. As I boarded our plane back to Mexico City and stood on the stairs, I declaimed, "I curse thee, Villahermosa. You will pay for ruining our vacation." Two weeks later the volcano blew up.

Please Return to Your Seat

by Mary Lou Brown

WHAT BETTER WAY to celebrate 18 months of remission from ovarian cancer post-chemotherapy than to head to London with some of my biggest supporters, my mother, sister and aunt.

At the airport I immediately lost my wallet at the departure lounge while my aunt left behind a jacket at the security checkpoint. Fortunately we were united with our belongings in the nick of time. On the plane we celebrated our departure by helping ourselves to the complimentary wine. Unfortunately my mother accidentally spilled a glass of wine all over my sister's clothes.

Although my sister was not able to remove any of her stained clothes, I decided to remove an uncomfortable pair of support hose worn to improve my circulation. In the restroom I removed my pants and was about to remove my support hose when turbulence prompted the pilot to order everyone back to their seats. I sat there half-dressed as a flight attendant began pounding on the door. Just as the attendant began inserting a key in the lock to force open the door, I was able to get my pants back on. Back at my seat my sister wanted to know why my panty hose were hanging out of my pocket.

After clearing customs I learned that the ATMs were down. Fortunately I was able to use the sweaty traveler's checks I had hidden in a money pouch tucked under my armpit. At the hotel the bell captain took our bags and we headed to the front desk where the desk clerk looked at our reservation vouchers and explained that we had no reservation. Two hours later we were assigned to a pair of rooms. After waiting another two and a half hours for our bags, I headed downstairs, found our bags and ordered the bell captain to put them on his luggage cart. The conversation was becoming a shouting match when an innocent bystander came to my rescue: "Hey Mate, I wouldn't mess with the little lady. I would do what she says."

The bell captain grew quiet and placed the bags on the cart. When we reached my room I was unable to unlock the door. After knocking for my sister I tried the key a second time and was finally able to push the door open, knocking my sister to the floor. As she tumbled her towel fell away, leaving her there in the nude. While I pulled the bags off the cart the bell captain hung out, waiting for a tip until I finally slammed the door.

Ship of Fooled

by Judie Kline

ON APRIL 30, 2002, my husband and I boarded the *SS Caronia* for an Atlantic crossing to Southampton. This ship is owned by Cunard, who bought out the White Star Line, which owned the *Titanic.* I sense a connection here.

Shortly after our arrival, I used the bathroom. I locked the door, and I might as well have entombed myself. The lock was stuck, and there seemed to be no ventilation. Some sort of engineer came to help and told me I hadn't used enough force to turn the lock and that the *Caronia* was an old ship.

That night, I awakened many times drenched with perspiration and gasping for air. The next morning I visited the purser to report the lack of air conditioning and was informed that the air conditioning in all cabins was in working order. The purser was informed that if this unbearable lack of air conditioning continued I would put on the lovely bathrobe given to each guest and sleep in the ballroom or disco where the air conditioning system had worked the previous evening. Two engineers showed up within minutes and informed me that the air conditioning was just fine in our cabin. I repeated my promise to the purser and invited them to join me in the disco or ballroom that evening—if they didn't mind bringing their own robes. Suddenly, they got to work and within minutes concluded that, indeed, there was no ventilation in any part of the cabin.

The system was somewhat fixed; however, I still had difficulty at night because the air conditioner was set to go on only after the cabin reached higher temperatures. Throughout the cruise the ventilation problem persisted in the laundry room, our particular deck and the elevators. Next was the elevator. The doors closed, the elevator went down a few feet, and the doors opened to a blank wall. The elevator continued in this manner until the doors finally opened to a real deck. This incident was reported to the security officer since I gave up on the purser. The concierge telephoned the next day and assured me that such an incident had never happened before and certainly would never happen again.

The next day, I had occasion to speak at length with a very nice crew member and learned a great deal about this ship. For one thing, that particular elevator does this stalling at least once every cruise and that most crew members take the stairs. Perhaps of greater importance was that a couple of cruises earlier than ours, many passengers became ill with respiratory problems. I was told that the Centers for Disease Control was still investigating the outbreak but that Cunard was voluntarily taking the *Caronia* out of the U.S. market and would cruise only around the British Isles. Our Atlantic crossing was to be the last. This decision was announced toward the end of the cruise.

Once off the ship, I felt like a new person released from jail. I could breathe in air that wasn't rationed!

After three days in London, we flew home. On the way back I began to cough. I was sick for a month with bronchitis, sinusitis, swollen glands and more sinusitis. It took three rounds of antibiotics to cure me, and I could not work for a month.

In fairness to this cruise line, I commend them for the entertainment, food and services rendered by those crewmembers who really do the work. We also met very nice fellow passengers. I did write to the president of Cunard and the answer included a $500 gift certificate to be used toward my next Cunard or Silversea cruise.

Pest Control

by Charli Ornett

THE CHIGGER-LIKE CRITTERS that had taken up residence under the skin of my legs and feet just had to go. My unwanted guests had moved in lock, stock and barrel when I was rough-ing it down in the rainforest a week before. All their tossing and turning and family squabbles made me itch out of my gourd. A miraculous anti-itch cream I found in Palenque kept me from scratching to the bone, but the bites had become oozing craters the size of cigarette burns. And they were spreading.

Now that I was back in civilization in the lovely town of San Cristóbal de las Casas in the highlands of Chiapas, Mex-ico, it was time to clean up my festering jungle souvenirs. I made a beeline to the Bio Farmacia in search of a roach motel's medical equivalent.

Now a farmacia in Mexico is not like a drugstore in the U.S. A farmacia glitters with glass counters and white-coated aides firmly planted between you and the goods. No brows-ing possible. While this is a great way to ensure gainful employ-ment, it is not so wonderful for the linguistically challenged tourist.

I sidled up to a customer-free counter and looked around for the lab coat doomed to serve the *gringa*. A thin, middle-aged man with sparse hair, aviator glasses and worry lines between his brows rose gallantly to the challenge, asking if he could be of help to me. *"Si, Señor!"* My exclamation point was both encouraging and eager.

"I have insect bites. They are not from mosquitoes. From the jungle. What do you have to clean them?" *(Tengo piques de insectos. No son de mosquitoes. Son de la selva. Hai estos que limpia los piques?)* Never mind that *"pique"* was misremembered French, in hindsight wasn't it close enough to the Spanish *"picadura?"*

The Señor nodded gravely and asked a woman behind him to fetch something. She returned with a tube of sunscreen. "No, gracias. I want to clean insect bites." Señor Anxious scuttled away and returned with insect repellent. That was progress. We understood that my problem had to do with insects. But it was too late for repellent. Maybe "cleaning" was our Waterloo. "Heal," that might work. But was that Spanish? *"Curar los piques,"* I tried. I leafed through my pocket dictionary while Señor Anxious-to-Please disappeared into the stacks for dandruff shampoo.

"I need *medicina* to *ayudar los piques!"* I hate tourists who shout.

Mercurochome appeared in his now sweaty palm. His forehead dripped with effort, eyebrows chased his receding hairline up his forehead. Well, maybe mercurochrome would do. I hadn't seen the thick brown glass bottle since grade school visits to the nurse's office. But the brown bottle jiggled my memory: Didn't hydrogen peroxide bubble gravel, germs and presumably, bug mandibles and eggs up and out of cuts and scrapes?

"Peroxida Hydrógene," I scrawled on a slip of paper, not sure if it was my pronunciation that was foiling communication. Señor Anxious's face lifted like a dog who's waited forever for his walk. He grinned. His eyebrows and shoulders

descended from their tense heights. His long legs gallivanted him to my side of the counter. He led me to a pillar of goods garrisoned by its own set of counters. This fort was guarded by a Panzer tank of a woman, with a helmet of peroxided locks. She was an advertisement for the shelves of hair coloring packages framing her brassy head. What she had to offer would dye my lower extremities rubia or rosa, but I doubted it would evict my unwanted insect tenants.

I thanked the Panzer politely and took pity on Señor Anxious who stood with empty hands dangling. I had run him through a linguistic ringer and exhausted his expertise.

In the end I bought a bottle of cane alcohol for 3 cents and fled with it to my hotel. When I unscrewed the cap the smell of rum flooded my room. I doused my wounds with the liquor of the Caribbean. It didn't sting. It couldn't be good for me. I waited an hour and still the alcohol didn't dry up the ooze or decrease the itching.

Switching to plan B, I went drinking. A woman at the bar told me she got the same bites down on the beach in the Yucatan but that they dried right up when she went swimming in a salt water lagoon. The lightbulb went on. And sure enough, rubbing Tequila salt into my wounds was my salvation. I am only slightly scarred to this day.

No Thanks for the Memories

by Michelle Walsh

MY PARTNER AND I were elated over our first trip to Hawaii. A week on beautiful beaches, sipping tropical drinks and letting the romantic atmosphere seep into our skin. We'd booked a resort on the Internet, boasting of spacious cottages, lavish breakfasts, nature trails, breathtaking views of the ocean and lots of activities. Then reality struck.

Our first three hours were spent driving in a pounding rainstorm trying to find our place. After miles and miles of forests and winding roads, we couldn't believe our eyes. The resort was run-down cottages in the middle of nowhere. Exhausted and hungry, we were so far from anything remotely resembling civilization that we resolved to make the best of it and spend the night there. It got worse. Our ocean view was nonexistent. Our stomachs were grumbling, but the nearest restaurant was a 45 minute drive, assuming we didn't get lost. Minutes after we hit the beds, we both started itching furiously. I broke out in tiny red bumps. The beds had bugs. Lots of bugs. At that point, we were so tired and hungry that we were bordering on delirium. We knew we couldn't stay there. I went to the front desk and explained the bug situation and their response indicated that this wasn't the first time they had heard this. They offered to have someone come and de-bug the room in the morning or give us a refund. We took the refund and hit the road for another two hours.

Finally in civilization again, we booked into a chain hotel, prayed for the best and fell to sleep in mid-conversation. The next day was spent driving around in more rain trying to find another place to stay. Our idea of staying in an exclusive resort with endless amenities was out of the question. Finally, we found a beautiful bed and breakfast, which was again in the middle of nowhere and far removed from anything resembling a beach. Breakfast aside, our only food option was a small convenience store that was about 20 minutes away.

The next day we decided to go on a whale watch because it seemed like the only thing to do. It had stopped raining and we were feeling optimistic. We drove another hour and a half to get there. On the boat I sat next to a little girl whose face was gradually turning every shade of green as she tried to fight off her nausea. As I turned my head to see the whale that everyone was shouting about, the girl vomited all over me. In response, I vomited too. I spent the next half-hour of the whale watch cleaning myself, on the verge of tears. That was probably the single most disgusting thing that has ever happened to me. Even more disturbing was the fact that the child's mother didn't acknowledge what had happened.

I took an obsessively long shower after we got back to our B&B. The next day it rained again, so hard that our windshield wipers couldn't keep up and it was impossible to drive. I speculated some vacation poltergeists were flying above and dropping 200-pound buckets of water on us at ten-second intervals. We spent the bulk of the day and night holed up in our room like refugees from our own vacation. Around 7 we ventured out for our nightly trip to find a restaurant. We came upon a seafood restaurant and ended up having a wonderful meal. Throughout the meal we pontificated about our experience and, ever the optimists, concluded that it would get better. The rain would stop. We would find a beach. We wouldn't let a bad start ruin the whole vacation.

Later that evening, I began getting excruciating pains in my stomach. At first, I tried to ignore them, thinking it certainly was that piece of cheesecake that did me in. As the pains grew more intense, I turned to my partner. In the haze of sleep, she brushed it off as possibly a bad case of gas. I began to drift off to sleep, but ten minutes later the pain was back. It felt as if I was being dissected with a steak knife from the inside out. I got up and crouched to the floor thinking that might make it go away. Instead I started to scream. I'm going to die. Oh my God! Help! I'm going to die! My partner jumped up and we got in the car to find help. We drove in the downpour for an hour and a half to the city where the closest hospital was.

I was admitted into the emergency room. It turned out that my gallbladder was the source of the problem. It contained a handful of gallstones and was twisted. The doctor informed us that it would have to be removed immediately. I was also told, "Thank God you came to the hospital tonight, because this is serious." Basically, if I had brushed it off as a case of food poisoning or a dramatic stomachache, I could have very easily died right there, or had an attack on the plane ride home.

I spent the rest of that night in the emergency room having my stomach sliced in three places and my gallbladder removed. The surgery went well, but I was immobile and still in extreme pain so I had to remain in the hospital for three more days. I spent the remainder of our vacation in bed, eating painkillers like candy, forcing down liquid food, watching movies and fading in and out of consciousness. It continued to rain the whole time I was in the hospital and rained until the very day we left. Mockingly, the sun came out as we boarded the plane. There was nothing in the world we both wanted so much as to get home.

Now, when someone mentions Hawaii to us, it's like living the trauma all over again. My souvenirs consist of three bright red scars that run across my stomach like some macabre map of a vacation gone horribly wrong. I also have the charming gallbladder snapshots provided by my doctor post surgery. They are not exactly the kind of vacation photos you'd want to email to family and friends.

We will not be vacationing for quite some time. In fact, thanks to our vacation karma we may just buy a swimming pool, plant some palm trees and call it a day.

Baksheesh in the Former USSR

by Sunny Lucia

WE PLANNED A TRIP to Russia in 1998 anticipating a culture of grandeur though little in the way of luxury. We hadn't anticipated being held hostage during an economic collapse.

Expensive business visas enabled us to travel without restriction. We had read that boats carried tourists from St. Petersburg to Moscow on the Volga River, so our daughter, Stephanie, and I spent an evening on the docks going ship to ship to find accommodation, and joined a tour group from Barcelona. "Great. I've come to Russia to practice my Spanish," said Stephanie. The boat director spoke only Russian, five guides spoke Spanish and Russian, and one spoke English. Stephanie was fated to a daily performance of language translation for her father and me for the next nine days.

The Volga River trip offered three meals at assigned tables in the dining room and a daily sightseeing tour. The stops included the islands Valaam and Kizhi, the cities Goritzy, Mandragvi, Yaroslavl, Uglich and then Moscow. A typical daily tour consisted of visiting churches and monasteries, with centuries-old fresco ceilings and walls, and the quintessential symbol of Russian Orthodoxy, the multiple-onion dome roofs. During the river trip, we watched tour guides grapple with the irresolvable expectations of the Western tourists. Freedom of movement is a concept not easily relinquished, and even in the smallest museum rooms the local guards regulated our every action. Businesslike orders of "stay in group," or "no talking, no pictures" and "no touch ropes" were steady, as were their weary, pinched, frowning faces and folded arms.

Guides methodically lectured for 30 minutes while our tour groups stood in the pouring rain. The feelings of suppression and exploitation were routine dinner conversation on the riverboat, as were the high costs and long, rain-soaked, dreary days. My husband, Steve, Stephanie and I decided to spend three days seeing Moscow on pre-paid tours and then we would exit Russia for Budapest via the Ukraine 10 days earlier than planned. As Moscow neared, I asked the boat director, Lyudmila, for information about buying train tickets to Hungary. We had grown wary of expensive "extra" tours in Moscow. I specifically asked which train station would sell us the tickets. Our intention and that request, like so much else in Russia, was fraught with difficulties.

Four days later Lyudmila informed us she had purchased our tickets and we owed her $495. When I saw the tickets cost $330, I asked for an explanation. The next evening while Steve and Stephanie were at the circus, Lyudmila came to our cabin with Natalia, the English-speaking guide. Lyudmila demanded the $495. I told Lyudmila that the 50 percent service fee was too high. Natalia translated. Lyudmila's face reddened as she insisted on the $495 fee.

"Help me understand," I implored, "because in Russia we have never been asked for more than a 10 percent service charge."

"The time frame was so short," Lyudmila retorted.

"Well," I replied, "the agency had four working days from 7 A.M. to 8 P.M. when the ticket office is open; this is not short notice."

I straightened my posture and looked directly at Lyudmila, confident that Natalia would reliably fulfill her role.

"It is from the InTourist; that is what they charge, you must pay."

"Since they are charging so much, where are the transit visas through the Ukraine?"

"What visas? No visas are needed to go on a train from Russia," Lyudmila angrily stammered.

"Lyudmila, I did not ask for these tickets, only information. Visas are absolutely required. And I must show your customs police receipts for all my purchases. Where is the receipt?" This was not true, of course. It was only a negotiating tactic.

"I have no receipt. This is price. Do you think I cheat you?" she began yelling. "Visas are not included. You must pay," Lyudmila growled, shaking her fist. The only card I had was to remain absolutely calm and repeat "no" again and again.

Lyudmila finally shrieked at Natalia, stood, threw papers on the bunk bed, stamped her feet, stomped out of the room and slammed the door.

Natalia told me that Lyudmila had said she would return the tickets and apologized saying, "Our tourist agencies are embarrassing. I am glad that you will not pay such a fee." Lyudmila stormed back into the cabin twice, squawked at both of us and stomped her foot on the floor. I gave Natalia a book in English and a set of pens as a gift, and we said goodbye. I dreaded another encounter with Lyudmila minus a translator but let the fear go since we were leaving on the boat the following morning after breakfast.

At 7:30 we were packed and ready to go.

Our plan was to taxi to the Kiev Railway Station and store our bags while we arranged our departure from the country. We got as far as the gangplank to a connecting boat when Lyudmila beckoned several deck hands, and four men blocked our path. When we tried to move on to the dock we were physically restrained. Lyudmila angrily addressed Stephanie and firmly grabbed her arm. Stephanie clenched her jaw, stood toe-to-toe with Lyudmila and said in Russian, "I don't understand you; if I speak English, might you understand me?" Lyudmila stormed away, waving her arms and called to the captain of the connecting ship, who came to the gangplank with two additional men. Seven men with folded arms and glaring eyes now blocked our way.

The men motioned for us to return to the lobby of our ship. We refused. For over an hour we calmly talked and stood with our bags. Then the adjoining ship's captain wordlessly stepped aside and opened his hand indicating we were free to pass. We nodded our thanks and scurried through the connecting ship, the now-opened dockside door, across the gangplank and away from the boat without looking back. We proceeded with an unmincing gait to the first main street and flagged down a taxi with an unspoken single agenda propelling the three of us—get out of Russia. Armed military were policing the bank runs and the government had pulled the ruble off of the exchange market. We couldn't use rubles or dollars. After hours of bad phone connections, runaround and piecemeal information, we put on our full American armor. We headed to the American Express office to charge air tickets out of Russia with no stopover in the Ukraine to Budapest. Six hour later our meal on Hungarian Airlines was the best fare we'd had in two weeks.

Digging for Roots at the Highland Games

by Cameron Burns

THE UNITED STATES has always been considered one of the greatest melting pots on earth, a place in which hundreds of ethnic, religious and political groups can coexist and integrate peacefully. Though far from any major ports or easy access to foreign lands, Colorado likewise has a decent mixture of interesting folks from faraway places.

That America is such a tremendous milieu of peoples leaves many citizens uncertain of their roots. When the family tree demands that you describe yourself in increments of 1/16th, it's hard not to have a wee identity crisis.

I'd long thought I had it figured out. Owning a name which is comprised of the titles of three sets of separate Scottish clans (Cameron, Murdoch and Burns), I thought I could at least label myself Scots-Irish, that handy catch-all title that means you're white, and the ancestors you know about came from Britain. Yep, I had it all figured out until I went digging for my Scottish roots in Estes Park.

Every September for the past 20 years, the town of Estes Park has played host to the four-day Longs Peak Scottish/Irish Highland Festival, the largest celebration of Celtic culture, arts and athletics in North America.

On any of the festival's four days, the finest bagpipe bands in the world can be seen marching around the town and its fairgrounds, while the eerie tones of the instruments bounce off the rocky cliffs of Lumpy Ridge and the high peaks of Rocky Mountain National Park. Huge men (and women) wearing kilts toss giant cabers and hammers around a baseball diamond, and all manner of Celtic dance is performed. Ancient military activities, such as jousting and horsemanship, are demonstrated to a crowd happily sloshed on single malt whiskies and expensive Scotch and Irish beers.

Thousands of Coloradans turn out each year, rain or shine. In 1999, the event was hammered by a four-day monsoon, which only added to the highlandish atmosphere and helped the whisky flow just a wee bit quicker.

The Games, as they're known, also attract a lot of straight-up weirdos: Guys in costumes from the Middle Ages, wannabe sorcerers and mystics and creepiest of all—the Deathrocker types, who look like they've just finished a refresher course in satanic sacrifice or come from a Marilyn Manson lookalike contest. The Games also attracted me.

I went partly for the whisky and partly to scour "Clan Row" for some insight into my family history. Every year, dozens of clan clubs from across North America bring whatever family artifacts and documents they can gather and erect tented booths along a grass alley on the west side of the fairgrounds. Most booths boast huge flags and coats of arms; some have detailed written histories telling the story of the clan. All of the booths have an endless supply of maps and charts showing where the clans are from and what their tartans look like.

As curious passersby wander along, they're likely to be hauled into a booth by the MacGillivrays or the Stewarts or the Hendersons and quizzed on their name, their family history and any ties they might or might not have to that particular clan.

At the end of the event, many members of the highly curious public walk away belonging to a family they never knew existed. Last year I met a guy named Wolchowski (or something that sounded like Wolchowski) who belonged to one or another clan with a Mac prefix.

"One sixteenth Scots-Irish," he told me. "Heck, I mostly come for the whisky."

Of course, family lineage, the spelling of names and exact histories is a game with some pretty loose rules.

The prefix "Mac," for example, is derived from a Gaelic word meaning "son of." The word has been shortened by many families over the years to the point where some use the prefix "Mc" or even "M."

"Names have a hazy history," wrote Scottish researcher Alan McNie in his series of books on Clan Heritage. "Sometimes they had more than one origin. Even the spellings of surnames were subject to great variations, shifting from usually Latin or Gaelic and heeding rarely to consistent spelling. In early records there can be several spellings of the same name. Undoubtedly contributing to this inconsistency is the handwriting in the official records, which was often open to more than one spelling interpretation."

That's why it's not uncommon to see names like Clark, Clarke, Clerk, and other variations lumped together with a common history. (Incidentally, the Clarks are claimed as a sept, or branch, by both the Clan Chattan and Clan Cameron.) One of my long-lost ancestors, a poet by the name of Robert Burns, changed his name from Burness to Burns—possibly to simplify it—in 1786.

My wife, whose father just happened to the president of Denver's Clan Donnachaidh (Robertson Clan) Society, seems to have her Scottish blood fairly well mapped out, thanks to her dad. With my name, I wasn't sure where to start. The Burns

Clan is not big enough to have its own booth, and because the Burns are a sept of the Campbell Clan, most people referred me to the Campbell booth.

A dozen strong-smelling big men in green kilts milled around talking loudly, cracking Irish jokes and drinking whisky. They were excited when I showed up and welcomed me into the fold like a cousin (which might not have been far from the truth). I felt like I belonged with these burly rowdies, but I felt a little off balance.

The Campbells, you see, have a bad reputation. In the latter seventeenth century, the Campbells and MacDonalds of Glencoe occupied neighboring lands. The two clans had suffered many differences and were considered archenemies, but at this point in time most clans were trying to negotiate peace with the English. In late 1691, the English decreed that all clans must sign an oath of allegiance to King William by January 1, 1692.

Although the MacDonald chief intended to sign, during a journey to meet with English representatives he was held up by bad weather and arrived six days late. In the meantime, the English ordered a regiment of Campbells to "fall upon the rebels (the MacDonalds) and put all to the sword under 70."

In the middle of the winter night of February 13, 1692, the Campbells massacred 38 MacDonalds in what later became known as the Massacre of Glencoe. The treachery is legendary to this day, because at the time the Campbell soldiers had been staying with the MacDonalds. Some pubs in Glencoe have warning signs near their entrances: "No Campbells Allowed." Hmm. Not the kind of thing you want to hear if you're planning on becoming a peat miner.

After disengaging myself from a hot, woolly drunken Campbell arm that seemed permanently fixed over my shoulder, I decided to try the Murdoch angle. The Murdochs are a sept of the MacPherson (or McPherson) Clan, which is a branch of a larger group called Clan Chattan (smaller families banded together for protection reasons). Since the Murdochs didn't have representation at the festival, I headed for the MacPherson booth. I learned a little history, the region of Scotland the MacPhersons inhabited, as well as other related clans.

But to tell the truth, the MacPherson Clan booth was pretty dull. Located at the quiet end of Clan Row—where the grassy field sort of tilted off toward a dumpster and a parking lot— the booth was manned by a small, frail, elderly woman who seemed to be doing little business. She was nice enough, but it wasn't as appealing as the party going on over at the Clan Campbell tent. I left and skulked past the Clan Cameron tent, en route to the MacGillivray booth.

Before arriving in Estes, my father had told me of a possible connection my grandmother had to the MacGillivrays. They had a nice flashy red and black tartan and were a friendly lot, with a sort of clinical precision about being Scots: We're from here, this is our tartan and this is our history. But honestly, they too lacked the sort of in-tent-rowdiness one hopes to associate with a Scot. None of them looked angry enough to take on English intruders in a downpour while wearing a highly absorbent form of skirt. I couldn't picture Mel Gibson leading the MacGillivrays against Longshanks in *Braveheart*.

I was stumped, so I concentrated on finding, then eating, lunch.

While much of the Estes Park fairground complex is devoted to Celtic culture (like Clan Row and the various venues hosting musical and dance performances)—about half of the event is devoted to good old-fashioned American-style Mac-Capitalism.

Indeed, an enormous inflated Coke bottle hovered over

the fairground's playing fields, while nearby a line of caravan-cum-foodstalls hawked everything from lemonade to corn on the cob. Under several large circus tents, vendors of Scottish products lined up their wares, and an American public eager for exotic goods responded by going into a sort of factory-outlet-style buying frenzy.

And why not? The range of purchasable items is pretty extensive: from swords and weaponry to CDs and tapes of Celtic music to videos depicting family histories and travelogues of Scotland and Ireland.

There are a half dozen or so professional kiltmakers who travel from Britain each year with vast quantities of tartan fabric in thousands of patterns, and who—for a hefty fee—will measure you, then sew a full-dress kilt to fit. I thought about buying one until I saw the price tag. They average around $800 a pop, and if you include the jacket, dress shirt-black brogues and dress socks, you're looking at close to $2,000. Maybe an old pair of tartan golf pants isn't such a bad idea.

It was while browsing through the remnants and sale tartans that I got the most help with figuring out my own ancestry. I asked a tartan salesman from Scotland if I could get away with Clan Cameron pants and a T-shirt saying Campbell on the front.

"Yer roots are as intertwined as a feeeld's worth of weeds," he said. "You could belong to any of them. Just pick the one with the best-looking tartan or the one yuuuu want to be a part of."

Sound advice, I thought. Find a pattern that matches my eyes or perhaps a clan with a fabric that's on sale.

But the business of tartans is as muddled as the names.

Tartans are known to have existed as far back as Roman times (a scrap of checked cloth dating to the third century was found wedged into the top of an earthenware jar filled with silver coin). The tight-knit communities found in rural Britain some 1,700 years ago were unlikely to have more than one weaver, and oftentimes the weaver used the same colors when producing woollen cloth (the colors being dependent on the natural dyes available in that particular are). Once outsiders had visited that community, or the group had taken part in a battle, certain checks of cloth became forever associated with individual communities.

After the battle of Culloden in 1746, the English banned highland dress. By the end of the eighteenth century, however, the ban had been repealed and tartan manufacture resumed in earnest, due in part to a sudden British enthusiasm for Scottish heritage and the establishment of a Highland Society in London. Thereafter, it was the clothiers who became the leading proponents of tartan. William Wilson, who owned one of the largest weaving businesses in Britain, took great interest in traditional Scottish fabric and began collecting samples of tartans from every area of Scotland so that his cloth would be truly authentic.

And most clans have more than one tartan. There are "dress" or ceremonial tartans as well as "hunting" tartans, which are often a similar pattern to the dress tartan but manufactured with more muted colors. Most clans also have "modern" tartans and "ancient" tartans. Like the hunting tartans, ancient tartans also tend to boast more demure colors, as they were and often still are made from natural dyes. When someone refers to a clan's tartan, they are generally referring to the dress version.

Finally, there can be any number of subfamily tartan variations representing specific branches of a clan. Within the greater Clan Campbell, for example, there are Campbell of

Cawdor tartan, Campbell of Loudoun tartan, Campbell of Breadalbane tartan and Campbell of Argyll tartan.

Many people consider the Campbell of Argyll tartan the true clan tartan as that particular branch of the clan was perhaps the largest and best known, but septs who were associated with other branches—the Orr family, for example which has been associated with the Campbells of Cawdor—might wear the Cawdor tartan.

Perhaps the most interesting thing about tartans is that they are subject to change. Though most clan tartans have been around and accepted for many generations, the clan chief can pronounce a new pattern (oftentimes a pattern with a minor change to the original) or completely disassociate himself with a pattern. The rest of the clansmen (blood relations or others who have banded with that family for protective reasons) then wear the tartan the chief has chosen. Today, there are some 2,500 registered tartans. Some are stunningly beautiful, some not so sharp.

The MacGillivrays had a keen check, but I later learned my grandmother's connection to the clan didn't exist. The modern dress MacPherson tartan was nice too, but there was no real clan at the booth, just the elderly woman sliding into the dumpster. The Campbell tartan itself was pretty nice, but then there's that massacre business. Clan Cameron was just a bad idea gone astray, and I felt slightly out-of-place with the Donnachaidhs. I gazed over at the nearby Este Park McDonald's restaurant and wondered what the employees were wearing.

In the end, I opted to start my own clan: the Cameron-Murdoch-Burns. There's only one member, but if you visit Estes this year, check out Clan Row. I'll be the one wearing the new clan tartan: pink polka dots on a fluorescent green background.

Nightmare Ride in Nepal

by April Thompson

AFTER TEN MONTHS on the road and a week in Kathmandu, I craved a quiet, open space free of exhaust fumes. I wanted to go far away, far from the scruffy tourists in two-tone velvet pants bought on Freak Street, from the Nepali men hawking hash and tiger balm on crowded street corners. I was ready for the jungle.

A swarm of Nepalis and their bully bags were waiting at the crossroads. Meeting the bus on its way out of Kathmandu, I hoped to shave an hour off my trip. A smoke-sputtering bus rolled up. Pink cursive letters on its side read "The Swan."

"Bardia National Park?" I yelled.

Its big-jowled driver waved me on. What luck! Hoping to blend into the tired upholstery, I took a seat with squeaky springs at the back of the bus. Several men vied to sell me a ticket, and I handed one the sum he requested.

Two toothbrushes dangled from a crocheted fringe on the windshield—the sign of a man married to the road. The driver vaguely resembled the actor on a film poster I had seen plastered around Kathmandu. Looking at his long, ragged hair and sallow skin, I wondered how long he had been awake, and if he would stay that way.

Perhaps Mr. Bus Driver used his horn to stay alert. He spelled out "I am bus driver, hear me roar" in Morse code beeps as he passed dopey-eyed cows grazing on garbage, slow girls in lemon and lime saris and boys on bicycles carrying boxes.

The horn dueled with a tape of a Nepali comedian. My attempt to meditate was like trying to relax at a Queensryche concert. I pinned my ears shut with my hands, then earplugs, to no avail.

The road folded into Nepal's lush, green hills, causing a boy and his mother to abandon their lunch. I gripped my seat and tensed a calf to keep from joining the men sitting on rice bags in the aisle.

Every few minutes we stopped at a dinky village or *chowk* (bazaar), where young, raspy-voiced salesmen circled the bus, peddling peanuts and pancakes through the windows. One boy ripped me off on a slice of coconut; twice I had to turn down shifty deals on oranges. I don't mind being pegged as rich, but I do mind being taken for a fool.

With every stop, a new character took over the seat beside me. One wild-eyed girl sat close and asked me *"Jane?"* ("You go?"), nodding to her house somewhere in the hills. A boy with intensely brown eyes babbled to me as if Nepali were the universal language. One old man asked if he could have my introduction. He kept pumping my hand and saying "essir, I'm sorry." My favorites were the schoolgirls with cocoa skin, gold nose rings and long, lustrous twin braids tied in ribbons.

An hour into the trip, a teenage kid plopped into the seat.

"How much you paid for the ticket?" he asked. "I saw he cheated 70 rupee from you," he said.

I sighed. Fooled again.

"And I hear you go to Bardia. This bus will not go there," he said.

The driver confirmed that I had two more buses to catch. My morning flight from Kathmandu was turning out to be a red-eye.

At last we reached the Terai's crossroads, flat ground to exercise the engine. Driver #1 passed me off to Driver #2, a dark, skinny man with a moustache and a jumble of teeth. At dusk, he dimmed the lights, put on some Indian pop and lit a cigarette and a pack of incense. The diva's voice swirled around the curls of smoke. It was sleepy time. I snuggled up to my shoulder and started fading away.

I woke to the skunk smell of marijuana—some kids had lit up a joint—mixed with someone's recurring dhal-bhat gas. Sweat was salting my back, but heat being relative nobody else was interested in opening a window. I had to pee like mad. My senses were in a state of alarm. I closed my eyes and breathed through my mouth. Sleep was no longer a possibility for me, though my seatmate kept nodding off on my shoulder. Insomnia consuming my personality, I stabbed him with my elbow.

Suddenly I felt something touch my butt through the crack in the seat. I let it go, perhaps a mistaken brush.

The toes toyed with my butt again. I squeezed the offending digits until my fingernails tasted blood. Then it moved to my breast.

"What the HELL do you think you're doing?" I screamed to the back seat. No reply.

I was pinching my own body parts by now, wondering if this nightmare ride had been real. All I could do was laugh in the face of discomfort, injustice, indignity, foolishness, optimism, fate.

By the grace of Kali, I did make it to Bardia National Park.

I spent days roaming *sal* forests draped with vines and laced with orchids. I battled blood-sucking leeches, rode a regal elephant, tracked paw prints and tiger poop, even glimpsed a gigantic dolphin. I refused to think about the dreaded ride still ahead.

An Algerian Wedding

by Tina Martin

A FORCED WEDDING! And the bride wasn't even pretending
that it wasn't. She sat there, sorrowfully, her head bowed, her
eyes lowered. I wanted to believe she was just deathly ill, but
her look often turned into a scowl of indignation that went
beyond mere dying.

I'd first mistaken her for an unhappy wedding guest several hours earlier, when I'd arrived as the only non-Algerian,
non-Moslem in a motor-caravan to get the bride. I was invited
by my dentist, the groom, whom I'd met during Ramadhan,
when after observing the fast during the day, I'd too zealously
feasted after sunset and broken a tooth. He expressed gratitude when I reclined in the dental chair without a veil cover-
ing my nose and mouth—a barrier he faced with his other
female patients.

After he had finished a temporary replacement of my broken tooth, he asked me out to dinner and assured me that the
rumors of his having a fiancee were totally unfounded.

"And when the wedding for this unfounded rumor takes
place," I asked him, "will you invite me?"

He laughed (beautiful teeth) and promised, "If I ever get
married, I'll invite you."

After several weeks of dating, he confessed that, in fact, he
did have a fiancee after all, but he kept his promise. His cousins,
who had been my students at the town's *lycee*, made me part

of their car in the caravan to get the bride in Algiers to transport her to the home of the groom's parents.

When we got to our final destination and were being
sprayed with flower water, the bride was escorted into the bedroom where all of us later went to change into our evening
dresses.

I saw her sitting on the bed, back to the door, hand to her
forehead. I wanted to sit down and say, "When I found out
that you existed, I told him he wasn't being fair to you." I
wanted to console her, side with her. But I wanted even more
to stay a safe distance from her.

After dressing, I was seated in a hall of women only, dancing for and with one another. Later the bride began to model
her trousseau of silk, satin, and velvet embroidered in gold,
which brought her in and out of the room several times.

Around midnight, the bride made her final entrance in a
wedding dress and accompanied by the groom, the first man
to integrate the hall. They were seated on a kind of throne on
the stage in front of musicians and belly dancers. On the bride's
left were seated aunts from the two families, and then several
uncles entered, standing on the groom's right.

The groom, smiling broadly, looked like a magician in a
black velvet suit, cape and shiny black shoes. *He* looked radi-
ant. The bride's eyes were lowered and she was not holding
hands with—or in any way joined to—the groom. After a
pause and to the background of the you-you-ulating, the
groom turned towards the bride and said something, perhaps,
"Take off your glove," because that's what she did. Their vows,
according to tradition, had been made a year earlier, when
they had become engaged. Now he slipped a ring onto her finger. After a couple of minutes, her mother whispered something to her, and the bride put a ring on the groom's finger.

This was our photo opportunity, and we took pictures of the half-happy couple.

There was no "If anyone knows why this man and woman should not be bound in holy matrimony, speak now or forever hold your peace." They just stood up and walked out of the room.

As some Algerians were driving me home, I commented that the bride was very pretty, and I could certainly understand why she looked so very, very tired. I was waiting for a response like "Yes, forced marriages are always so fatiguing" or "I can't stand brides who put their antagonism towards the groom before being good hostesses." But they said nothing like that.

I agonized all weekend and would have agonized for longer except that, by some happy coincidence, the next week my students brought me a copy of a French-English magazine that featured a story about Julie de Ternante, who had died of a broken heart on her wedding night.

"Her parents," the article said, "had forced her to leave the man she loved and had chained her for life to some awful, crawling louse. As it was all a long time ago, when parents were parents, she did not dare say no. She just dropped down dead. And now she wanders about all night among the cedar trees on her lover's estate in Louisiana, USA."

The story was the perfect opening for the wedding day tragedy I'd witnessed, and I began, "You know how happy and smiling brides always are."

The students gasped in unison.

"Oh, no!" they said. "A bride must always look serious and sad. She mustn't talk to anyone and must keep her eyes low."

Even if she's not dying of a broken heart and being forced to marry some awful, crawling louse?

"Yes!" they said in chorus.

And it was later confirmed that it's tradition for the bride to look gloomy, even bored. That was just good etiquette.

So I stopped worrying about the bride and groom until the groom wrote me a letter telling me his wife was pregnant, and he really missed me.

I re-sealed the letter and wrote on the envelope: "Does not exist. Unfounded rumor. Proceed to live happily ever after. The End."

Husband at the Wheel

by Mary Baca Haque

WHEN ONE'S HUSBAND wants a more adventurous way to travel, the wife needs to look at this from all perspectives.

One last time, the husband convinces her to take a road trip ... this time to Ixtapa, Mexico. Reluctantly, she agrees, in the back of her mind asking, "Wouldn't it be much easier for the family to fly?"

The comforts of an airplane look much more appealing. A husband's reckless driving is difficult to enjoy with eyes closed, the routine of passing turned into a horrifying experience for the entire family.

That beloved spouse may have a habit of nodding off once he gets relaxed. Has anyone seen a pilot nodding off while flying?

The wife finds herself listening while he points out the distance on the map, estimating with confidence that the breathtaking drive from Guadalajara, Mexico, to Ixtapa, Mexico, will take five to six hours. Whereas, the wife thinks to herself, by airplane, this trip will take a mere two. Reluctantly, the wife prepares for the journey.

We decide to take our brand new Audi that can fit all four of us comfortably. Unexcitedly, the wife pulls the cooler out of storage for packing sandwiches. In the back of her mind she thinks of the two-hour trip by airplane, that delicious bag of peanuts with an added soft drink. In addition, the wife knows she is not the one in charge of the cleanup. Those polite stewardesses take care of everything!

The preparations continue. You must map out the route because the wife knows that her husband will *not* ask for directions! The children need to be situated, stop for gas and use the bathroom one more time before venturing out on the highways of Mexico.

The highways of Mexico are deceiving. The line on the map may look straight, but once the husband arrives, confusion sets in as he encounters the swirling, curving mountain roads. He takes the curves with speed and husband-like precision.

The daughter's face has grown pale. Carsickness was something the wife did not prepare for. After all, the map said it was a straight direction, and there are no sickness bags conveniently provided or flight attendants to take away the mess.

After this episode, the family continues impatiently to Ixtapa. The husband's ability to drive has somehow diminished; the wife's threats to kill him when the family arrives seem to have no effect.

The beloved husband continues his quest, plowing over unseen speed bumps at 70 miles an hour. The family is suffering from blows to the head by this time. He is on a mission indeed, passing semitrucks on a one-lane local mountain road. Within a couple hours, the carsick daughter manages to do her thing out the car window two more times.

By arrival at the hotel, the car is on its last legs, the family virtually exhausted. The man at the hotel takes the bags politely.

It was, as the wife says time after time, "HER LAST ROAD-TRIP."

With the husband.

Hurry Up And Wait

by Sharon Fleischer

MY HUSBAND, SON AND I were scheduled to travel from Harrisburg, Pennsylvania, to Vail Eagle Airport in Colorado on a ski vacation. We were to return a week later, traveling from Denver to Harrisburg.

When we boarded the plane, the pilot announced there would be a 30-minute delay due to weather problems in Chicago. The delay lasted two hours. Our pilot announced that we shouldn't worry about missing our connecting flights because all flights going out of Chicago would be similarly delayed. Because we never had experienced a delay of that length of time, we believed him and made no attempt to change our connecting flight.

When we arrived in Chicago, we found our connecting flight had left. We went to the gate for the next flight to Vail and became standby passengers for that flight which was scheduled for 3 P.M. The airline personnel told us we were the first three standby passengers and would most likely be on the plane. However, the flight was delayed several times and left Chicago at about 5:30 P.M. and with no seats for us.

We finally were booked on a flight to Denver with a shuttle connection to Vail. When we arrived in Denver, we went to the Express desk for the connecting ride, but were told they had no record of us being scheduled and all the remaining vans for the night were filled. By now it was midnight in Denver and we had no transportation to Vail and no luggage. Luckily we met a group of people looking for others to share a limo. We went with them and arrived in Vail at 2 A.M.

The next day we located our luggage at the Vail Eagle Airport and were told it would be delivered to our hotel, but we couldn't be guaranteed a time. They told us if we wanted our luggage that day, we should come to the airport and retrieve it ourselves, which we did. We were reimbursed for this transportation as well as the transportation from Denver.

Our return home was not much better. Checking in at curbside, we were told that our return flights were canceled. Since we missed our original flight to Vail, the remaining part of the trip was canceled because we were listed as a no-show. Ultimately we were booked on a flight and we had a pleasant trip to Chicago. As we were ready to board for the flight from Chicago to Harrisburg, it was announced there would be a delay because of bad weather in Harrisburg. We immediately went to the desk and listed ourselves as standby passengers for flights to Philadelphia, because there were no seats available on flights to Harrisburg until the next day. Finally we were booked on a 6:30 evening flight to Philadelphia. The flight was delayed, but we boarded the plane when it was announced. Before leaving the terminal, we were informed there would be another two-hour delay due to weather problems in Philadelphia.

Later during take-off, we abruptly came to a stop and returned to the terminal. The pilot announced that a light indicated an electrical problem with two of the main engines and a check of the system would be carried out. Later, a second take-off was aborted due to the same electrical problem.

Returning to the terminal for the second time, the pilot announced that the maintenance crew would be called in. We were allowed to leave the plane while the maintenance crew was working. After about half an hour, we were told the problem was corrected. I was still very apprehensive and spoke to the co-pilot. He told us there was a problem with one of the voltage regulators and the maintenance crew now bypassed this piece of equipment. He said it would be replaced later. I immediately decided to leave the plane. Many other passengers agreed. The pilot finally decided to change planes because we were flying into bad weather. By now it was 11 P.M. and we were hungry. The airline had nothing to offer us and all the terminal restaurants were closed. There weren't even any vending machines.

Because of all the delays, our flight crew had gone beyond its duty day and was forced to retire for the night. A new plane and flight crew arrived. We were given the option of spending the night in Chicago or leaving on the replacement aircraft. We chose to take the flight because our son was due back at college near Pittsburgh the next morning. The flight was great. We were served dinner on the plane at 1:30 A.M. and arrived in Philadelphia at 3:30 A.M. Since our car was in Harrisburg, we had no way to make the final 90-mile journey home. Luckily, another passenger on our flight, who lived in our hometown, offered us a ride. We arrived home at 5:30 A.M. It felt good to be back safe and sound.

When in Rome

by Lester Catonese

I DON'T KNOW how many of you have visited Italy, or what you thought of it if you have. But for two Italian-Americans, namely my wife and me, it was indeed a strange place.

My story about our travels to Italy with friends Sal and Diane Pecoraro is not centered on one single episode, but instead covers several incidents. They still give my wife and me a chuckle when we think about them, years after they happened.

Incident 1: We go to dinner at a restaurant in Frascati. After several earlier meals in hotels in which we were given hard Italian bread and jam, we asked the waiter for some butter. Out he comes—with a five-pound slab. All the kitchen workers stuck their heads out to see what we planned to do with it. Talk about buttering up the tourists.

Incident 2: Every time I said my last name, the locals would respond, "Oh, mafioso." I'm of Sicilian heritage, but frankly I was taken aback by this. While in Lucca visiting a relative of my wife's, I asked him why everybody kept saying this. "Your name means from Catania, Sicily, which is one of the hotbeds for the Mafia. And we have just seen the movie *The Godfather*. I would guess you're getting good rooms and service."

We were.

Incident 3: While visiting friends in Rome, we visited a Capuchin Monks Cemetery next to the American Embassy.

In the chapel were the bones of over 1,000 monks, some of them skeletons dressed in robes. Rooms were full of bones and stacked with skulls. A pretty deadly visit.

Incident 4: From Rome we drove down to the Amalfi Coast, then to Positano, a city built on a cliffside. At a small seaside restaurant I ordered one of my favorites—calamari. As I took a bite I noticed a pop and a crunch and had my wife, who speaks Italian, ask the waiter. It turns out that the calamari are served whole, with heads intact. Growing up eating my mother's wonderful calamari, I've never even realized the things *had* heads! Next time I'll stick to the pasta.

Incident 5: We were driving across Sicily and got a flat tire. After awhile, a policeman stopped and asked what was wrong. We told him about the flat but by this point it was fixed and he didn't believe us. Only after opening our trunk did we convince him—and then we noticed a second officer across the street with a machine gun aimed in our direction.

We learned later that policemen had been ambushed along this road, and they were taking no chances that our "flat" might be a ruse.

Looking for Lodging in All the Wrong Places

by Roger Rapoport

ONE OF THE MOST frequently asked questions travel writers hear is, "Why do I need to pay for a guidebook when I can use the Internet for free?" Ever since Priceline.com refused my request for a $300 refund because my on-crutches daughter couldn't make her flight, I've viewed online travel very carefully. Unlike travel agents, who can fix problems and get you your money back, the Internet can actually create problems.

For example, there was the time I was in Madison, Wisconsin, at an Internet cafe/laundromat scrolling through an online travel directory that was years out of date. Recommended establishments had closed, doubled their prices or changed their phone numbers.

On a sales trip, I blanched when my computerized driving directions to a bookstore told me to turn right and left at the same intersection. The fact that so much of what passes for impartial advice turns out to be either paid advertising or publicity means that the Internet often lacks the impartiality or objectivity of a guidebook.

Even when you have a PDA like a Palm or Handspring in the front seat of your car, it's often much quicker to find what you need in the pages of a guidebook, particularly when the author has actually bounce tested the mattress at the inn you have in mind. But it was only when I reached Jackson Hole, Wyoming, that I came to fully understand the limitations of the Internet miracle.

I had called from Rock Springs seven hours earlier to let the owners know I would be late. Since I knew I had excellent directions, there was no need to reconfirm the inn's location. The full moon made it easy to navigate around the corpses of deer hit by less fortunate motorists. And my recording of *Hamlet*, with a cast led by Kenneth Branagh, was perfect accompaniment for a snowy mountain drive. Rosencrantz and Guildenstern were dead by the time I crossed the Snake River and descended into Jackson Hole.

When I arrived in town, shortly after 2 A.M., no one, not the cab drivers outside the Cowboy Bar, hotel desk clerks or guards on the graveyard shift at a gated development could pinpoint the location. Calls to the inn were no help because the switchboard was closed for the night.

Perplexed, I headed to the Best Western at Teton Village, where the night clerk and I looked at a MapQuest printout pinpointing the alleged location of my bed and breakfast on Raven Haven Road.

During the next two hours I searched vainly for Raven Haven Road checking out every other bed and breakfast in the area, all unmistakable thanks to brightly lit signs. No one could find a street map of this neighborhood just east of town save for a tourist giveaway map that pinpointed all lodging in the region except my inn.

With the sun rising and airport shuttle vans arriving to pick up the morning passengers, it was now all down to the Internet. The Best Western clerk and I studied the MapQuest printout and shook our heads. "It can't possibly be there," the clerk told me. "That map is way off. Look, I know where it is. Just head back toward Highway 22 about six miles. It's on the left, back from the highway. You'll see it."

Armed with the inn's web site printout, I now knew what I was looking for. I checked every single street, driving up and down side roads, searching for Raven Haven Road. After half an hour of checking every address on the left side of the road I hung a U and noticed a small sign parallel, not perpendicular to the highway. Flicking on my brights, I saw the B&B sign I'd been looking for, on the *right* side of the road. Turning down the side road to the inn at 5 A.M., I now understood why I had missed the road over and over again. The single Raven Haven Road street sign was missing and unaccounted for.

Glancing down at my MapQuest printout I saw the free Internet map had misplaced the B&B by about four miles. It's really true that you get what you pay for.

Uppity Surf

by Jim Kravets

NINETY MILES off the west coast of Sumatra, the tiny Indonesian island of Nias is heaven for professional big-wave surfers. Twenty-footers wrap around a submerged rocky shelf and zipper evenly closed over a distance of nearly half a kilometer. The raw power and consistency are hypnotic.

I had never surfed before I arrived on the island two weeks earlier, but I liked the title "Surfer" better than my one at the time, "Punk." The transition was simple. I splashed benignly about on waist-high waves falling off a surfboard I rented for a dollar.

"Are there any rules?" I asked a pro from Melbourne.

"Only two," he said, pronouncing it "anly." "No more than one person per wave, and never turn your back on the ocean. But it's surfing, mate," he said and winked. "Just have fun."

"And dangers? What if you hit the bottom?" I asked.

"Impossible," said the Melbourne pro. "It's 40 feet deep out there. If you're held under, just remember: There's a flotation device—your surfboard—tied to your ankle." He referred to the leg-rope, or leash, surfers use to remain connected to their boards. "Just grab the rope," he said, "climb it to the surface. . .and you're saved! *Tidak ada masala!*"

He grinned, patting me reassuringly on the back.

Tidak ada masala means "no problem" in Bhasa Indonesia, the national language. It's something of a country-wide

245

motto. I said it all the time myself, almost continually even. "No problem" was a good attitude, I reasoned, for the experienced, veteran traveler I was so quickly becoming. Road washed out by landslide? Well, *tidak ada masala*. Typhoid? Hey, a little typhoid never hurt anyone, *tidak ada masala*. It would still be another six weeks before a compassionate teacher in Java corrected my pronunciation. I had not, evidently, been saying "No problem" but something more closely approximating "Not smelly" or "Not unanimous."

Correctly pronounced, *tidak ada masala* is the perfect phrase for those tempted by the seas that surround Nias. The ocean looks lovely. It demands much. It invites you into its bath-warm waters. Then it separates you from your drawers. Ironically, the same turbulent waters that attract visitors, previously helped keep Nias invader-free. For centuries the difficult approaches conspired with its rugged terrain, malarial climate and warlike population to isolate Nias from the mainstream of Sumatran culture. Headhunting and human sacrifices were practiced as late as 1935. My guidebook said, "A magnificent megalithic heroic culture flourished on Nias well into the 20th century."

"Magnificent megalithic heroic!" I repeated these words to myself one early morning as I left the surf village of Lagundri to climb high into the jungle. The humid air was thick with vomit, or so it seemed. Papaya trees grow everywhere, and as the fruit decays on the ground the papain, a digestive enzyme naturally occurring in the resin, provides a constant post-party ambiance.

The day's flat surf made Lagundri an extremely tense place; surfers paced and seethed on the shore like businessmen with cancelled flights. I opted out of the pacing and headed for the village of Bawomataluo in search of Nias' *menhirs,* large stone monuments perhaps as old as 800 years, that were erected in the jungle villages during communal feasts to enhance the status of the aristocracy or as memorials to the dead. Masons created these stelae and obelisks in accordance with the ancient religion of the island's first inhabitants who arrived between 3000 and 5000 B.C. The villagers have long forgotten the origins of these megaliths or even the meaning of the inscriptions. German Lutheran missionaries saw to that when they finally gained access to south Nias over 100 years ago. My objective was a stone column: a head-high pyramidal structure with a decidedly curious purpose. It is the column used for *fahombe.*

Despite the toxic testosterone levels endemic to the surfboard set, Westerners were not the originators of fab *x-treme* sports. Bungee jumping, for instance, was inspired by the vine jumpers of Pentecost Island in Vanuatu (formerly the New Hebrides) in the Pacific Ocean. In *fahombe,* young Niah warriors ran full speed down the central village runway, sword in one hand, torch in the other, and jumped over two-meter-high stone columns covered with sharp spikes and pointed bamboo sticks as training for nighttime attacks on the fortress walls surrounding rival villages. In its charming Neolithic way, this exercise was also used to prove a young man's readiness for marriage.

The final approach to Bawomataluo is up 88 steep stone steps. Not deterrent enough, apparently, as I learned too late that the village is on every Sumatran package tourist itinerary. Village children first give the traditional Niah greeting of "Hello money!" and then swarm, hard-selling figurines, beads and other souvenirs. I was offered a hand-carved chess set, a kazoo, ladies batik shorts, a live chicken (a magnificent megalithic heroic chicken), a plastic Amex travelers check wallet, a bag of *krupuk* (fried prawn crisps—Indonesia's answer to pork rinds), a Fa brand shampoo bottle filled with *arak,* a local rice moonshine big with emetic fans and a black visor with Lufthansa embroidered in black on the brim.

Bhasa Indonesia provides 12 ways to say "no" and I ran through them all, invented some new ones and reverted to a few in Spanish to deflect the onslaught. Bawomataluo, however, is worth it.

Massive pile structures with posts buried in the ground and soaring roofs with opening skylights are the distinctive features of a unique architectural tradition that has no parallel in other parts of the Indonesian archipelago. For stability in the seismic western islands, Niah homes employ a rare strategy of using thick logs as diagonal struts or braces arranged in the form of the letter V. Bawomataluo also delivers the megaliths, 287 to be exact. Huge stone *menhirs* in the form of benches, circular seats and 18-ton stone chairs, where the dead were once left to decay, fill the main courtyard.

In the middle of the central runway I found the *fahombe* column. The sharp spikes and pointed bamboo sticks were absent, but even without them the column was unmistakable. At over six feet tall it's imposing and even a little ominous. I wondered if I could jump it.

Maybe. Probably. Sure. I don't know about the bit with the sword and the torch but otherwise, yeah. If I wanted to I could do it. If I had to.

The villagers watched me sizing up the pylon and smiled. I know that smile. It's a sweet, almost pitying smile. It's the same smile I give my two year-old nephew, Sam, when he tries to munch the dog. Disturbingly, the column itself seemed to be giving me the smile as well.

These days *fahombe* is performed mostly for tourists groups and costs about $120 for a private showing, so I resigned myself to buying a bag of Indonesian prawn/pork rinds as my souvenir and returning to Lagundri. I caught a glimpse of the activity, however, as *fahombe* is featured on the Indonesian 1000 rupiah banknote I handed over for the snack.

Within the short time I'd been on Nias I'd already distinguished myself. And I didn't need tough-guy stone columns or swords to do it. One morning, still ill with one of the infinite varieties of stomach disorder readily available in Asia, I'd decided to surf anyway. Sitting among the other surfers in the line-up, I felt the unmistakable and nonnegotiable call of impending gastro-intestinal evacuation

Demonstrating what might be considered an uncanny *lack* of oceanic knowledge for someone on a planet two-thirds covered by water, I paddled out a few hundred meters, did my business and then returned to the line-up. When the now well-dispersed contents of my distressed bowel arrived barely a minute later, I learned an exception to the first rule of surfing. I was left alone with my jetsam, while five surfers shared a single wave, heading toward shore without contention or delay. Word spread, and with the Indian Ocean off limits, everyone went shopping. Only a shark could have done as much for local retailers.

Days in the surf village of Lagundri settle into a routine of eating, surfing badly and the regular small humiliations that result from such a steep island learning curve. Did you know that some coconut palms are protected by territorial stinging ants? *Tidak ada masalah!* You will quickly learn this on your first attempt at climbing one wearing only shorts.

Occasionally, Indonesian tourists arrive, most on package tours from Java. Disgorged from the bus, they stumble around on the beach in sensible shoes aiming cameras. For them, the Westerners seem to be the subjects of interest and they cheerfully click away at anyone foreign. For a local flavor photo, one female tourist positioned her two young children at a table next to a French surfer named Claude. Revolted, Claude got up and left. Witnessing this affront and feeling benevolent, I offered my posing services and sat down with the children. The mother, revolted, grabbed her children and left.

The air temperature in Nias is the same as the water: exactly 98.6 all the time. The steady breeze can only be described as soft, not in strength but in texture, and the constant humidity somehow amplifies gravity. Nothing—clothing, hair, books—ever dries, no cuts ever fully heal, and all of the business dealings are with 12-year-olds. Mostly boys, they circulate 24/7 selling bananas, pineapples, John Irving books, cigarettes, toilet paper and coconut bread.

"*Bagus?*" Wayan, my 12-year-old sundries vendor, shouts out to me as he made another orbit wielding a stalk of bananas his own height.

"*Bagus,*" I reply. *Bagus* is an all-purpose Indonesian word meaning, "Right on."

Unfortunately the youth retail contingent does not, however, sell surf wax. When rubbed on the deck, surf wax creates the high-friction surface necessary if you want to stay on the surfboard for any length of time. The most common brand is "Mr. Zog's Sex Wax."

One evening I asked Wayan if he could get me some surf wax. He swallowed, looked around furtively and motioned for me to follow. Wordlessly, we snaked through the darkened village, down a dirt road and arrived at a bamboo lean-to next to a rice paddy. He told me to sit at a wooden table illuminated by a single lamp hanging overhead. The pressurized lanterns on Nias burn lamp oil or kerosene, but these fuels are expensive. So the locals just use gasoline, and the villages are essentially illumined by slow-burning Molotov cocktails.

In a few minutes he was joined by an older Indonesian man, saying, "*Yaho'wo*," the traditional Niah greeting meaning "strength." He introduced himself as Wayan; three out of five men in Indonesia are named Wayan. He wore the casual ensemble of choice for both Southeast Asian men and women, a sarong, which is a single piece of thin, beach-towel sized fabric wrapped around the waist. Sarong are often handmade with intricate, traditional batik designs. Wayan's sarong is cut from a bed sheet with a Tom and Jerry motif; Tom repeatedly chases Jerry with a large cleaver. Wayan sat with the light behind him, deliberately shrouded in silhouette.

Abruptly he said, "So, you look for Sex Wax."

"Yes. I need a package."

He shook his head and sighed, "Sex Wax very, very hard to find on Nias, very, very hard to find." As if the scene wasn't *Godfather* enough he actually ended his statements with "my friend." "Sex Wax is gold on Nias, my friend."

"Okay, well I only want one," I said. *"Berapa harga?"* I asked using the Indonesian for "what's the price?"

"Sex Wax come from Aussie. Very, very far away, my friend." He paused, breathing through his nose remorsefully, if it is possible to do so. The Molotov cocktail swayed a little in the breeze, the surrounding jungle rife with night sound. "Everybody want Sex Wax."

"Okay, how much?" I asked again.

"Very expensive, my friend. Very expensive."

Negotiation in Indonesia is inherent in every transaction. It is not merely the route to a final price but an age-old ritual choreographed as an expressive dance. Impatient Westerners insult their hosts with their haste.

I looked at the table helplessly, counted a few beats, and

delivered my lines, "But I must have it, I must!"

Wayan liked this.

"*Bagus,* my friend. *Bagus.*"

For the hockey puck-sized bar that costs $1 in the U.S., I ultimately paid Don Wayan 20,000 rupiah or about $8. This same sum would buy two weeks of beachfront accommodation, 150 pounds of bananas or a bus ride the length of the island three times.

Every day between 10 and 3, *perahu,* outrigger canoes with sails, slide into Lagundri Bay filled with red snapper, tuna, *ikan putih* (white fish), *ikan merah* (red fish), barracuda and many others exotic and bizarre. Ask and point and the fishermen will call everything "snapper." It's the only English name they know, and more important, they realize that all Westerners like snapper.

For about a buck you can buy a fish the length of your arm, a snapper, say, and have it cooked for free at your *losmen* (bungalow)—barbequed in a banana leaf and served with rice and *sambal* or chili. Provided you donate the 70 percent you can't finish to the owners.

Sometimes the outrigger *perahu* sail by when I'm out in the water. They move slowly in the light wind and I can paddle over to one and buy a fish on credit right there in the ocean. The fishermen smile, say, "*Bagus, bagus*" and make the classic surfing posture: front arm outstretched and the head ducked. Then I'll ride the next wave in with the fish on the board. For the fish it's a strange day.

Lagundri is unique among the world's big wave surf spots. Usually, large surf carries a self-regulating feature. Paddling a surfboard out from the beach through the break or impact zone is generally only manageable by those who have the skill to be out there in the first place. It's a life-saving filter on days with big waves. Weaker surfers and punks are left to flail about in the shallows. But in Lagundri there is something called "the keyhole." The keyhole is a rocky shallow reef that juts out perpendicular to the shore providing the point for the famous Nias "point break." To access the surf all you have to do—all anyone has to do—is walk out to the keyhole at the end of the point past where the waves are breaking and hop in, *tidak ada masalah.*

Unfortunately such a hop is irreversible, resolutely irreversible—tragically irreversible—because you then have to make your way back to the beach the only way possible: through the surf. The keyhole allows any punk at all to jump in right next to the pros.

An analogous setup would be stepping out of bed directly onto Soldier Field, taking a hand-off from Doug Flutie and quickly fulfilling all of your organ donor responsibilities with the enthusiastic assistance of the Bears defensive line.

For weeks the surf has been small, playful even, and a hop into the keyhole has resulted in no great threat. But overnight a swell arrives. Waves explode offshore with a force that shakes the bamboo *losmen* high on the beach. Surfing a 20-foot wave might be compared to jumping off a burning two-story house, landing squarely on your feet, and then having the blazing house chase you down the street. Or maybe jumping over a two-meter high stone column covered with sharp spikes and pointed bamboo sticks with a sword in one hand and torch in the other. Does jumping off a burning two-story house, landing squarely on your feet and then having the blazing house chase you down the street prove your readiness for something? Marriage? An identity? Medication? I didn't know.

For the experience level necessary to be in the water today, my two weeks of small-wave frolicking leaves me, by a conservative estimate, a decade shy. But with a mindless hop from the keyhole I'm in the water.

The ocean is sentient. The messages it sends are often whispered, indirect, carried on a current or suspended in mist. Other times, however, the sea's communiqués are harder to miss, even charitable. This is illustrated by my first wave today, which neatly strips me of my shorts and what feels like most of my body hair.

"Go home, punk," is seldom more clearly articulated.

I heed the warning, whimper audibly either "not smelly" or "not unanimous" and paddle crazily for shore—not merely turning my back on the ocean, but mooning it as well. So much for the second rule of surfing. The universe, evidently, takes a dim view of repeated transgressions.

Victims of violent crime often cannot describe their attackers. Similarly, I have no memory of the next wave itself, only what follows—I'm alternately dragged and bounced along the sea floor. Obediently, I pull the rope that tethers the surfboard to my leg anticipating sweet ascension from the deep. Instead, I'm soon holding the severed and decidedly surfboardless opposing end.

Eventually I am washed up onto shore. Sensitive travelers careful to learn the customs of their host country please note: few gestures are more universal than a freshly lacerated naked man trailing rope from one ankle lavishing the beachfront with bile.

The proliferation of "extreme" lifestyle media and easy-access adventures create chronic self-aggrandizement. Are you a mountaineer simply because you are on Everest? Are you a warrior because you chucked yourself over a two-meter high wall? Hey, buy all the SUVs you want. Attempts to shortcut an established workup system are unfortunate conceits. The delusion usually ends abruptly.

Merely floating on a surfboard in high seas does not make you a surfer, any more than running into a burning building with an ax makes you a fireman. To some degree, both activities are all the accreditation you need for the title "idiot." Much of the distinction "surfer," or "fireman" for that matter, is awarded with one's ability to exit the situation gracefully. Or at least with your shorts. Fools may indeed rush in, but only surfers and firemen sashay out.

Five miles back from the ocean, 1200 feet above the shore, through a dark jungle a young warrior moves quickly. Down a pathway, his bare feet accelerate off stone, his eyes fixed ahead. Escape velocity, he springs upward, one knee forward, body taut, alert without sound, face half-illumined in yellow torchlight, metallic glint, a sword in starlight. Mid-flight his body rotates, 15 degrees, only slightly, a confident aerialist. Altitude: two meters, malice averted, wall cleared. With landing assured, a secret smile, a look skyward. Upward flight resumes. Descent respectfully declined.

Publish, Don't Perish

If you have a story you'd like us to consider for the next volume in our series, use this book as a handy submission guideline. All stories must be original, true and well-written. Your submission can be as short as 500 words. Try to keep your story under 3,000 words. We don't have writer's guidelines for the series. Reading this book and others in the series, easily available at bookstores or libraries, is your best bet. Send your story to RDR Books at 4456 Piedmont Avenue, Oakland, CA 94611. Include a postcard addressed to yourself and we'll confirm receipt. Be sure to send us a copy of your manuscript and hold on to the original. Even though we are in the business of writing about other people's problems, you can't hold us liable if something terrible happens to your manuscript, such as a fire at the post office or a skunk that gets loose in our office. You can email us at trouble@rdrbooks.com. Attachments don't always open. As a backup please paste your story into the body of an email. Our fax is (510) 595-0598.

Here are a few tips from our editors.

1. "I" stories, me, me, me, are tricky. Consider a "you" story where you write about other people who shared your unhappy experience. Instead of a monologue, consider dialogue.

2. Direct quotes are a good idea.

3. Laugh at yourself. You may have been part of the problem.

4. If you wish, show your story to another writer, editor, librarian or bookseller before you submit it.

5. Try to shorten the story and see if you like it better.

6. Read a lot of travel humor.

Bon Voyage.

About the Authors

Lee Arnold

When not traveling, Lee Arnold is a librarian and archivist in Philadelphia. Travel essays on Cuba, Mexico, Grenada and Guatemala have appeared in *Philadelphia Forum, Pathfinders Travel* and *Delta Epsilon Sigma Journal*. He is a regular reviewer of travel literature for *Library Journal*.

Brian Abrahams

Brian Abrahams is a Chicago-based writer and consultant in marketing and fundraising. The fundraising part of his career is probably an unconscious reaction to how poorly writing pays. But he's not sure because he can't afford the therapy to find out. He has studied Japanese, Wolof, French, Spanish and Hebrew, but despite these efforts he can only speak broken English. The rest of his time is spent as the husband to one and father to two. (Oh yeah, there are also two cats in the mix. But what's a one-word description for your relationship with a cat?)

Judith Beck

Judith Beck writes both fiction and nonfiction. Her most recent acceptances for nonfiction have been at *Prairie Schooner, Creative Nonfiction's Brevity* and *Andre Codrescu's Exquisite Corpse*. She has had several short stories published and is presently finishing a novel.

Ralph A. Bolton

Ralph Bolton has traveled throughout the world. His wife of 52 years has often accompanied him on business trips in North America. In the early 1990s they decided to see the rest of the world. Their first overseas trip took them to Egypt where they were rammed by a ferryboat while sailing on the Nile river. Despite trips interrupted by earthquakes, emergency landings and riots they have retained their optimistic outlook on life.

The Boltons have 3 children, 11 grandchildren and 1 great grandchild living within "eating distance" of their home in western New York. Bolton has also been a Bible teacher for over 40 years.

E. Peabody Bradford

With the exception of a decade in Illinois, Peabody Bradford has lived her entire life in Northern California. She currently resides and practices clinical psychology in San Francisco.

Loretta Graziano Breuning

Loretta Graziano Breuning has been a Professor of International Business at California State University, Hayward, since 1983. She has written widely about international trade, and manages a Sister City relationship between Piedmont, California, and Piemonte in Italy. The anti-corruption movement is her research interest, and her article "Ten Ways to Refuse a Bribe" was published in the *Transparency International Annual Report*, 1998. She has drastically curtailed her high-risk lifestyle and limits herself to domestic baklava.

Mary Lou Brown

Mary Lou Brown is a registered nurse who graduated from the College of St. Mary's Nursing in Omaha, Nebraska. In 1990, in order to do more traveling, she became a Traveling Nurse. Her first assignment took her to California, 12 years ago, where she enjoys traveling, reading, films and music.

In remission since 1998 from ovarian cancer, she marks each new year by watching the sun rise on the first day of each new year.

Priscilla Burgess

Priscilla Burgess is a freelance writer and project editor. She has published travel articles, profiles and columns in addition to her on-going relationship with *Fodor's Travel Publications*. Currently, she is project editor for a health book and one on outdoor sports while her novels are making the rounds in New York.

Cameron Burns

Australian-born Cameron Burns is a Colorado-based writer, photographer, designer and communications specialist. He has authored or co-authored five climbing guidebooks. His essays and articles have appeared in such books as: *World Mountaineering (UK)*, *Ascent*, the *American Alpine Journal*, *The Walker Within*, *I Really Should Have Stayed Home*, *I Just Should Have Stayed Home* and *The Best of Rock & Ice*.

Les Catanese

Les Catanese is a graduate of San Jose State University School of Business. He has been married to his wife, Valerie, for 46 years and they are the proud parents of four and grandparents of four. Catanese worked for Eli Lilly Pharmaceuticals for many years.

Mark Cerulli

As an award-winning writer/producer at HBO, Mark Cerulli worked on the promo campaigns of major movies and specials. He has also scripted episodes of two Nickelodeon series— *Hey Dude!* and *Clarissa Explains It All;* produced/directed DVD "making of" documentaries on *Halloween, Halloween 4* and *5;* and co-produced docus on the James Bond classics *Goldfinger* and *Thunderball.* When he's not in an edit room, he loves to travel!

Audra Crane

A Southern California native, Audra Crane developed a taste for the more unsteady and uncomfortable forms of transport and travel on her father's much used sailboat. After completing college and a teaching credential she took off for five globe-trotting-on-the-cheap years. She has written a collection of travel tales under the title, *The MisAdventures.*

Lacy David

Lacy David was born in Canada and defected with her baritone ukulele to California during a 58 below zero blizzard. Her songs have been recorded by almost every pop and country artist on the Billboard charts, and she won an Emmy nomination for the "Happy Endings" theme on CBS, plus numerous gold and platinum records. She also wrote themes and songs for 34 TV shows and movies, including *Eight is Enough* and *Violet*, an Oscar winner.She just finished a funny novel called *Mondo Condo.*

Carol Dickerson

Carole Dickerson grew up in Denver, Colorado, and took her degree from Washington's Evergreen State College. After working for the State of Washington for many years, she retired in 1996. Dickerson started her own business called Away You Go, driving people in their own cars to the airport.

Inette Dischler
Inette Dischler is a Principal Learning Consultant at the University of California, Berkeley. She grew up in Chicago, moved to Florida for graduate school and now lives just 50 miles from the site of her story. She still loves to travel, but is more inclined to keep her adventures on the ground.

Erica Etelson
Erica Etelson is an attorney and freelance writer. She is at work on her first novel.

Julia Niebuhr Eulenberg
By the time she was three months old, San Angelo, Texas, native Eulenberg had crisscrossed her native state with her parents twice. Her passion continues with a special focus on Europe.

Joyce Evans
Joyce Evans is a comedy writer trapped in the body of a secretary, working a dull job in Marin County, California. She won a two-week trip to Holland with an under-50-word essay. The Holland trip was awesome and she met both Queen Beatrix and the owner of Heineken beer who sponsored the contest.

Donna Feuerstein
Donna Feurstein is a full-time wife and mom, part-time kickbox instructor and medical transcriptionist. She holds a BS degree in Animal Science.

Sharon Fleischer

Sharon Fleischer is a registered nurse residing in Pennsylvania. An avid skier, she frequently visits Vail, Colorado, with her family.

Amy Forkner

Amy Forkner is an emergency room nurse and an officer in the Army National Guard in Cheyenne, Wyoming. She is an avid writer, having penned four novel-length manuscripts and several short stories.

Jake Greenberg

Jake Greenberg is an auctioneer living in Marin County, California. After graduating from Boalt Hall Law School in 1972, he traveled to North Africa, Asia and the Middle East, importing textiles and tribal carpets. In 1992, he founded the Berkeley Travel Club, a group of 25 hard-core travelers who meet regularly to share their adventures and misadventures.

Mary Baca Haque

Mary Baca Haque is an American who has lived in Guadalajara, Mexico, with her family for the past four years. She is the author of a bilingual children's book, *Madalynn the Monarch and Her Quest to Michoacan*.

Candace Hisert

Candace Hisert is a retired English teacher who gives tours and lectures at the California Palace of the Legion of Honor. She has participated in digs in Pompeii ('94) and Petra ('96), where she discovered a capital of a column. Hisert also does outreach programs in several Bay Area schools.

Larry Jer
Able to say "why me?" in several languages has been more useful than Larry likes to admit. Currently following the road well-traveled, he and his wife, Jun, enjoy a fixed address in the Pacific Northwest but will shed their city suits once again when the nomad gene comes out of remission and therapy kicks in.

Kim Klescewski
Editor Kim Klescewski has edited a number of RDR Books including *The Wannabe Guide to Music, I Really Should Have Stayed Home* and *Foiled: Hitler's Jewish Olympian.*

Judie Kline
Judie Kline retired from the San Francisco Unified School District after teaching for 29 years. She now does substitute teaching in the local school district.

Jim Kravets
Jim Kravets writes freelance magazine, newspaper and guidebook features. His subjects include natural leavening of bread, showerheads, and lunch-time betrayal. He is an avid consumer. He lives in Northern California.

Sunny Lucia
Sunny Lucia is a veteran adventurer who began independently exploring the globe at 40 years of age, after an executive career and raising two children. She took her backpack and soloed through China for a month. She found towns not on maps, rode in every mode of transport, was spat on and invited into homes. Lucia has traveled with her husband on freighters, rafted wild rivers and hired donkey carts in 38 countries. She has written a book on travel for couples.

Donna Marchetti

Donna Marchetti lives with her husband and son in Cleveland, Ohio, where she is a fulltime writer. Her articles have appeared in the *New York Times, Los Angeles Times, International Herald Tribune, Michigan Living* and many other newspapers and magazines. The author of the books *Around the Shores of Lake Erie* and *Lake Michigan,* she has a special affection for the Great Lakes.

Tina Martin

Tina Martin's travel adventures began when she was eight years old and "accidentally" flew alone to New York City to join her father at a psychology convention. That experience taught her the importance of welcoming unexpected detours. After finishing college, she applied to the Peace Corps and was sent to Tonga for two years, after which she used her Peace Corps readjustment allowance to travel to Spain, where she taught English in Madrid for a year and got free French lessons, leading her to go to Algeria, where she taught at a girls' lycee for two years. After she returned to the U.S., she got married and had a son, and began teaching at City College of San Francisco, where—between trips to Japan, Cuba, Chile and Oaxaca—her ESL students have made it possible for her to travel around the world just by coming to class.

She's written three plays, three novels, and numerous short stories, which she keeps in a trunk for her son to inherit along with the rest of the house.

Eileen Mitchell

Eileen Mitchell's wings have been somewhat clipped of late since adopting Elvis, "he ain't nothin but a hound dog," an ex-racer greyhound. She spends much of her time devoted to greyhound adoption and writes a self-syndicated pet column about the joys, trials and tribulations of pet ownership. She hopes to tour Machu Picchu and the Amazon one day and when the time comes, will prefer to face the jungles alone rather than risk another roommate from hell.

Charli Ornett
Charli Ornett art directs magazines and lives in the San Francisco's Mission District. She is embarrassed to say that she is linguistically challenged in all five of the languages she has tried to study, but vows to keep trying with Spanish since she loves Mexico and Spain.

Renée Owen
Renée Owen is a writer and psychotherapist with a practice in San Rafael, California. She received an award from Artist's Embassy International and won first place in an RDR Books contest for her travel essay on Mexico. She participates in public readings of her works with the Redwood Writers and is collaborating with her husband on setting her poetry to music. While currently obsessing about her next trip, she's working on a book about her travels.

Nadine Michele Payn
Nadine Michele Payn is a clinical psychologist with a practice in Albany/Berkeley, California. She hosted a popular psychology call-in show on KGO radio in the early '80s and was a contributing editor to the *Berkeley Insider Magazine* in the mid '90s. Payne began traveling at the age of 15 and loves to write about her many adventures and misadventures around the globe.

Roger Rapoport

Publisher of RDR Books, Roger Rapoport is the author, editor and co-editor of numerous books including *I Should Have Stayed Home, I Really Should Have Stayed Home, After The Death of a Salesman, The Getaway Guide to California* and *Hillsdale: Greek Tragedy in America's Heartland.* He has visited over 2,500 bookstores in the past ten years including many with cats that enjoy being petted.

Kellie Schmitt

Kellie Schmitt writes travel and features articles for the *San Jose Mercury News* in California. She studied at a university in Buenos Aires, Argentina, where she wrote for the *Buenos Aires Herald* and traveled throughout South America. She lives in San Francisco and spends time hiking and painting.

Jillian Shanebrook

Model and author Jillian Shanebrook is a graduate of the University of Michigan. She has worked around the world and regularly appears in leading magazines at home and abroad.

Stefan Sharkansky

Stefan Sharkansky is a computer software developer. A wisconsin native, he also attended schools in Kenya, Israel and Australia, and still travels whenever he gets the chance. He now lives in San Francisco with his wife and children.

Jean Sigler

Jean Sigler, a lifelong resident of Omaha, Nebraska, has worked as a special education teacher, a wallpaper hanger, a bookkeeper and as the executive director of an agency that serves people with developmental disabilities. Jean has spent the greater part of her life smoking cigarettes, watching TV and eating fast food. Three years ago she decided to get healthy and began swimming, biking, skiing and hiking. Her new lifestyle has led to adventures like hiking the Grand Canyon.

Thomas O. Sloane

Thomas O. Sloane is emeritus professor of rhetoric at the University of California, Berkeley. He and his wife Barbara, a former English teacher at Piedmont Middle School, have now traveled extensively on six continents and set foot on the seventh.

Thomas E. Stazyk

As a business traveler, Thomas Stazyk earned gold elite status in the frequent flier programs of three different airlines. But nothing compares to his experiences as a leisure traveler in his second career as a student and writer.

Eric Steiner

As a traveler, Eric Steiner is rather accident prone. Fortunately, he has a better track record as a business man and grandfather. He is retired and lives in San Francisco, but continues to tempt fate on trips to various parts of the world.

April Thompson

April Thompson is a San Francisco-based freelance writer who covers travel, spirituality, and environmental and community issues for magazines nationwide. She visited Nepal on a year-long solo journey around the globe.

Karen van der Zee

Karen van der Zee has dined on fertility goat sausage in Kenya, seen her Palestinian butcher's bedroom in Ramellah and lunched at the palace of an Ashanti chief in Ghana. Some of her most disastrous cooking adventures were published in the *Washington Post.* She also has 35 romance novels to her credit and is now finishing a humorous nonfiction book about living the expatriate life in Africa and other fun places, tentatively entitled *Madame, Your Green is Missing.* Married to a globetrotting development economist, she presently enjoys new adventures in Armenia after spending three years in Ghana, West Africa.

Michelle Walsh

Michelle Walsh is a writer and activist from San Francisco, where she lives with her life partner. Originally from the East Coast, she says that San Francisco has swept her off her feet, and that she continues to be inspired by it on a daily basis. She hopes that her next vacation will not involve bugs, rain or emergency surgery.

David Wright

The author was left by aliens in a small farming community in southern Illinois. After being raised there by the kindly family who found him, he fled the heat, humidity and insects of the Midwest for a better life in Wyoming. He currently resides there with his wife, two step-children and the human clones he has produced in his basement.

I Should Have Stayed Home

The Worst Trips of Great Writers

Edited by ROGER RAPOPORT *and* MARGUERITA CASTANERA

In this hilarious anthology 50 top travel writers, novelists and journalists, including Isabel Allende, Jan Morris, Barbara Kingsolver, Paul Theroux, Mary Morris, Dominique Lapierre, Eric Hansen, Rick Steves, Tony Wheeler and Helen Gurley Brown, tell the stories of their greatest travel disasters. Most of the writers of these original essays are contributing their royalties to Oxfam America, the international relief organization. Guaranteed to whet your appetite or make you cancel your reservations.

ISBN: 1-57143-014-8

$17.95 ($23.95 Can)
TRADE PAPERBACK
256 PAGES

I Really Should Have Stayed Home

The World's Worst Vacations

Edited by ROGER RAPOPORT *and* BOB DREWS

This collection of travel disasters might make you rethink those vacation plans. Before you pack *your* bags consider some of the many ways that the trip of a lifetime can backfire. In this hilarious anthology of vacation horror stories, families are humiliated at Orlando theme parks, incarcerated on jets in Detroit blizzards, shipwrecked in the Caribbean, and hospitalized in Cancun. This book is guaranteed to make you unfasten your seatbelt for the belly laugh of the travel season.

ISBN: 1-57143-081-4

$17.95 ($23.95 Can)
TRADE PAPERBACK
300 PAGES

I've Been Gone Far Too Long

Scientists' Worst Trips

Edited by MONIQUE BORGERHOFF-MULDER *and* WENDY LOGSDON

In this hilarious anthology, 26 research scientists go off the deep ends of the earth. Travel with a young researcher in Dian Fossey's camp as she is handed a gun and told to go out and shoot a gorilla poacher. See how a scientist reacts when he discovers a poisonous bushmaster in his bidet. From bush pilots and endangered species to Land Rover nightmares, this hair-raising book will keep you up past dawn. This book is a tribute to the courage of an intrepid band of researchers who have risked all to bring home the truth.

ISBN: 1-57143-054-7

$17.95 ($23.95 Can)
TRADE PAPERBACK
296 PAGES

After the Death of a Salesman

Business Trips to Hell

By ROGER RAPOPORT

In this sequel to bestselling *I Should Have Stayed Home* and *I've Been Gone Far Too Long,* business people tell of their greatest travel disasters—from the emergency room to the paddy wagon. Read this book and you'll be happy you weren't traveling with: oilman Jack Howard, cruise scout Marcia Wick, bookseller Monica Holmes, conductor Murray Gross, investor Jack Branagh, or publisher Cynthia Frank. Dedicated to the memory of Willy Loman, this tribute to corporate road warriors offers an amusing view of everything they don't want you to know in business school.

ISBN: 1-57143-062-8

$15.95 ($21.95 Can)
TRADE PAPERBACK
224 PAGES